This is the story of one man's service in the British South Africa Police of Rhodesia during his service of nearly fifteen years (1965–1977). In many ways it forms a sequel to the author's book *Mad Dog Killers*.

The struggle to keep Rhodesia out of black nationalist hands started in late 1964 and ended with the Mugabe regime in 1982. It is a story of a policeman engaged in that war as a member of the paramilitary BSAP Support unit, the Police Anti-Terrorist Unit and as an ordinary member of the force that had always been designated the country's first line of defence. Most of the service was on remote, rural district stations, often on the "front line".

The account tells of one man's learning to be a policeman and later a police public prosecutor and also about the eccentricities of some of the circuit magistrates. A policeman has a lot to learn about life. In the BSA Police he was expected to jump in at the deep end from the start.

It is also the story of the strange struggle by Rhodesian-born policemen in a force where the majority were English-born, at a time when Rhodesia was in rebellion against Britain. The author's senior officers, though fiercely loyal to the force, were British and required to join the rebellion. It tells of his resentment at the lack of drive by senior officers in the fight against terrorist atrocities.

There is additional insight into the utopian life in Rhodesia, especially in rural areas, when it was still possible to hunt buck for the police mess rations, where there was no electricity or other modern amenities, and where the single quarters were in ancient buildings enclosed by a wraparound gauzed-in veranda – a life now gone forever. It is also a story of a young man who grew up in Salisbury and of his sexual excesses and sadness.

The British Queen Mother was patron of the force all her life and was very proud of her association with it.

Ivan Smith was born 1941 in Fort Victoria, Rhodesia. He grew up on a farm before doing his national service after leaving school in 1958.

After some cowboy and mining work, he spent two years in London and Copenhagen. In 1964 he signed up for a six-month contract as a mercenary in the Congo. He joined the British South Africa Police in 1965 and served fourteen years in the paramilitary Support Unit and the Police Anti-Terrorist Unit during the protracted Rhodesian 'bush war'. He emigrated to South Africa in 1984, where he worked in the security department at the University of Cape Town for sixteen years.

A lover of hunting and fishing, he has written for various outdoor magazines for over forty years. He lives in the small village of Joubertina in the Western Cape of South Africa.

# BUSH PIG DISTRICT COP

## Service with the British South Africa Police in the Rhodesian Conflict 1965-77

**Ivan Smith**

Helion & Company

G G Books UK

Co-published in 2014 by:
Helion & Company Limited
26 Willow Road
Solihull
West Midlands
B91 1UE
England
Tel. 0121 705 3393
Fax 0121 711 4075
email: info@helion.co.uk
website: www.helion.co.uk
Twitter: @helionbooks
Visit our blog http://blog.helion.co.uk

and
GG Books UK
Rugby
Warwickshire
Tel. 07921 709307
Website: www.30degreessouth.co.uk

Designed and typeset by Farr out Publications, Wokingham, Berkshire
Cover designed by Euan Carter, Leicester (www.euancarter.com)
Printed by Lightning Source, Milton Keynes, Buckinghamshire



Cover: Bruce Allen and 'C' Troop – Support Unit, Makuti. (© Bruce Allen)

ISBN 978-1-909982-29-1

British Library Cataloguing-in-Publication Data
A catalogue record for this book is available from the British Library



For details of other military history titles published by Helion & Company Limited contact the above address, or visit our website: http://www.helion.co.uk

We always welcome receiving book proposals from prospective authors working in military history.

# Contents

# List of photographs

# List of acronyms

| | |
|---|---|
| APA | African Purchase Area |
| BSAP | British South Africa Police |
| DC | district commissioner |
| i/c | in command |
| JOC | Joint Operations Command |
| KAR | King's African Rifles |
| OC | officer commanding |
| P/O | patrol officer |
| PATU | Police Anti-Terrorist Unit |
| S/O | section officer |
| SAP | South African Police |
| SB | Special Branch |
| TTL | Tribal Trust Land |
| VAT | Voluntary Anti-Terrorist |

# Map

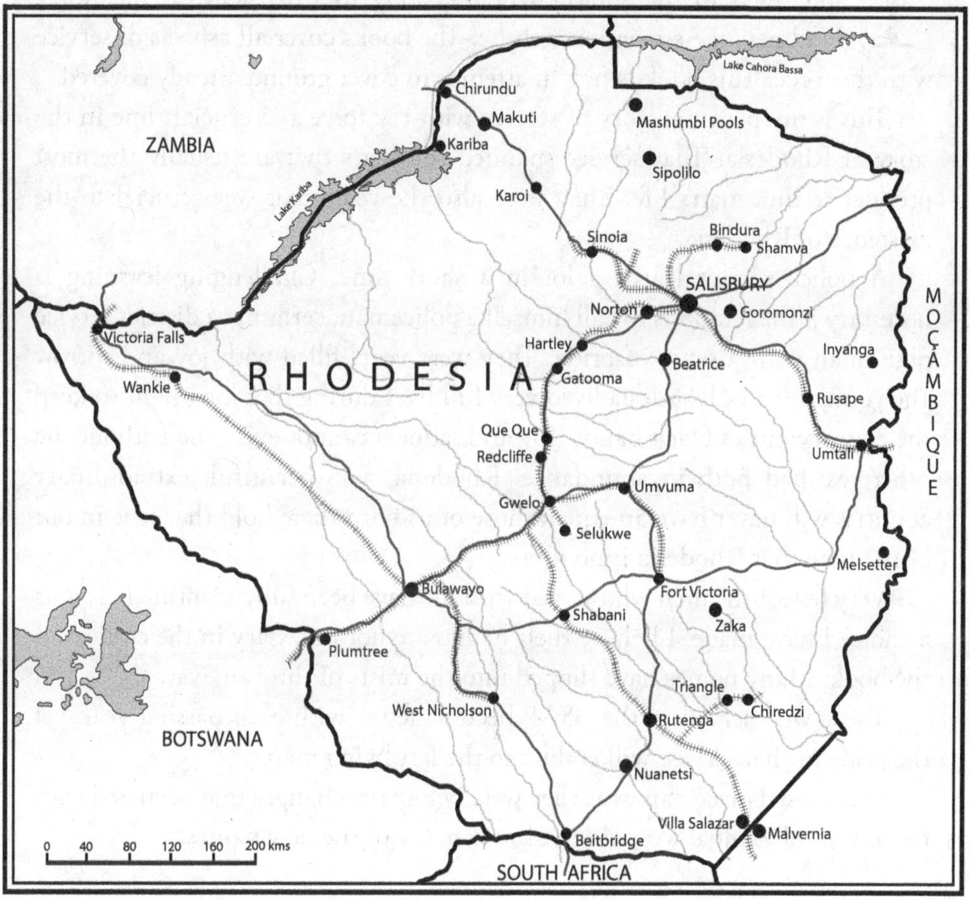

ZAMBIA
Lake Kariba
Lake Cahora Bassa
Chirundu
Makuti
Kariba
Karoi
Mashumbi Pools
Sipolilo
Sinoia
Bindura
Shamva
SALISBURY
Norton
Goromonzi
Hartley
Gatooma
Beatrice
Inyanga
Rusape
Umtali
Victoria Falls
Wankie
RHODESIA
MOÇAMBIQUE
Que Que
Redcliffe
Umvuma
Gwelo
Selukwe
Melsetter
Bulawayo
Fort Victoria
Shabani
Zaka
Plumtree
Triangle
Chiredzi
West Nicholson
Rutenga
BOTSWANA
Nuanetsi
Villa Salazar
Malvernia
Beitbridge
0 40 80 120 160 200 kms
SOUTH AFRICA

# Preface

There are many books about the British South Africa Police, and anyone interested in the subject will find long lists of them on the BSAP Regimental Association website. The books cover all aspects of service with the force. This book is not an attempt to cover ground already covered.

This is my personal story of service with the force at a crucial time in the story of Rhodesia. That service spanned the years that are usually the most productive in a man's life. They were also the years that were crucial to the existence of Rhodesia.

A police recruit learns a lot in a short time. Challenging learning is necessary if the recruit is to call himself a policeman; certainly a district service policeman with a sense of pride. They were years filled with joy and sorrow. The young men of Rhodesia lived very full lives during that long fight to keep the country out of black hands. Joy and sadness cannot exist one without the other; we had both in abundance. Rhodesia, as a beautiful, extraordinary country, will never have an equal; those of us born there hold that true in our hearts now that Rhodesia is no more.

Very few of the men who served with me have been fully identified. That is a choice I have made. I believe their names are not necessary in the context of the book. Many names have slipped into the mists of time anyway.

Those who served in the BSAP become fewer with each passing year, yet the pride in that service will endure to the last living man.

I have used place names as they were before the changes that occurred with the advent of Zimbabwe. I do not know many of the new names.

Joubertina, Eastern Cape
November, 2012

1

# The match is made

It is almost impossible to discover where something originated. Human beings carry millions of years' worth of genetic material in their makeup and the start of human evolution goes back to the original big bang. All human beings experience the world through five senses. Those senses report only what has taken place; no matter how fast the senses react to stimuli, all that a person's brain can record is what happened in the past, even if that past is but a millisecond back. It is the same for events that affect the lives of men. All have their origin in past: a past that is sometimes close, sometimes far. All human beings are a product of the environment they find themselves in and over a lifetime modify their behaviour to adapt to the environment, genetically passing on that adaptation to their descendants.

Maybe it started here. In the mid-1800s, John Lee moved with Umzilikazi to what became Matabeleland. Lee was linked to the British Royal Navy and had married a relative of President Kruger of the Boer Republic. Umzilikazi fled the bloodletting at the death of one of the Zulu kings and took his followers to what became Matabeleland and Lee was given a vast farming area as a reward for loyalty. The king granted the farm as being in size the land a horse could be ridden around in a day. That he did not specify how fast it had to be ridden brought Lee and his sons into a long dispute with the king's indunas. Lobengula eventually took over the Matabele kingdom. In the new kingdom, Lee was still the king's customs and immigration officer. To Lee's homestead, in the 1880s and 1890s, came the old hunters who moved through Central Africa decimating elephants and shipping long wagon trains of ivory back to the south. In the wake of the hunters came traders and missionaries. That was one beginning.

John Lee refused to join the war against the Matabele instigated by Rhodes, so the BSA Charter Company confiscated all his property. Having invaded the land by force, the Charter Company had the bare-faced cheek to say that Lee did not have proper documentation to his land. At least Lee kept his honour in that affair, unlike so many others at the time. For example, two members of the mounted police of the same Charter Company, forerunners of the BSA

Police, were given a sack of gold by Lobengula to ransom his freedom after his kraal was burnt down. He and his entourage were heading north to the Zambezi, but the troopers decamped with the money. One trooper was caught and punished; the other went back to England and became a landed squire with his share of the loot.

Maybe it also started here. On 2 September 1887, Jesuit missionaries from Belgium, including Father Depelchin, arrived at the kraal of Lo Bengula (their spelling), son of Umzilikazi. They found at the royal kraal a fair collection of English priests and traders including the king's favourite, Fairburn, who later convinced the king to make a treaty with the English and Rhodes. The Jesuits went through many trials, but persisted with their mission.

This is taken from the diary of one of the missionaries:

> By this you will understand that one of the best means of entering a little into the minds and hearts of these barbarous tribes is to teach them, with devotedness which is proof against all trials, the elements of the arts which are useful in life. We must drag these people away from their savagery that is to say from laziness, from improvidence, from complete lack of industry; we must teach them in a practical manner to enjoy the fruits of a Christian civilization and of Christianity. They are completely materialistic; it will therefore be necessary to provide first for their material needs, in order to lead them subsequently little by little towards that life of the spirit, towards the sublime virtues of Christian morality.

Those diaries and other writings were published in the annual papers of The Rhodesiana Society, which became available to me fairly recently. The Society was formed to preserve old Rhodesian documents and historical writings. The extract is from the 1959 publication. Colonel A.S. Hickman MBE was a staunch member of the Society. He worked his way up from constable in the British South Africa Police (BSAP) to being its commanding officer. One of his sons commanded the Rhodesian Army and his other son was in the BSAP. We were stationed together in the 1970s at Sipolilo. During the Rhodesian war, the hearts and minds were what each side contended for.

A further starting thread was woven when Skipper Hoste met Cecil Rhodes and was offered command of a troop of mounted infantry in the expeditionary column then being formed to advance into Mashonaland, a vassal state of Lobengula. Hoste had been a passenger liner captain plying trade along the

East coast of Africa. Chicanery by Rhodes had obtained a concession from the king to travel beyond Matabeleland and take out minerals in the land of the Mashona, whom the Matabele described as 'our dogs'. The BSA Chartered Company expedition crossed the Shashi River into Matabeleland on 6 July 1890. They crossed the river on horseback, three abreast, and Hoste was in the first row. Skipper Hoste's troop then cut a path through the forests for the wagon train from the low veldt up the high plateau near the Zimbabwe Ruins, a plateau that makes up the centre of Rhodesia. On 12 September, the wagons were halted at the site of the future Salisbury and the next day the British flag was hoisted with ceremony on a hastily erected sapling flagpole. Hoste and a friend of his, Tyndale-Biscoe, had rigged the pole, the latter hoisting the flag that morning. There was no sign of native kraals or local inhabitants anywhere near the chosen spot. This is important to note and refutes later nationalist claims of natives being moved off the land.

In a very few years thereafter, the Charter Company carried out part of Rhode's plan to occupy all of the land to Cairo, by taking by force all of the land south of the Zambezi River. The strife with the natives, when it inevitably broke out, was quickly put down and the Company got on with exploiting the natural resources. That exploitation went on into the 1920s and made them millions, not only at the expense of those few white men who made the new country home, but also the natives. An early census gave the numbers of natives at about 200,000. A 1952 census, just fifty years later, counted just short of 1,000,000. The country was big and empty. The natives had no technology before the white men arrived and were limited to living by subsistence farming near water, and that limitation was a natural curb on population numbers.

Sir Charles Coghlan, an Irish lawyer, moved from South Africa to Rhodesia in 1900. He entered politics and from 1909 struggled to get home rule for the country, meeting Winston Churchill and various other British politicians. Both Smuts and Churchill tried to convince him to join Rhodesia to the Union of South Africa after the Anglo-Boer War and the Unification of the Boer states. Before a referendum on the matter, Smuts even toured Rhodesia trying to convince voters to do so. There followed a long political fight, but on 1 October 1923 at seventeen minutes past noon, Rhodesia was granted home rule with a constitution of its own. He became Rhodesia's first Prime Minister. Coghlan then fought another battle to finally get rid of the BSA Chartered Company. He won that battle also, but at great financial cost to the fledgling colony. Even after he had won the fight, the Company still held hegemony over the railways and mines for many years and only gave them up at further great cost to the settlers.

All the threads that had gone before fused for me when my service in the British South Africa Police began in July, 1965. The previous events and circumstances continued to affect contemporary Rhodesia and reach to this day into Zimbabwe. At the age of twenty-three, and by then eight years out of school, it became a matter of urgency to find a steady, respectable job. Seven years of aimless wandering had taken in the copper mines in northern Rhodesia and short spells of living in London and Copenhagen as well as a six-month stint as a mercenary in the Congo. It was patently obvious that life had to take a more solid course. This was not what I thought, but what others thought for me. It was time to begin working for a living. Does mankind today have any choice other than to buckle down to earn a living? A reckless devil-may-care few still manage free lives, but not many are that brave.

A recruiting poster for the British South Africa Police promised an interesting life in the outdoors. The BSA Police had been formed when the BSA Company Police of Skipper Hoste and his contemporaries was disbanded in the 1890s. It was a police force that served Rhodesia with pride and distinction; a force that had tradition and much skill by the 1960s. The timing and location of my application form-filling are lost. Very early recruiting posters had asked for 'sons of gentlemen who can ride and shoot'. The 1960s posters called for fit young men between the ages of eighteen and thirty who wanted an adventurous and responsible life. A few short weeks after applying, the Police Training Depot, a large area next to Government House on the northern edge of urban Salisbury, became home for six months. Six months in a recruit camp had already been served as a Territorial in the Rhodesian Army.

The recruits were taken into the Training Depot in squads of about thirty men at a time, and at any given time there were some six squads in Depot. The squad which became mine, the fifth for 1965, was made up of three Rhodesians, two Kenyans, one New Zealander and an ex-northern Rhodesia policeman. The rest were recruits straight out from England. Those recruited in England were sent to Cape Town on a Union Castle liner and then by train to Salisbury. At the station they were collected by a mule charabanc, a specially built wagon with rows of seats, canvas roof and drawn by eight mules. The English recruits' first impression of the modern vibrant city of Salisbury was a ride in a mule wagon. The mules had special handlers who drove the wagon and wore khaki overalls and wide-brimmed floppy hats. A lot of the vast depot was maintained by mule and horse-drawn machinery and transport. It was only in the mid-1950s that horses were withdrawn from police stations where they had served as transport for patrols.

The recruit accommodation was a large tower block with one man to a small room. The female recruits lived on their own separate floor. The Depot was a sprawl of parade squares, sports fields, officers messes, canteens, lecture rooms, sports club, stables and horse grooming lines where lines of chains were anchored to posts under spreading jacaranda trees. There was a guardroom near the main entrance, where recruits did duty day and night. The entire complex covered maybe fifty hectares. There was a parade ground outside the other-ranks mess, a double-storey Victorian building and another where ceremonial drills took place, at the edge of which stood three flagpoles. The three flags were the Union Jack, the BSA Police flag and the Rhodesian flag. A detail from the native police depot next to the white recruit depot raised and lowered the flags at the end of each day. At the same time, a single bugler from the police band, stationed at the native depot, blew reveille and lights out and all the other calls of military camps, day and night.

The training was much like basic military training. Like the Territorial Army, the police basic training was done by instructors with loud voices, vicious tempers and sadistic tendencies. At 5am physical training, then marching and arms drill all took up large portions of the day; lectures in law, police procedures and typing class only a small portion of the day. After the first six weeks riding instruction began and then at 4am the morning ride started. The horses had to be brushed down, saddles polished and all the squad mounted and ready for the riding instructors by 5am. Grooming required the horse's tail and mouth be sponged clean and any recruit caught doing the rear end before the mouth was put 'behind the guard'. The recruits were also responsible for the readiness of the instructors' horses. The early morning rides took in the suburbs of Salisbury, on footpaths through heavily-bushed veldt of which there was still plenty then, and sometimes through the heavily-treed avenues of the residential urban area.

That was a good time to be alive. A cool winter morning, with the magic of a strong horse and the smell of the earth and rotting leaves, the purple jacaranda trees dazzling the eye in the morning light and the heavy carpet of purple snow flowers across the tar road. Pretty women on balconies waving and smiling as the muted thunder of multiple shod hooves rumbled through the streets. Then a split-arse gallop back across the grassy fields to the stable lines and a 10am breakfast in the Depot mess. All horses had at that time been withdrawn from outlying police stations, but there were still fifty-odd in the Depot stables which were used for ceremonial purposes like the opening of Parliament and the Police Display, an annual event, apart from teaching police recruits to ride, a discipline deemed necessary for the character.

Ten pounds came off the salary of forty-two pounds, six shillings and eight pence for mess and accommodation. Uniforms were supplied free. What other basic wants were there to be covered? Uniforms were mainly made to measure by the Police Tailor, housed in a hanger-like building, where there worked a preponderance of homosexuals. The yearly issue of uniform to all ranks was distributed to all station personnel from there. The leather leggings were hand-made by the Police Sadler, the leather being shaped round lasts made to mimic human legs. The leggings were originally issued for riding but were worn with shorts by all officers except office workers. Drinks and food were very cheap in the messes and at the Sports Club or Police Reserve Club. All the sports such as rugby, cricket, tennis, golf, cross-country, track running and squash were freely available and there was a swimming pool. An annual police boxing championship was also held.

The Police Armoury was also in the Depot and had a side room covered in a comprehensive display of hand guns; all four walls carried hundreds of different makes and types of revolvers and pistols, attesting to man's ingenuity in things of war. The Lee Enfield .303 was withdrawn and the new FN assault rifle in 7.62mm was issued one morning after arms drill. Number 038, the thirty-eighth such weapon to be issued by the police, was issued and remained my weapon til October 1977. It was an early model with wooden butt and fore piece. It had a fully automatic change lever which, many times over the years, was supposed to have been replaced with a single shot only option, but never was. Each time an armourer called at the station it was hidden away. It had no flash eliminator, but as it was used on interprovincial range contests, it had a fine Parker Hale ring and foresight fitted to replace the coarse military one. That rifle was carried on Police Anti-Terrorist Unit duty for nearly fifteen years. It was something trusted to protect life and it never failed. On normal police duties no firearm was carried; that was always a matter of pride in the force.

The training stretched over a period of six months. Money from the stint in the Congo had come in. As in any training camp, bands of friends were formed and those friendships endure to this day. Things got hard for our merry band on the early morning PT. Most nights the lax curfew was evaded and revelry in a nightclub went on till the early hours, ending with breakfast of chicken-in-a-basket. I was rich. There were consequences. The PT instructor made his way slowly up the assembled ranks, sniffing. Those reeking of tobacco and beer were singled out for twice round the assault course. A hard way to freshen up after a debauched night is to be physically driven to vomiting and then taking a long shower before a solid breakfast. Those were truly the days for the young and strong. It was an all-new and enjoyable adventure.

Looking back to Depot is like looking back to junior school days. Did anyone learn anything? The lectures on law and police procedures went over most heads; the terms used were alien, like a new language to learn. Some learnt to ride horses, but many already knew how. My days of working on a cattle ranch after leaving school and riding a horse from sun up to dark for months on end meant there was not much the riding instructors taught me. It was another squad in Depot who were chosen as the display squad, and they spent a year riding horses at The Police Display which travelled around the country and appeared nightly at various agricultural shows. There was a pretty, harassed single woman who taught typing; that was one skill that served us all well, as police dockets had to be typed. At Depot, friendships formed that endured these fifty-odd years; 'Johnny' in New Zealand has stayed in contact all these years from that faraway place and so have several other squad mates not seen since that time.

The events put in motion in the early days of Rhodesia came to a point on 11 November, 1965. The Prime Minister, Ian Smith, and his cabinet exhausted all other means of keeping the country out of black hands and declared independence from Britain. The declaration was merely restating the Home Rule treaty of 1923 that took Coghlan most his life to get from the English. It was politically inconvenient to Britain to see the truth and war was declared on the colony by Britain and its allies. The Rhodesians in the squad were happy with things and proud and defiant, the way most Rhodesians remained until the bitter end and the coming of Mugabe. The day after the declaration, the squad were put on parade with all the others in Depot, and the Depot chief inspector took the parade.

He stood under the flag poles where the buglers usually sounded off and in his great big voice said that all police officers owed allegiance to only one flag: that one on the left. The one on the left was the Union Jack, then still flying, and an uneasy, confused murmur ran through the ranks. The chief inspector got red in the face, suspecting defiance of his order and then turned around, noticing where the men were looking, and saw that he had called 'left' instead of 'right' forgetting he had his back to the poles. The one on the right was the blue and gold flag of the BSA Police. And it was serving in that well-respected force that kept most of the police members going, although quite a few of the new recruits from England resigned on principle and went home. For the rest of us, the fifteen-odd years of working under almost wartime conditions had begun.

This was the swinging sixties and there were girls. In Depot there were many 'camp followers'. My own circle of females was wide, as I had grown up in Salisbury and had two sisters whose friends called at the house. Then there was the fame of being an ex-mercenary, which attracted women and was easy to take advantage of without a conscience. From Depot it was off to Driving School which was situated at the old Cranborne Airfield barracks. After WWII, the barracks had been turned into a temporary depot for settlers from England while they found their feet. The recruits at Driving School were popular with the local ladies, as almost each night there was a rock and roll party at the mess canteen. My collection of women was wide and varied and 'sowing wild oats' took on a meaning; one popular bar song was 'Wild Colonial Boy' and seemed as though it had been written especially for me.

To elaborate on a subject that will crop up again, my harem was many, and collected over the years of living in Salisbury. My pre-teen days on the farm saw me work at a man's labour, which built and hardened my body from very young. At the age of eleven, opposition rugby teams objected to me being included in the under twelve side. When the ball was handed to me I trotted to the try line with an assortment of small boys hanging on to my leg, arm and jersey, being dragged along and over the line. Being fit and strong ensured my place in all the high school sports teams and hero worship from the schoolgirls. Being blond, blue-eyed and handsome (all young men are handsome) helped add members to the harem. After school it was rock and roll, but also rugby for the Salisbury Sports, who were the league champions, competitive squash and tennis. Summer days were spent at the pool, doing double twist pike dives from the high board.

After leaving school, a stint on the Copper Belt and in the Congo honed my brawling skills, boxing having been one of the sports I enjoyed since being a junior in high school. When a rock party was the night's entertainment and a gang-brawl the almost inevitable after party activity, previous long experience in such matters made sure my reputation was enhanced. All of that added up to success with women. Success builds success. Women like confidence in a man, and confidence comes to a man with success with the women. There was always a wide choice of good-looking girls at home, visiting my sisters and vying for the older brother's attention. My fellow policemen stood in awe at the number of the harem. They assumed the escort for the night had been seduced that day and that each day the seduction was repeated. In fact, the women were almost always those from earlier years. None had been parted from in anger, so could be called on at any time. All through the years, though, early learnt confidence attracted women; that and blue eyes.

There are always payments to be made for living a fast life. The future is not reachable, but in 2011 at the age of sixty-nine, my careless times of those long ago days reached out across the years. A son made contact with his father. He had been married twice and had four children. His mother never mentioned him and she went to another city to give birth and put him up for adoption. He was raised on a farm near Battlefields and moved to South Africa, and finally in his forties, felt the need to make contact with his father. She was eighteen and our meeting is totally lost in those same mists of time. At that time, policemen were not permitted to marry until they reached the rank of inspector. The salary was just over forty pounds a month. She did the right thing, the only possible thing. Like the future, the past is not reachable... Life always extracts the dues owed.

Cranborne and Braeside were the next door suburbs. Mention those places and, in my mind, the tropical sun shines all year and the warm rain falls in golf balls for an hour, so the red dust turns to earth scent and boys jump into the mini-rapids at the side of the road. Home from Nettleton School to kick off shoes and grab catapult, or later a pellet gun, and roam the pristine forest along the nearby Makabusi River till dark, hunting and fishing, or go for a long ride down bush footpaths on the bicycle. The suburb came into being during WWII with the Cranborne air field and attendant tin huts. The brick houses near the airfield were first occupied by pilots. Nettleton School was housed in a collection of the same tin-sided, wooden-floor huts once used by the RAF. My mother was a teacher there for decades. The old military swimming pool was home during the summer. It was where I learnt to swim and how to kiss a girl, how to do a double twist jack-knife dive and to walk on my hands.

Hatfield was next to Cranborne. In the late 1940s, my father owned Hatfield Farm and the family moved there from the farm Condor in the south-east of the country near Fort Victoria after WWII. He sold the farm to his brother, Eric, or rather traded it for a De Soto sedan. Eric ran a dairy and eventually bought farms in Nyabira, north of Salisbury, where he built the largest private dam in the country. Eric was the commander of the RAF Rhodesian wing during the war in Ethiopia and his command trained Ian Smith (no relation) to fly. Another member of the family once owned the land on which Salisbury's main commercial and military airport, New Sarum, was built. My brother did twenty years in the Rhodesian Air Force and his father-in-law was a wing-commander with the same force. My brother-in-law also flew jets with the Rhodesian Air Force for twenty years. Cranborne was established as an RAF airfield, and Braeside, the suburb housing air force staff; the playing fields of my carefree youth. The Police Driving School now was in the centre of where my childhood memories were made, housed in the old Cranborne barracks.

My motorcycle licence dates from 1955 and bikes have been a lifetime enjoyment. At the age of sixty, a non-stop trip from Cape Town to Johannesburg did not un-nerve me and the ride back was also a pleasant trip. My first bike was a BSA Gold Star that cost seven pounds, spread over three months and that was followed by various bikes til the age of sixty-five. I miss riding bikes; steel joints preclude it. My car licence is dated 1959. Driving School required each recruit, with or without licence, to do a six-week course on a motorcycle, then another six weeks learning to drive a Land Rover, which was at that time the usual station transport. Having shown some talent for driving, probably because at the age of about seven I was driving farm trucks, another six weeks on B-cars, urban patrol cars, took place. To pass that advanced driving test a written exam required 100 percent pass and answers to be word-perfect as in the book, followed by a very rigid practical driving test.

For working days on end the police recruits rode Matchless 500cc single cylinder and BSA Gold Star 600cc twin cylinder motor cycles down bush footpaths, along gravel tracks and at times cross-country. There, down near the Makabusi, a dozen motorcyclists played just as freely as we school kids had played in earlier years. There was a collection of deep craters where the brick works had been and where earthworms for fishing used to be dug. The track led down into the crater and up the far wall. John was one of those eager extroverts who would charge headlong at everything. He did not know that the track up the far side turned at right angles to the river and then ran along the high bank. Without a pause he charged down the track, across the mud at the bottom and churned at speed up the other side, flying several metres into the air off the riverbank and into the middle of a deep pool. A crane had to be called to recover the bike from the river.

B-cars patrolled the streets of the major cities day and night. In 1966, they were the big and powerful Austin Westminster, which had shortly before replaced the Vauxhall Velox. The B-car course required hours of high speed driving round the suburbs, usually chasing a bandit car driven by an instructor. There was also a long-range top speed drive out of Salisbury to Inyanga in the Eastern Highlands and then on secondary roads to Umtali and on back to Salisbury; a distance of over five hundred kilometres. That was part of the final practical test. The instructor sat next to the driver, urging him to go faster all the way there and back. It was dangerous and very enjoyable. On the way home, near Rusape after dark, a small buck was caught in the headlights. My revenge on the pushing instructor was to tell him I was going to run it down for biltong. That, at 160kph, would have been interesting. At the last moment, with the urgent shouts of the instructor causing mirth in the back seats, the car was braked and swerved. Well, I thought it was funny even if the inspector was suddenly subdued and sullen.

While still a recruit, Christmas arrived and it was decided that more policemen were needed in the busy streets in the centre of town. So for a week the beat for us raw recruits became the crowded Salisbury pavements. The uniform worn was khaki tunic, dark green shirt and tie and riding breaches, Sam Brown belt, leather riding leggings and cleated drill boots. That was the Number One dress at the time, usually reserved for High Court days. The peaked cap with big badge on front shaded the eyes. Walk up and down was the order, and that was what we did. The cleated boots made the hard pavements very slippery, and the sudden grins of recognition from girlfriends and ex-school mates brought on a certain coyness. I had not yet got used to wearing a police uniform. The recruits carried no radio or other means of communication with the Central Charge Office. What was required of an actual policeman was still very hazy; walk about, sure, that was easy, but what if a crime happened?

This was the first time that a hare-brained scheme affected my life, but not the last time. The plans were laid in some high-ranking office far from the front line. From a distant administration office the plans all looked good. In the BSA Police, it was the lowest ranks that were the worker ants. The brass thought of something and orders were passed along down the line. The junior European rank was patrol officer and below that were the African sergeants who passed it on to the constables. When possible, the patrol officer passed the work on down, but many orders were such that he had to carry them out himself. This extra police on the beat over Christmas was one such far-fetched plan. Headquarters staff had hatched the plan, in itself a good one, but there were no spare policeman in the force. No station or post had more than the minimum staff, so the untrained recruits from the Depot were put in place. How much damage was done is hard to say, but the embarrassment of it stayed a long time.

One morning, there was a commotion in a shop door with people running out and shouting that a shoplifter was running away. The thief was quickly lost in the crowds. A small group gathered round the policeman in his impressive uniform, expectantly. There was no way that he was going to chase down after the bare foot thief along the pavement and skid and fall with the hobnailed boots. Another cardinal sin; there was no notebook or pen in the top pocket. Recruits had not yet been issued with those vital items. Reassuring the watchers, the recruit went inside the shop and borrowed the phone at the admin desk. He then had to ask the clerk for the charge office phone number before dialling and reporting the matter to real policemen. The by-then grinning watchers were told the police were on the way. It was a very long, long week walking that Christmas beat.

There is one thing that holds true for police work – only long years of experience shape a recruit into a good policeman. The extremely varied matters that are run-of-the-mill police work make sure it is a long time before a policeman has dealt with and learnt it all; in fact, to learn it all is not possible but one does learn how to handle an unknown factor. The prohibition in place in those days, of policemen not being able to marry until the rank of inspector, was put in place because junior ranks were usually posted to remote places not suitable for family life, and also because junior ranks certainly could not afford a wife. Not only that, but it was also the junior ranks that did most of the actual work in crime investigation and patrolling and the hours were very long. The prohibition was relaxed and by about 1970 had fallen away. The long hours, especially on small and remote stations never fell away.

As an unmarried man, this principle affected me throughout my career. At first, postings to remote stations were done because they were unsuitable for married officers. There were many other junior ranks that were unmarried and a there was a wide choice of men to post. When the marriage probation was relaxed many S/Os and P/Os married and the pool of unmarried men became fewer. That meant that I and the other few bachelors were kept on remote stations longer as the pool shrank; a closed circle really. There were very few single women in the remote areas, so the single men had no choice but to stay single. If the single officers met and married a woman while on leave or in other circumstances, it was impossible to take the bride to some of the stations, especially as the insurgency intensified. The choice narrowed down to marry or stay on the remote bush station.

The training on the B-car was the equivalent to the London Police Hendon Driving School course. Qualifying meant posting to Salisbury or Bulawayo Central, where the cars patrolled the streets day and night. This meant the crews had to work day and night shifts. The tower block on the edge of Salisbury Depot that housed the single officers included a dining room, pub and a swimming pool in the lawn outside the main entrance. There was a long rambling building of single rooms next to it called the Annex. It was easier to sneak a woman into one of the rooms at the Annex, so they were sought after. Women in the single quarters were frowned on, and not allowed. They were sometimes sneaked in up the outside stairs. Night shift with the B-cars started at 11pm and finished at 8am. It was nearly impossible to sleep in the early evening before shift, when men were coming back from office work and the pool and pub were buzzing. It was likewise at eight in the morning when men were leaving for work. The long corridors magnified sound and no-one cared about the poor buggers on night shift. The night shift came round every three weeks and was exhausting work. Driving deserted streets in the dark hours of the morning having slept only an hour or two was very hard.

B-cars were dispatched when the control room received reports of a crime from the charge office. All reports were handed to B-car crews initially. Fighting and assaults filled the hours after the bars closed; housebreaking and car thefts after midnight. Peeping Toms worked in the get-out-of-bed hours. Then there were the non-stop traffic accidents and the odd house on fire. In the major towns there were Police Traffic officers, but they worked only office hours. The car crew was a patrol officer and a constable. The constable was essential when locals who could speak only Shona were involved. Shona was my second language, so my man could be left in the crew room. He normally fell asleep in the car anyway. At times it was necessary to switch on the blue light and siren and put to use all that training, but very seldom. The wise, more experienced drivers knew that there was a very small time of arrival difference between edge-of-seat driving and quick driving.

At one stage of Rhodesian history, women were shipped out in some numbers from Britain to create gender balance in the colony. There were many young women in the early days of the country who crossed the oceans looking for a better life in the sun and a husband. Many of those women were nurses whose work hours were long and hard like those of the police. They were at one time called 'the sunshine nurses'. An enduring bond between nurses and police formed. Those swinging sixties days of my early service saw the bond still in place. Nurses came to police mess parties and police went to those held at the nurses' hostels. Salisbury General was in the central suburbs and night shift nurses had 'breakfast' at midnight when they took an hour off to refresh and relax. Nurses worked six months on night shift and then had a long break. Most weekday nights, midnight and the hours after were a slack period for the patrol cars.

The constable was glad to be left to doze in the crew room at Central and I had stopped under the jacaranda trees just after midnight. Three white-uniformed nurses, pretty, young and bright, had made themselves at home in the Westminster. There was animated conversation. They were asked not to press the button on the radio mike wedged between the front seats and accidently transmit to the control room, and then they got curious about the blue lights, the roof-mounted spotlight and the siren switch. Could the car do a hundred miles an hour? Would I show them what that speed felt like? There was a long road from the hospital towards Mablereign, where the houses were set far back and the yellow sodium streets lights aided the headlights. The pedal went to the floor and each gear held to the maximum engine revs. The nurses switched on the blue lights and the siren and flashed the spotlight at trees. The clock was registering nearly 170kph when far ahead brake lights flashed and a robot turned amber. It had been anticipated that the car ahead would cross on the amber and not stop. The big car was braked heavily, the nose dipping and the tyres smoking. At the robot, the driver of the car ahead reached to adjust his rear-view mirror better to see who had screeched up from behind to within a hair breadth of his back bumper.

In the B-car it was a battle to switch off the siren and lights and pull the nurses back inside. They were leaning out the windows shouting, laughing and waving to the stopped car's occupants. The roof light in the car ahead came on and the driver took a note book and pen from a pocket and wrote down the B-car registration number. The driver's bullet head identified him to me. It was the chief superintendent commanding the Salisbury District, with his wife, probably on the way home from a late night dinner. The B-car was slowly reversed till there was space to make a three point turn and the ride back to the hospital was sedate. The nurses could not stop laughing and begged me to return the next night. The chief had a reputation as quite a lad and he was relatively lenient. He only issued a verbal warning and there was a slight smile on his face at the sheepish explanation I gave the next night, standing across from his massive office desk.

Some people take a while to learn. Relations with the nurses inevitably progressed to a more intimate stage. There was an area near the National Archives on the Borrowdale road behind the Depot known as Gun Kopje that later became a suburb for the wealthy and was renamed Gun Hill. There was once a pine forest there, used as a 'lover's lane'. B-car drivers took clandestine nighttime liaisons into the pines. The Salisbury urban commanding officer had several times issued orders prohibiting parking in the forest. It came to pass that in the after-midnight hour my B-car was deep in the forest and my shorts with the heavy belt and my shirt and cap were off and she was in the same state. Sometime before, one of the B-car drivers had been in a similar state of excitement and had accidentally transmitted the action over his car radio to the control room. The microphone for the radio clipped to the dashboard but was usually left wedged between the two front seats. It was easier to reach there. Recalling that, I disengaged and half sat up to remove the mike from between the seats and in so doing noticed in the rear view mirror a vehicle in the gloom some distance behind. It was coming slowly forwards without lights. It was a grey coloured Austin Westminster, the car the duty officer drove.

Slapping a cap on to go with the boots and leggings, I engaged gear and drove, and she grabbed for her clothes, giggling. That was one time all the high-speed driving training was used to the full. The difference was, when training drivers were not dressed only in cap and boots as now was the case. The lights of the B-car were left switched off to make it almost impossible to see the rear number plate. Street lamps gave enough light and once on the Borrowdale road, progress was at full engine revs. The duty officer tried valiantly to catch up, but urgency lent speed and once the other car was out of sight, the B-car was driven into a yard with a high hedge and the rest of the uniform quickly pulled back on. Her laughter was almost hysterical by then and she was still at it when I dropped her at the General. The duty officer and control were calling repeatedly on the radio for any car in the Borrowdale area to identify themselves. Did I identify myself?

In our school days there was as saying, 'Salisbury by the Kopje, smooth like Spice, Sharp like toffee'. Old Spice was the preferred aftershave of young blades. Sharp was an imported English toffee. The kopje was the small mountain in the centre of the capital the pioneers had mistakenly stopped at, thinking it was the Darwendale Range. At one time it was the rich, mainly Civil Servants, who lived near or on it. My brothers were born in a house in Rotten Row, at that time a sought-after road but, in the 60s, part of the older side of town bordering the industrial area known as The Cow's Guts. It was also the red-light district and nightshift B-cars prowled the mean streets in a half-hearted attempt to put a stop to prostitution, which was illegal but seldom prosecuted.

The kopje was not the usual giant's castle of massive boulders that occur in profusion all over the country. It was a sugarloaf-shaped mountain covered in msasa trees, thick undergrowth and spear grass. At the top was a topograph, a circular wall with plaques indicating the direction and distance to all the worlds' major cities. There were two separate tarred roads to the top and on any given night pangolin and porcupine could be seen from the roads. At night there was a view of the lighted streets of the city below reaching to the horizon and it was also a spot favoured as another 'lover's lane'. This sort of place was usually used by those who were engaged in illicit relations.

Being near the mean streets, it was also a dangerous place. Robbers lurked with gun and knife to pounce on those distracted by passion. The B-cars patrolled routinely at night. In the early hours before dawn on a hot summer's night the constable shone the roof spotlight on a car parked at the topograph. The light showed the parked car as empty and that needed closer inspection. As the B-car stopped next to the parked one, a back door flew open and a stark-naked man galloped off down the road. He was chased down by car. As the B-car closed on him, the man stopped and shoved his hands up above his head; not a nice sight in the headlights, all naked and hairy.

'Please don't shoot me, please don't shoot me.' Then he did a double-take and saw it was a police car driven by uniformed police. 'Oh, Christ,' he said dropping his hands to cover his tackle and leaning close to the window, 'I thought you were her husband.'

The constable shone the light back at the parked car and a female head showed the back seat to be now occupied. 'Sir,' the constable said. 'It is best you put your pants on and go to your house.'

The B-car drivers did not investigate the crimes they attended and recorded in any depth. The initial report they handed in was allocated to others to follow up. In a very short time, the novelty of the work was turned to drudgery by the long hours and repetition. Each shift was the same. Check the vehicle and tools. Tick the extensive checklist and sign it. Make sure the torch battery would last the night and that pens and notebook were ready. Drive out of Central and prowl the streets waiting for a radio call to go to a crime scene and record the initial report. Return and type the report and hand it in for passing to an investigation team. Stop drunken brawls Friday and Saturday nights. Pick up the pieces at accident sites while waiting for the Traffic Branch to come and make the plans and photographs; the endless night shift draining energy through long weeks of very little sleeping time.

It was a great day when the first transfer came to a station. It was to Marlborough Police Station on the Mazoe Road on the outskirts of town. The single quarters there was full and so my mess was at Mablereign, the neighbouring sub-urban station. This was where learning what it was to be a police officer started. The major crime in the area was housebreaking and theft. The cases reported were dished out in the mornings by the station inspector to the patrol officers. That P/O had to investigate, collect evidence and make an arrest if possible. If a matter went to court the case docket had to be completed to the prosecution stage. Each morning, the case dockets were checked by a senior, usually the station section officer and he added instructions. When investigations reached a dead end, or a case had been to court, the docket was closed and filed. Serious crimes were reopened each year to see if anything new could be added to the docket. There was also routine patrolling and visits to empty houses at night; women alone could also request routine visits. The work started at 6am with 'stable parade', at which cleaning and refuelling of the station vehicles was done. At 4.30pm the offices closed, but then the duty member took over. The station charge office counter was manned all night by constables who took any after-hours crime reports and then phoned the duty member, the P/O nominated as duty member for that week. He had to work for twenty-four hours a day if required.

A steep learning curve began there and in a police force learning never stops. There is always something new and strange to deal with. The rudiments of correctly investigating a crime and gathering evidence come only after much practice. An early case involved a persistent thief who targeted chickens from the many residential properties in the Marlborough suburb which was semi-rural. The chicken theft cases piled up each day and were amalgamated into one docket, which was put in my desk in-tray. Nothing seemed to work, but then one early morning a different approach saw me and a constable checking round the servant's quarters which each residential property had. The quarters normally were at the back of the properties and were accessed via the sanitary lane. The lane was a feature of all Salisbury houses. It was a narrow dirt road that ran between properties and was used by the rubbish trucks to collect bins in the morning. At the one house central to the area of the thefts, a bin stood next to the rear gate and servants quarters and round the bin was a litter of chicken feathers.

A feeling of success flooded over us as we arrested the occupant of the servant's quarters and also discovered the bin was almost full of feathers. A month later, dressed in Number One uniform, I faced the prosecutor at the magistrate's court. The prosecutor who took the case was a tyro like me, but it was not evident just yet. All eighteen cases of chicken theft over several months were charged to the accused, who now stood half-smiling in the dock. The final evidence given in the case by me was that a search had revealed a large collection of feathers in the bin next to the accused's living quarters.

The magistrate leant over his high desk. 'Tell me, Patrol Officer, what relevance to the case is the finding of chicken feathers in a bin?'

'I supposed them to be from the stolen poultry, your honour.'

'Is there any way of linking chicken feathers to stolen birds? Maybe something I have missed?'

'Not sure, your honour.'

'In his plea the accused stated he was the cook for that house and the feathers came from birds slaughtered for meals. Can you show that that is not so?'

How that docket ever got through the S/O, the station inspector and then the prosecutor is hard to say. Sometimes the obvious is blinding. That was the first time a flea was lodged in my ear by a magistrate, but far from the last time. Sometime magistrates were hard to please. The daily grind of investigating petty crime and minor road accidents was beginning to become routine. Then came the day the duty P/O for the week fell to me for the first time. At 4pm on Friday night everyone gathered in the single quarters to drink beer and play darts. The man on duty was forbidden to drink. Several times that night the constables in the charge office required assistance and not much sleep was had. At 5am they again put the phone through to the mess. The voice on the other end informed me that there was a naked and dead man lying next to the main Sinoia road.

Now things were getting interesting and the silver body-box was loaded on the roof of the Land Rover station wagon. The roof racks were specially made to fit the box snugly. The duty sergeant came with me and soon the scene was reached, about a kilometre from the station. Mablereign area started at a bridge just a short way south of the scene. In the long grass next to the road on which traffic was passing was a naked man with his testicles cut off and his throat cut. His clothes were nowhere to be seen. On closer examination, he turned out to be still breathing. Totally at a loss, the experience of the sergeant was all there was to rely on. The thing to do, he said, was to call the CID from Salisbury Central. That police detail reluctantly agreed to come out to investigate. Meanwhile, there was nothing to do but stand and wait. Nothing I could think of anyway.

By the time the CID inspector had arrived the ambulance men were loading the injured man. The inspector wanted to know who he was, and we had no clue. Then where were the victims' clothes? Surely there would be papers in them? We still had no clue. Who had called the crime in? A motorist on his way to a day's fishing. His name was on the initial report. There is no worse feeling than realizing you know almost nothing about the job you are required and expected to do. For weeks, reports were required and questions asked. There was nothing that could be added to the answer 'I really don't know'. Eventually, the man was identified and months later the assault was traced to a gambling and drinking game at the back of a nearby house. The man's genitals were never located. Not enough evidence was found to arrest anyone and after months in hospital the man died from pneumonia. The docket was filed as murder and would be kept until all possible witnesses were old and dead.

Another day dawned and again the 5am phone call came. This reported a man attempting to hang himself from a tree next to the road, close to that previous disaster. The constable grabbed the man by the leg and pulled him down from the fork of a tree he was busy attaching a noose to. What was he doing, I asked him in Shona. His wife had run away with another man, taking his children and all his savings.

'Well, listen here. You see that bridge back there?' Being facetious might deter him. 'Yes? Well if you still want to hang yourself go back down the road and over the bridge.'

'Why?'

'Because that is in Mablereign police area. I don't want to have to cut you down. They can.'

Two or three passers-by had stopped to watch the police action. They and the constable laughed heartily. The man was left standing at the side of the road, looking sheepish. Later that morning, the station inspector called me to his office.

'Did you earlier this morning go to an attempted suicide?'

'Yes sir.'

'And did you also tell the man to go hang himself in the Mablereign area?'

'Yes sir. But it was meant to be a joke.' The terrible sinking feeling.

'Well, you silly bugger, they have just phoned me and he did just that. They are not happy. Not happy at all. Let me have a full report at once.'

Apart from learning police work, there was police culture to adapt to. The force was a closed community most of the time. Each and every station had a local pub where members met socially after working hours. If there was no police pub, as sometimes was the case at small district stations, there was certain to be a sports club in close proximity. Sports clubs were the social centres of district stations. Pubs in the urban police stations were where officers met after work. In that way, these pubs were similar to the English local; a place to gather and talk and play darts, snooker or cards and bar games. Most weekends there was a party at one or the other of the police pubs with invited women and dancing. Officers played hard and worked hard; the story of police all over the world. However, excess the night before was never an excuse not to be up at 6am for 'stable parade'.

At single quarters parties, very often the big, stainless steel body-box was filled with ice blocks and used to cool the beer supply. It caused the officers a lot of mirth when a female visitor asked what the real purpose of the box was and grew hysterical at the beer bottle in her hand. Men are callous at times.

# 2
# The preliminary rounds

There has been a lot of misinformation put out about the war that was fought in Rhodesia and a lot of this is so old and in such volume that today, so long after it all happened, it is hard to show the truth to those who were not there. It was a long, long war, contrary to what the victors claimed later. It did not start in the 1970s. In September 1964, Dube Ranch homestead in Matabeleland was attacked by a gang of insurgents. It was late at night and the house was fired on with automatic rifles and grenades were thrown. It was a total failure as a military action, but it was a triumph for the nationalists in that it marked the start of the long fight for black rule. Some of the weapons used that night, and abandoned by the gang who fled in terror at their own audacity, were Lancaster sub-machine guns. This was a year before the Smith government cuts ties with England.

The Lancaster was an English WWII weapon manufactured with the Sten gun, both a cheap and easily-made weapon produced in haste after Dunkirk. It differed from the Sten only in having a large capacity magazine and it was issued to sailors and marines for close combat aboard a ship. The guns were withdrawn from the British Army and disposed of by being buried at sea in the English Channel. The attack and information about the weapons was secret and known only to those in the top echelons of the police. The facts came out years later. Almost immediately after that first attack, the terrorist gangs were armed with the AK 47 and other communist bloc weapons. Could it be that the English had a hand in that first insurgency? That is very likely, given the way they negotiated with the Smith regime.

Secrecy about what was going on was the hallmark of the BSA Police. They were, from the time of the pioneers, tasked with being the first line of defence and guarded carefully what was seen as a privilege. The army and air force were isolated from the 'war' for many years and all insurgency dealt with by the police. This attitude meant that it was not until the terror gangs were flooding into the country in great numbers that the rest of the Rhodesian military forces became involved. The BSA Police was run by senior officers who were British. They served to pension and then went 'back home' to England. Those men were loyal to the BSAP, but were, certainly when a final choice had to be made, more loyal to England than the BSAP or Rhodesia. This was something that worried me for all of my service. I was a Rhodesian and considered a rebel by the English and yet my senior commanding officers were British at the core.

Early on in my service, just after leaving the Central Police Station and B-Cars I was 'volunteered' for the first but not the last time. A unit of mixed police reservists, mainly farmers, and regulars was put together and designated Voluntarily Anti-Terrorist (VAT) units. A ten-day training hike in the Umvukwes ranges north of Salisbury followed. The group of men were given maps and had to make their way to certain points distant from each other to test map-reading and bush-craft. Large mountaineer-type backpacks were carried, loaded with food and water for those ten days. The exercise was really a test of bush skills and the ability to live alone and off the land. The Mashonaland bush was like home to me, especially as it was then the season in which the wild fruit trees carried ripe fruit, so the jaunt was a ten day holiday. I had grown up in the high veldt bush.

At the end of the exercise, those taking part were called to Police Headquarters to a meeting with senior staff officers. They wanted to know what could be done to improve the effectiveness of the intended VAT units. My suggestion that the unit be issued with fully automatic assault rifles, sub-machine guns and grenades was met with outrage; policemen do not carry assault rifles. When it was suggested camouflage uniforms be issued, they asked how the camouflage would work with the blue police helmet that had 'Police' printed in large white letters on the forehead. Were the navy blue riot trousers and jackets worn in the bush not good enough? Those officers were fully aware that the terrorist gangs were coming into the country in numbers and were heavily armed. That information was kept from those of us who were to go into the field; it was too secret to tell to the fighting men. They had never had to deal with a situation where 'riot dress' was not the appropriate uniform either.

At about this time, the order came to shift to the Support Unit. As that meant getting out of the office, it was an order welcomed by me, but I had again been 'volunteered'. No-one had asked me if I wanted to go.

There is a story about an officer in the Kings African Rifles (KAR) in Kenya who attended a party in Nairobi. A sweet Swedish woman asked him what the KAR actually was and he replied, 'White officers with black privates.' To which she murmured demurely 'Oh, how exotic.' That was a line I used at times when asked the same question when in the BSAP Support Unit. Most of the time it went over people's heads but one night at Makuti, a voluptuous Australian gym mistress slipped her hand under the table to unzip my trousers and had a look. 'You're lying, mate,' she said. They were, and they were also a unit of very fit, hard-playing and hard-working men. Orders came one day at Marlborough to report for the required stint of nine months in the unit. The Support Unit was then, in about 1967, a body of some one hundred permanent men, with eight or so white members who were not permanent. In later years, it expanded to battalion size and had permanent officers. But at that time it was used in various roles and not only as an infantry battalion as it later became.

The Unit was very proud of its drill parade marching skills. In full dress, the men wore tasselled fezzes and black boots and belts over the khaki shorts and tunics. They showed off their exceptional and practised skill in official parades such as the opening of Parliament, overshadowing other units. The Unit supplied the guard for entrance gates to Government House; men who stood in the box at the gate with gleaming bayonets fixed. There was a regular three-month stint in Bulawayo on 'riot standby'. Recently, the Unit had also been given the task of guarding the restriction camps where detained nationalists were housed. One camp was at Villa Salazar on a remote stretch of the Mozambique border and another in an isolated area in the Midlands. In the mid-1960s, the Unit also started anti-terrorist work in the Zambezi Valley. Most of the insurgent gangs at that time crossed into Rhodesia from Kaunda's Zambia and so Makuti, on the Zambezi Escarpment south of Chirundu on the main road north, was made a Support Unit base and sometimes the upper end of Lake Kariba at Milabezi was also patrolled. After the Portuguese left Mozambique, the easier border to cross was that one and operations shifted from the north of the country to the north-east.

Those early terrorist incursions were small, a handful of armed men struggling across the immensity of bush each side of the Zambezi, across areas infested with dangerous animals, tsetse fly and mosquitoes, trying to reach a populated area. Again and again, the gangs were tracked down by Rhodesian forces, usually PATU or Support Unit and after a brief firefight, killed or captured. Sometimes the gangs were also hunted down by Rhodesian Army units, mainly the Special Air Service. These widely-spaced operations were kept secret from the general population. They were treated as police matters and the army was still resented by senior police officers for interfering in their domain. The obsession with secrecy was taken to extremes, so even those engaged in an operation were not told who or how many enemies they were facing. It was far too secret for junior ranks.

The first police camp at Makuti consisted of a tent camp; two large marquees used as mess hall and storeroom and many smaller living tents. It was situated on the hills south of the motel, which was also sited on the hills just north of the road that branched off the main road north and wound down the hills of the escarpment to Lake Kariba. There were 'long drop' toilets behind thatched fencing, and a caravan under a spreading msasa tree did duty as an office. The Support Unit was self-sufficient when out in the field, carrying all they needed in seven-ton trucks, with the men travelling in convoys of specially fitted Ford 250 vans. Each Ford carried up to ten men, two in the seats in front and the rest in the back cage which was fitted with wooden benches. They were four-wheel drive capable.

Each time a troop took over from the one going back to Salisbury barracks, every item in the storeroom had to be checked and signed for at a formal handover. Counting picks and shovels, buckets and rope, riot shields and batons, ration packs and cooking pots took up almost a day. It was a rare thing if the handover did not find at least one item missing, and then detailed reports had to be written. Normally, the first day at Makuti was used to settle in and clean the tents and camp area. The first impression of the camp was that it was a wild and lovely place. There were all the free-roaming wild animals of the land there and wide views of far mountains and valleys and in spring the msasa trees covering the slopes put on new leaves and then the hills were extravagant paintings in all the pastel shades; pale green, light yellow, orange, pink, crimson and russet. The scent of flowers filled the blue sunny days and warm nights. Far off elephant trumpeted and nearby flocks of birds sang.

The first time at Makuti with the Unit was not the first time I had been to the small settlement. When mining on the Copper Belt, trips to Salisbury for a weekend, driving all night, were often done to attend rock-and-roll sessions with a favoured band, and the restaurant next to the petrol station at the T-junction to Kariba was then a favoured stop for pie and milkshakes. The motel sprawled over the top of a hill and a narrow tar road went winding up to it. It was also not the last time, as over the years the post was home base while on Police Anti-Terrorist Unit work and also one of the stations to which I was posted. Over the years, the tent camp grew into a fully-fledged police station.

While the insurgency came mainly from Zambia, it was decided that the tent camp would become a permanent police camp. A dozen houses for married black policemen were built, and then a charge office block with several office rooms and a small veranda at the entrance lined with flower boxes. Unlike the black staff, only single white officers were posted to the station. Two four bedroomed houses were built. They were spacious and modern when compared with other police stations built many years previously. There was no electricity as the main power lines from Kariba did not come near. The messes had gas stoves, paraffin fridges and a wood burning 'donkey boiler' for water. During the day, a small generator supplied power for the station wireless and at night a bigger one was used for the change office, mess and security floodlights. It was quite a handful for the senior officer to keep all the required fuels on hand. Everything was ordered from Sinoia which was two hundred kilometres south, and the weekly railway bus brought the station order and mail bag. Food and personal items ordered from the shops in Sinoia for various police staff were delivered the same way.

There was a small trading store hidden away on a ridge near the road run by an Indian, where it was possible to obtain almost anything except fresh food. The station was built on a hill south of the motel, near the main road. Further south on the side of the same hill range was a collection of tin huts where the tsetse chamber staff lived. The chamber was a large barn of tin, with gauzed-in windows recessed into the sides and sliding doors, and all traffic exiting the tsetse fly area had to stop in the chamber. The doors were shut so the only light came from the cage-like windows. Any tsetse on the car flew to the light to be later captured. Then an insecticide was sprayed inside the vehicle. That went on until the late 1970s when tsetse fly traps, poison impregnated material shaped like a small buck, which worked and decimated the fly, were put in place. The tsetse fly had kept human beings out of the area and with them gone, rapid settlement took place. In today's Zimbabwe the area is no longer game rich and it supplies most of the firewood shipped to the dysfunctional cities.

Each of the four sections of a Support Unit troop at Makuti went out to patrol a different area. Each section was made up of about ten men, the patrol officer, a sergeant and eight constables. The patrols were normally fourteen days duration and all requirements were carried in packs; food, water, ammunition and weapons and short-wave radio with batteries. The big packs were heavy and if a base was made in the bush from which the patrol worked, they were left there. Often the patrols did not have a set base and walked many kilometres a day cross-country, carrying the packs. The Unit patrols in the Makuti area were normally 30 kilometres in a day. The day began at dawn and ended at dusk, and every hour or so a short rest was taken. The patrols were mainly done in the vast valley which held the mighty Zambezi, the river that was the border with Zambia, but at times the hilly land at the top of the escarpment was patrolled.

During those mid-1960 days, the gangs crossing into the country were ten or so strong and came at intervals of many months apart. When their presence became known, an operation was put in place and the gang chased down and uprooted. The operations were police actions and the army did not get involved until the incursions became a flood after the Portuguese left Mozambique. In the early days, a command was established at the Makuti Police Station, and after the gang had been mopped up, the station reverted to a police camp. The border with Mozambique was long and there was no big river or lake to cross. As the focus of operations shifted to the east, once-busy Makuti station went back to sleep and the single section officer left there as the member in charge (i/c) had the two big single quarters houses to himself.

On that first Support Unit visit to Makuti, orders were to patrol eastwards from the main road following the base of the escarpment for a week and then to circle back covering new ground. The patrol was to look for boot prints and follow any found to contact and capture or kill any insurgents. The Support Unit stick patrolled split into two separate sets of men. A stick was five men walking in a diamond shape with the P/O at the centre. A second stick had a senior sergeant at the centre of it. At first light, the patrol started out and as the day got hotter and hotter, rests became longer. At midday, a two-hour break was taken in the shade. When the sun dipped, the patrol went on till dusk. Then bedrolls were placed round a campfire, the men ate and slept, and predawn were away again. All day it was the heat and humidity of low country, dripping sweat, black skins reflecting. All day it was slapping biting flies and buzzing mopani bees irritating the ears and nostrils. Looking and searching and all the while feeling that it was all for nothing and only blind luck would bring any contact with the enemy; a contact that all the Support Unit men wanted badly, and had trained all their lives for.

The black members of the Unit were all hard, fit and superbly disciplined troops. When not out walking long distances, they trained for combat. At home base, each morning there was an early morning run in formation with rifles at the port, then foot drill, and then map-reading marches or sports, range work and un-armed combat. Many of the older men had served in the Malaya campaign; all of them were keen fighting men who were fiercely loyal to the Support Unit. When at the Salisbury barracks, they delighted in brawling with the lesser class of ordinary policemen. All spare money went on beer and women, so they were craving meat when out on patrol. Living on ration packs for weeks on end without red meat was morale sapping. The valley teemed with game. Warthog and impala were taken and at the campfires at night the entire animal was eaten in one sitting, roasted on the open coals and salted. In reality, those early patrols were a jaunt of the safari kind that today rich men pay heavily to duplicate. To the men of the Unit, a patrol without a contact, it was just routine, boring work not suited to warriors.

The beauty of the Zambezi Valley is of a savage and hard kind. Along with the heat and stretches of dry rocky land where the baobab grows, there were the forests of mopani, grey, fragrant and yellow and then great fields of tangled thorny bushes where the elephant and buffalo with thick hides fed. The rocky sides of the escarpment higher up were covered in densely-packed trees, mostly msasa and Rhodesian teak, and up there were always the noisy baboons' bouncing booming voices echoing off the forests. The smell of it lingers in memory like the perfume of some woman; a wild smell, sharp herbs and rotting leaves, wet dog and a hint of rose. At night, the stars were bright enough to throw shadows under the trees and when the moon rose it was yellow from horizon to horizon, a giant brilliant ball, shrinking as it climbed the purple vault.

The Makuti Motel was a popular stopover for travellers going both north and south. It sprawled over most of a hill north of the T-junction of the road north and the road to Lake Kariba. It was an hour's drive to the bridge at Chirundu, across which the rest of Africa began; it was an hour's drive down the side road to Lake Kariba and the holiday playground of hotels, casinos and world-class fishing. Travellers going both north and to the lake, especially if they left Salisbury late in the day, stopped for the night. Travellers coming out of Zambia or further north stopped at the first place that still clung to European standards. The police, the game rangers and the tsetse control hunters of the area all made the long men's bar their local. There was a more formal ladies bar next door.

The motel buildings were several long rows of rooms with a place for a car undercover next to each. The buildings were terraced and spread out over a vast, "treed" lawn, and in the middle of the room blocks was the main building. The road winding up the hill ended in an open parking place next to the main building and that was the dining room, lounge, reception, kitchen and bars;

two of them, one formal and the other not. The veranda ran the length of the building, wide and furnished with tables and chairs. Below the veranda was the swimming bath, which was the social centre of Makuti. Day and night and in all seasons, people gathered at the pool. Except for a week or two a year, the weather was hot or very hot and the pool was very welcome comfort.

My uniform had not been changed for the two weeks the Unit had been on patrol, nor had I washed or shaved for that time. It was late evening and the steak, egg and chips served hot from the motel kitchen was a strong magnet. On the veranda, sitting on chairs round a big table, was a gathering of men and two women in bikinis. Suddenly the steak, which had been haunting me for days, was no longer all that important. The ladies were voluptuous; it turned out that they were physical training teachers from Australian high schools. Voluptuous is the only word that fits the two of them. A bit more curves and flesh than skinny women, with all women's assets in the right place and in ample, firm quantities.

There was a vacant chair at the table and upon sitting it became obvious that there had been lots of drinking going on. Australians hold their drink better than most, but the Rhodesian men at the table were from the bush and not normally hard drinkers. They were being unnaturally loud and behaving badly to the point of being obnoxious. My normal drink was vodka and Coke and Wendy across the table held her glass up to show me she drank the same, so I ordered for both of us.

'Come on, please, come and see the view from my room,' Jack said his face red with strain. 'Why won't you come look at the view?'

'My hunting camp is down on the river, you would like it there,' said Taff. 'Please come down river with me.'

And so it went for half an hour: clueless over-eager men, whose brains had been fried by a combination of abstaining a long time and then drinking; that and the straining bikinis. Meanwhile, the vodka and Coke warmed me, as it does after a long dryness, as Wendy looked questioningly at me across the table and the gabbling.

'Let's change the subject,' I cut in, loudly. 'What do you think of Yevtushenko's poem Babi Yar?' It was the only one that came to mind. It was a shot in the dark.

Wendy gave a squeal of delight. 'Do you know his work? Come let's go down to those chairs by the pool where we can talk about his poetry. Too noisy here.' She stood up and men's eyes popped out on stalks. Most Australians can hold their liquor and she certainly could and it was very much later when we staggered up the hill, arm in arm.

There were lions in the hills all round the motel. The males loudly proclaimed territorial rights early evening and again at dawn light; there were at least three resident prides. Lions hunt mainly at night. The grounds of the motel were infested with scavenging hyena. Hyena like easy pickings and the motel kitchen, waste bins and rubbish tip, in a deep nearby gulley, were hyena magnets. Often hyena scared the guests on the path from the main building to the rooms. It is not all that safe outside the rooms at night. Wendy's roommate was in the room, but she would not wait till another more suitable time and the lawn was good enough. If medals were given for upholding the honour of all males, gold should have been awarded that night. Not for the actual performance, but for the degree of difficulty that attended it. The danger as well as my rough and ripe state over-excited Wendy; and she probably mixed me, the lions and the hyena together in her imagination. It was a rather heroic hour; at least I thought so. It was my pale, bare buttocks which were exposed in the dark night as a target for the strongest jaws in the wild, an inviting target exposed while complying with the demands of an overexcited, strong woman.

A further patrol interrupted the affair and a game ranger from Mana Pools took Wendy and her friend down to his camp on the Zambezi River. It rained after they arrived at the camp and he told them the road was too muddy to use, so they were stuck there for a while. That was a lie I would not tolerate and went down to Chirundu and made use of the police patrol boat, telling the inspector a Support Unit informer down river had information on an incursion. The game ranger was strutting his stuff with a fishing rod from the jetty, with the tanned and voluptuous females on camp chairs behind him when I drifted the boat to the landing. His face would have made a famous picture if there had been a camera. Wendy squealed in delight and she and her friend flung their clothes and carry-all bag into the boat and waved him goodbye. There was a war on after all. The two followed me to Salisbury, but all too soon went on with their hiking tour of Central Africa.

The patrol that allowed the game ranger his chance had been to Lost Horizon Mine. That mine was a collection of thatched huts on top of a hill overlooking a wide sand-bed river. There were open seams on the ground where mica had been taken out. It was in the remote Chiwore Wilderness. Jack Finn, one of the last old time prospectors, had roamed the Zambezi Valley and environs long before anyone wanted to take any interest in the area. Till the

1950s, the area was open Crown land, hot and dry for most of the year and guarded by tsetse and mosquito, but in later years the valley became controlled and regulated. Jack spent many years, even after the government put in place rules, doing as he pleased. He opened and ran several small mines throughout the area, but always sold them soon after and moved on.

The Support Unit stick had moved into the abandoned mine huts and made them a base from which to wander about in the sea of mopani and baobab scrub, where many small sand-bed streams criss-crossed, streams that rose in the hills of the escarpment and carried water only in the rains. It took all day, grinding along a track in mostly low gear, four-wheel drive to get to the mine from Makuti and in the late afternoon I shot a young kudu bull drinking at a pool in the sand of the riverbed below the hill. The stick took all the water cans and went off to bring in the meat and fill the cans. A lot of meat was hung in the cooking hut, the one with a fire in the centre surrounded by rocks. The rest of the night was spent fighting a war with a raiding party of hyena. The end of the skirmishing came when, using the powerful lantern torch, the pack was looked over in the beam until the big matriarch was identified. After she dropped to a bullet from my FN rifle, her marauders slipped away in leaderless panic, and it was possible to get some sleep. It was then long past midnight.

The next morning the unit went off to patrol down one of the meandering riverbeds, the objective still being to look for signs of human beings crossing the river sands. The map showed permanent water at a bend in the river, and that was the point where water bottles would be refilled for the return. By 9am it was forty degrees in the shade and water was vital to life in these hot months. The sergeant and his four men were thirty meters ahead of me and my four men. Human beings long ago lost the ability to observe what would be obvious to wild animals. Near midday and nearing the promised water-hole, a spot was found where there were lion pug marks and recently passed urine still curled the sand. To an animal that was a clear boundary; to the thirsty human beings, only the water ahead mattered.

In Shona the word for lion is 'shumba', the word for water 'mvura'. The sergeant turned and shouted and was heard to be saying 'mvura', indicating that he had found the water-hole. A lioness was growling at the leading men and he had shouted 'shumba'. Yes, we know there is water, so go on, was the signal to him. The Support Unit men were absolutely iron disciplined; if the P/O said 'go on' they went on. The day-old cubs were hidden in the reeds on the bend and the lioness came out in fury at the blatant intrusion.

Her deep rumbling growl, which the rear men had not heard, changed to a yowling, hissing roar and her tail stood up like a poker. The front men turned and ran at my command; big mistake, as cats instinctively chase runners. My own half-section turned and joined the fleeing men. The lioness cantered along the bank, shoulder high and alongside us, checked and launched. Her target ducked and her talons hooked into his backpack, which was half shrugged, half torn off in an instant and the retreat speeded up. After a quick killing bite to the pack, she charged in earnest, paws thumping the ground as she galloped at full stretch. As her body came alongside and a metre away, I triggered the rifle, firing several shots blindly. One bullet cut her back leg sinew and she was reduced to a three-legged hop. When a gap had opened up between the rampaging lioness and the men, the order to fire was given and several scattered volleys ended it.

It was a jittery bunch of men who went back to the reed bed to look for the cubs, intending to take them to game rangers. A giant black-mane male stuck his head out of the reed bed and snarled, his fangs like carving knives. A detour up the river, back along and down some distance away eventually found the water. The four hours back to Lost Horizon were a subdued walk. Every man was concerned for the young cubs; their fate would not be pleasant but no-one wanted to tangle with the black-mane. No sign of terror gangs was found, that day or any of the rest of the patrol. That pristine wilderness endures to this day, albeit with fairly frequent incursions by licensed hunters. On those wonderful, wild days we were paid to do what modern safari guides charge clients stiff fees to copy. Yet then the only desire in all of us was to get back to Salisbury as fast as possible. Truly, youth is wasted on the young.

Another tour of duty with the Support Unit took us back to Makuti some months later. Over the years it was a patrol base on many occasions and then a home station. My service with the Police Anti-Terrorist Unit spanned nearly all fifteen-odd years of service and as the tempo of incursions from Zambia grew, Makuti was often the base from where PATU went out into the valley hunting the gangs. It was a beautiful and wild place and even today when on fishing trips to the Zambezi and Kariba, it is found not to have changed much. There are signs of more settlement, a consequence of winning the war on the tsetse fly and the chamber on the road has gone, but the police station has not changed. The Indian-run general dealer still stands forlornly on a hill between the police camp and the motel. There is still the petrol station at the turn-off to Kariba and probably the hyena and baboon that plagued the camp forty years ago are still doing so today.

When the Support Unit was back in Salisbury and the black troops were at home in their Police Depot housing, the white members had very little to do. The only formal duty for the home troop was Government House guard and the troop sergeant handled that. There was an office next to the drill square and it was manned by the commanding officer, a superintendent who was assisted by an inspector. What they did was a mystery. The only time they were called on was to sit at hearings, where the rumbustious men were charged with drunkenness or assault, usually both. The white members did not do the couple of hours foot drill each morning, but did do the early morning, before breakfast run at the head of the troop. The afternoons were filled by map-reading compass marches in the bush near town or on the shooting range. The commanding officers took part in none of those activities.

Another of the duties assigned to the Unit was riot standby in Bulawayo, the country's second city; that was a tour of three months duration. Since 1960 and the rise of nationalism, there had been orchestrated rioting at various times in Bulawayo and when rioting was widespread, the local police needed reinforcements. It was a popular duty as there was seldom reason for a call-out as it was not often that a riot reached the level where a couple of police officers with tear gas launchers could not cope. The troop travelled by train overnight and arrived at the Bulawayo main police camp bleary-eyed and hung-over from spending most of the night in the dining car pub. The inevitable counting of stores took place at a snail's pace. After that duty there was no official task except to be ready for an unlikely call-out. The troop commander had the job of keeping his men in top physical shape.

Bulawayo in the mid-sixties had many fine bars and nightclubs. For some reason, women were the standard barkeeps in the city, most of them attractive. The troop commander was a section officer known as Uncle Reg, a mild man with a quiet hesitant manner. The patrol officers were Brother Bruce, a maniacal toper and raconteur who has remained a friend over the last fifty years, Brother Doug who later joined the Selous Scouts, and a nugget of a man, Brother Ken, devastatingly handsome and fair haired, and me, Brother Ivan. Uncle Reg and Bro Bruce were heavy drinkers who were in the end ruined by the demon drink, as so many colonials were. Bro Bruce is a lifelong alcoholic, and has fought the demon all his life, in those distant days their dependence was not yet apparent.

So the nights went by in congenial company and in atmospheric bars where, for instance, the bar lady tore telephone directories in half at request and wore rabbit fur shoes. If she liked you she would invite you to lie face down on the carpet and walk on your back massaging it with the soft fur on her feet. The five of us would shower and change into civilian clothes at about 6pm and head for the nightlife in a Land Rover. In the early hours, a return was made to the camp and bed, usually to the accompaniment of raucous singing. Bro Bruce was left behind one night and drove himself home in a borrowed fire engine. It was returned to extremely annoyed firemen the next day with apologies. Another night, while on the way into town, a frantic man waved down the Land Rover and stuck his head in the driver window, reporting his car stolen and just then vanishing down the avenue. Uncle Reg told him to call the police, slid the window closed and drove off.

Without the physical exercise, the way of life could have been very damaging to health. With no formal duties, a training roster was made and posted on the board. At dawn, a couple of kilometres were run as a troop, white members leading the three ranks with drill later in the morning and an hour or so of first-aid lectures or law instruction to the other ranks, followed by a route march or sport to fill the afternoon. One favourite sport was 'murder ball', probably invented by the Unit and certainly only played by them. Similar to football and played with that ball and goals, it differed in that the ball was carried to the opponent's goal in any manner desired. The only other rule was that no biting, eye-gouging or kicking in the gonads was permitted.

The troop sergeant, as the senior, longest-serving man, was always the selector and referee. It was stick versus stick and there were only two field positions, the goalkeeper and the rest. The white stick leaders were always nominated for the keeper's job. That way the troop could take revenge on the bwana for sins in the past. The ball was thrown into the middle of the field and with a battle cry the ranks clashed and old scores were evened with boot and fist, and the howling mob scrummed towards the goal. There the ball was forgotten and with screams of glee, the bwana was assailed by the men of both sides. A wise stick leader learnt to search for the ball in the melee, ignoring the bumps and slaps, and carry it into his own goal. That way the troop sergeant had to curb his mirth and blow the whistle for a goal. Uncle Reg, who never took part, eventually would take mercy on the rest of us and tell the sergeant to blow the final whistle.

The early morning run in boots and long trousers went out the main camp gates and round several city blocks of light industry that side of town. There was a very big native township also that side of town and each morning there were many workers on the roads, some on bicycles but many walking. The sight of a body of policemen running called for ribald and crude comments from the workers. They could not be blamed for not being able to distinguish between normal police and the roughneck Support Unit members: the black-boots. The Unit wore black boots as opposed to the brown ones of normal policemen. The Unit men were not the sort to take insults lightly, and naturally the name-calling gained momentum when some reaction was seen.

Uncle Reg had a good idea what would happen, but gave permission anyway. The troop sergeant had suggested that it was good training if, on the morning run, the riot shields and batons were carried. The shields were aluminium, a metre round with padding inside for the arm in the carry loops. The edges were sharpened, a special Unit trick. The batons were hard-wood pick-axe handles. The troop, carrying the shields and batons, wheeled out the gate and the sergeant started a song to keep rhythm with; a war cry relished and loudly sung. A section of workers, confident that previous shouted insults would cause no retaliation made a mistake of repeating them that day.

Without waiting for permission, the troop sergeant ordered the troop to disperse the crowd. The crowd, far and near, guilty or not, were dispersed with gusto and energy. By the time Uncle Reg and the rest of us shouted orders to reform, the road ahead and behind for a long way was littered with shoes, hats, bicycles and an assortment of other stuff. In each direction, the distant reaches of the road were crowded with hard-running workers trying to put distance between themselves and the now beaming Unit members. The troop formed up and went on, the marching chant now deep and happy. For the rest of the duty tour, the morning run was given a wide, open road and respectful silence.

As variation, the entire troop went off to the Matopo Hills. They are a vast area of granite-outcrop mountains and hills, a place always held as sacred by the Matabele, where tribal leaders had been interred in secret caves and where oracles lived. Rhodes and Coghlan are also buried high on granite massifs there, and a stone cairn nearby marks the final resting place of Major Allen Wilson and his patrol, who were all annihilated by the Matabele near the Shangani River. They fought to the last man. The British always thought highly of soldiers who fought to the death. Is it not better to make sure the others die for their country? The hills are a great big mysterious and wonderful wild place, and the troop strolled along from the green foot-hills on up into the great rocky places and then down again to the gentle farm lands where the thorn acacia bush grows interspersed with tufts of scrubby grass: ideal cattle and game country.

A night was spent at the top of the massive granite mountains and the rock world spread to the horizon in all directions, a grey sea under the cobalt vault of the sun. The ponchos were pegged on each corner to form small tents and sleeping bags rolled out. The native troops' ration-packs were also used by the white officers and dinner, eaten under a rose-red, green and gold sunset, was stiff mealie-meal porridge called 'sadza' in Shona, and a relish of bully beef and mixed tinned vegetables, coffee and hard biscuits. The white's ration pack differed in having rice in place of the maize meal. We preferred the maize meal as it was more filling. The walk that day had been up high mountains and the fire died down early and the men went to ground. In the night, the peak became the home of Thor, the god of thunder. A tropical storm blew in with the sudden wind and lightening repeatedly slammed the peak we had chosen. The rock must have been laced with iron or another conductor. Deafening and blinding strikes smashed and caused tremors in the very rocks under the troop. Nothing was ever as loud or as frightening in the raw power of it all; grenades or gunfire mere tinkles in comparison. And then a rage of falling rain, blown away as fast as it came, leaving the men calling out to each other in small relieved voices. It was well that everyone was too frightened to move, standing up would have made a person into a good conductor rod.

The soft buttery sun the next morning saw the troop winding down from the granite heights, past sweet-smelling dams and herds of cattle. Red streams of impala flowed, arching away through the thorn trees just higher than a man's head. It was in this area that the strife between the Matabele, then the rulers of all the land, and white men lately come and covetous of what they saw, began. There we were, a troop of forty paramilitary police, the native members hard and fit and fiercely loyal to the white commanders and the police force, practising for the new war that had been going on at low intensity for a couple of years. Earlier that year, a gang of insurgents ripped through the province, killing several headmen in the tribal areas and two government agricultural advisors. The BSA Police PATU sticks deployed, caught up with them while the Support Unit was making ready to join the hunt from Bulawayo, and accounted for them all. The natives were again fighting the natives, each sure of the righteousness of the cause. Not for a second was there ever reason to doubt the members of the Support Unit, who were very sure of the righteousness of what they were fighting for.

A stint back in Salisbury Depot, the Unit headquarters, was quickly followed by a tour of duty at Villa Salazar. There were then two main nationalist factions in Rhodesia: the Zimbabwe Africa Peoples Union, ZAPU, and the Zimbabwe African National Union, ZANU. Both laid claim to being the voice of the people. That split was between the Matabele and the Shona, and it was one that endures to this day. Before Rhodes, the Shona were regarded by the Matabele as their private property. Impis sent out by Lobengula raided far and wide and Shona men were killed, the women taken as breeding stock and the younger children assimilated into the Matabele Tribe. Rhodes and his Company rescued the Shona and others from the vassal state. Now the Support Unit was opposing both sides of that ancient divide, a return to the days when the Shona were slaves and the Matabele ruled by bloodletting could not be allowed. The Unit's task was clearly to prevent that and the black members were adamant about that. Near the hamlet of Villa Salazar, a restriction camp had been put up for the more active members of ZAPU. They were restricted and held without trial under the emergency measures the armed insurgency had made necessary.

That small hamlet was sited on the border of Mozambique, where the railway line to Lourenço Marques crossed. My first visit to it had been as a schoolboy in about 1956, when a friend who had joined the Customs Department had been posted there. There were, back then, three small houses in a clearing in the ocean of mopani scrub interspersed with dark green, massive evergreen trees and baobabs. The houses had tin roofs and stood in an unfenced, cleared area of white sand. There was a boom on the sand track that crossed the border, but it was never manned. The Portuguese side was a small railway village of some twenty houses. There was an ornate cathedral-like railway station and a motel. The only access road ran along the railway and was once used by fisherman going to a big dam just across the border but it is doubtful that there were ever more than a dozen cars a year on it.

That school days trip was made at the time before the hand of government extended to the distant bush places. The Chefe do Posto, the government head of that part of Mozambique, was a drunken sot who spent his time shooting any wild animal that crossed his path. He gave me permission to shoot a bull elephant and he introduced the local ivory poacher as a buyer. They were sworn enemies, but both saw a profit in the transaction. The poacher was a giant with a pot belly who lived in a native style village of huts on the edge of Malvernia, as the Portuguese railway village was called. The settlements were named after premiers of the respective countries at the time the railway went through. Lord Malvern was the Rhodesian head and General Salazar the Portuguese one. The elephant hunt was carried out alone and bare footed, and that bull is etched in the memory banks. The tusks bought me a fortune of ten pounds, about a tenth of what they were worth, but more money than I had ever seen before. That hunt was one that marked the end of an era. It was probably the last time a free-ranging elephant was hunted with official permission and at no cost. It was an apex hunt for me in that it was done alone with no food or water reserves and with only a native axe as a knife. There are no longer any places where such a hunt could be done. I hunted other elephant in later years, but they were on licence and under strict regulation.

Salazar was another place in Rhodesia that was remote and wild and beautiful, a place where the African sky heated a vast, dry forest; a place where game trails wound through the trees to secret pans that only elephant knew held water all year. It was a place where a man would wander to his death from thirst and starvation as surely as in any sand desert, a good place to put men who needed to be isolated from society.

The road from the South African border runs north to the town of Fort Victoria. About half way along that road, near Nuanetsi, the railway line running to the coast in the east crosses the road at Rutenga. That railway runs straight and level through the sandy mopani veldt. There were almost no bends and virtually no inclines. At night, the headlight of a train heading towards Salazar can be seen three hours before it arrives at the border. Just before the border there is an airfield in the mopani sea at a spot called Bole. There, an air sock flew near a tin shed. The airfield staff total was one Shangaan with a wheel-barrow, pick and shovel and apart from filling in ant bear holes he was required to clear the runway of impala, buffalo and other impediments before an aircraft came in to land.

The troop boarded a Dakota at New Serum, on the military side of the airport. Once on board, the majority of the black members took blankets out of their packs and once seated, covered their heads. Some of the men who had done parachute courses and had their wings loudly jeered the scared men. The runway was long and the take-off smooth, but the summer air made the flight bumpy and many of the covered men gave shouts of alarm. The runway at Bole was short and not smooth. The Dakota bounced back into the air twice before finally making solid contact with the ground and then braked sharply so the tail section lifted high before dropping. It was nice to leave the plane and step onto solid ground. The wild aromatic smell of the veldt filled the senses as the terrible noon sun beat down. The tour at Salazar lasted six weeks.

The outgoing troop drove the transport that met us at the airstrip; a quick handover and equipment check and then they were in turn driven to the waiting Dakota. As the silver plane wallowed up into the sky herds of buck, mainly impala wandered out of the trees and went back to grazing the grass on the strip. The Shangaan waved as he stored his barrow for another month or two. The hamlet of Salazar had changed since my first visit; that was clear as it came in sight. There was a prefabricated police mess, a fairly large house of slatted sides and tin roof. There was a large collection of rondavels made of tin, with glassed windows, scattered over a large clearing. The huts were used as offices, storerooms and clinic. There was a large one with a second tin story on the roof which housed a cooling plant and it was insulated for use as a cold room. The Customs and Immigration houses were still there and near them stood a brick house for the animal health inspector. Three more brick houses stood a little way off from the old government ones, houses for the small Rhodesian Railways staff. Most of the railway staff lived over the border.

The camp housing the restricted nationalists had first been built next to the police camp. That too was a collection of tin rondavels, living huts, cooking huts and bath huts. There was a large oval pole and grass construction with several rooms that had been built for the ZAPU leader, Nkomo. As the incursions intensified, the nationalists were moved further from the railway line and village. A barrack-like camp was built in the mopani sea about three kilometres away. There were a dozen long tin buildings with cement floors, a water tower and smaller tin huts for kitchens and toilets. The barrack clearing had a single roll of barbed-wire round it, knee high, in which there was a simple garden type gate. Outside that fence stood three tents for the use of the Support Unit members tasked with guarding the camp. At any given time any inmate could step over the wire and walk away without much trouble. The remote tree fastness was the gaoler. Then again, apart from being removed from contact with the general population the detainees had a normal life, probably a better life than the average tribesman as they had three meals a day, hot water and dry and secure housing. They were allowed to arrange their own activities.

The guarding of the barracks required one Support Unit stick; a white officer, sergeant and eight men. It was arranged that the duty would fall to one section for a week. The rest of the troop back at the police camp did nothing. The old restriction camp huts next to the police camp were taken on as base for the troop. The Nkomo building was the P/O and S/O's bedrooms and a bar counter was built of empty glass beer bottles. Having to work only one week of the month meant that there was plenty of time to savour the European culture of the Portuguese village across the border. The social life there revolved round the railway station, the motel where imported wine and beer was served and the 'Cockroach Club'. That was the railway club, a big barn of a building with a stage at one end, a long bar counter at the other and tables and chairs in-between that were moved to form a dance floor. The liquor bottles behind the bar got the place its name. Each time a bottle was lifted from the shelf, roaches scattered. The railways subsidised the food and drinks and the Rhodesians were granted honorary membership.

At the fenced barracks, one of the three tents was for the section commander, the rest slept on stretchers in the other two tents, four to a tent. There was a chair, table and stretcher in the commander's tent, and a paraffin lantern, which when full and turned down low burnt through the night. As there was an assortment of wildlife in the vicinity, it was wise to have a light in the tent. On the ground were snakes and scorpions, hyena, lynx and honey badgers. Leopard, lions and elephant wondered by in the night. One man sat on a stool at the gate next to the tents, awake day and night and he too had a lantern and a loaded gun to keep him safe. The inmates closed the doors and windows of their tin buildings at nightfall.

There were some chickens belonging to the inmates and they were cooped at sunset. In the day they roamed the barracks and often scratched and clucked to the tented Unit clearing. The stick commander's tent was behind the others and not so visible from the other side of the wire. A permanent whip trap was set up just inside the tent flaps, baited with maize. At least twice a week chicken was on the menu; the restrictees blamed the wild cats or badgers. There was a fairly extensive flock at the barracks which supplied eggs and was fed on mealie meal porridge left over from inmate meals. That small diversion aside, the days on guard duty were slow and long.

At regular intervals the inmates gathered near the guards' tents and shouted insults at the Support Unit members. It was a ritual and the Unit members gave as good as they got. As with all insults, some barbs went deep and caused resentment. The camps food supplies for the hundred-odd men came by train weekly and large quantities of meat were kept in the cold room at the police camp. A daily delivery of supplies was made by the regular police to the restriction camp. Any sick men were taken to the clinic where a trained male nurse dispensed medicines. The restrictees obviously were as bored with the situation as we were. Almost each meat delivery provoked protest; it was an excuse to needle the police. The supply was too little or the meat was off. A minor riot began inside the wire. Stones were thrown onto the barracks roofs; stones were thrown carelessly so that some targeted the Support Unit guards. Without waiting for orders the duty sergeant formed a wedge armed with pick-handles and shields and the men galloped into the small riot. The revenge was taken on some of those whose insults had struck home, and the clinic nurse was busy for a while. All was quiet until the next round of insults and riots: so do bored men amuse themselves.

The long slow days left scope for heavy drinking. The police mess had a small bar counter and beer was delivered on the down train. A record book was kept at the mess bar of beers consumed and payment was on pay days. The police bar was in business from 5pm till late. On its own it was not too much. The problem was that the Portuguese did not keep any specific bar hours. The railway club only opened in the evenings as the barmen were volunteers. The motel served food and drink on demand. The main problem was the massive, marble-counter bar at the Gothic railway station. Chico's Bar was run by the owner and his wife on an all-day and all-night rotation. The locals sat at night playing dominoes and sipping wine or liquors, aghast at the antics of the Rhodesians who treated each visit to Chico's as a holiday to an exotic country. Many of the police drank beer at their own bar in the evenings and then crossed the border to have peri-peri chicken dinner and drink strange wines and liquors into the early hours.

Uncle Reg went to bed each night with a six-pack of dumpy beers. During the night he quenched his thirst with four of them. On waking, he smoked a couple of cigarettes and then drank two beers slowly before getting out of bed to shower. Then he wondered about for a while in the sun before announcing that he had to go to the shops across the border for eggs, potatoes or something else. By 10am he was sitting in Chico's and he slowly and steadily drank beer till 4.30pm when the police bar saw him until later when he again crossed back to drink more. After midnight he took his six-pack home to bed. Some years later he was discharged on 'medical grounds'.

Bro Bruce drank his entire salary 'on tick', but still managed to cross the border and drink at others' expense. He was a charming and witty raconteur and most did not mind paying for him. One afternoon, he drove the Unit Land Rover back overland. It appeared at the edge of camp through the trees and crashed up a steep red anthill till it tipped over the top and stuck with all four wheels off the ground. The door opened and Bro Bruce fell out and crawled, owl-eyed to the house and sprawled face down and asleep on the floor of his room.

Bro Bruce took to running with me each afternoon and afterwards cutting wood for exercise; a habit that he fell into and used to keep fit for all his life and which probably keeps him alive. He fought alcoholism all his life and became a magistrate on leaving the police, but he took to taking vodka to the bench in the water carafe and later worked at the Cape Town city security department in between spells of rehab. He now lives in Scotland with his long-suffering wife who is an Anglican priest. She was one of the nurses of the B-car days and later became a teacher. He recently broke into the church vestry and stole the communion wine.

The main social event of the two settlements was the twice-weekly train to the coast. The train was a mixed goods and passenger one and the camp rations came down from District Headquarters on it. The Portuguese garrison troops turned out in numbers. Long before the arrival of the train they strutted along the railway platform, preening and using the station windows as mirrors to comb and oil their hair. When the train came in they walked up and down till female passengers were seen and then they gathered outside that compartment in numbers, leering. At the same time as leering, they tried to pretend they were just casually glancing. These garrison men did not see females of their own kind for years and it showed.

The restriction camp rations needed two seven-ton trucks to carry them from the railway station. With the detainees and police all counted, there were about two hundred men and the meat ration alone was one pound a day per man. The big freezer room was stacked full. Also hanging in the cold room were usually three or four small antelope, as each night the police went out and hunted along the track next to the railway line. There was never enough meat for the police officers. The train also returned from the coast with prawns in fifty kilogram frozen packs. The railway catering staff bought them at two shillings a pound at the coast. A prawn feast, with demijohns of cheap red wine, took place in the police mess once a week and the two pet baboons and the camp dogs joined in. The down train also brought the mail and letters from home.

In good weather, the train coming down could be seen from three hours out, the headlight like a search light low in the evening sky. The track was straight and level for some hundred kilometres. A driver was nominated and a group of policemen piled into a truck and headed up the line to join the train. The nominated driver donned reflective traffic sleeves and far up the track stood on the railway line and signalled the train driver to stop. The drivers played along and soon the policemen were ensconced in the dining room, lining the bar and socializing with passengers. One jovial Irish driver often came back from the engine to drink with us; the railway line was straight and level, but one night the engine hit an elephant when the driver was in the bar. Luckily it was not derailed. Train engine one, elephant nil.

There was a senior inspector in charge of traffic in Bulawayo. The Highway Patrol Jaguars and their drivers fell under his command. His nickname was Piggy. As a sideline he produced pickled boiled eggs and onions in five litre glass jars and sold his produce to police bars. The Highway Patrol roamed far and wide over Matabeleland and Midlands checking on traffic offenders on the roads. The motto was 'Piggy's pickles are delivered countrywide by uniform drivers'. The Vila Salazar police bar had an ample supply of both eggs and onions.

One hard night saw me overeating the pickles with beer and then crossing the border to continue the binge on cheap red wine and anise liquor followed by peri-peri chicken. In the early hours, we all fell on our beds in the old Nkomo hut. A few hours later saw me standing outside the huts barking long and loudly at the ants. An acidic mess spewed over the straggling lawn. In the days and nights that followed, the solids were scavenged by small creatures, but the liquid soaked the ground. The scraggy grass yellowed and died and a bare earth patch marked the spot. A decade later the site was revisited.

The flight back to Salisbury was again bumpy. It was a relief to say goodbye to Salazar. Usually the wild places were what I enjoyed, but the fleshpots were calling. A spell of malaria had put me in hospital in Fort Victoria, and the excess drinking and late nights with other men had paled. It was a rough place to be stationed. It was a wild frontier place but not a place to live for long unless you were suited to being chaste. Shortly after getting back to Salisbury the stint with the Unit ended. In later years when the war intensified, the Unit became a military battalion and postings of white officers were voluntary and permanent. In my time, it was hard playing and even harder work, and although we chased and hunted hard, not one contact with the enemy gangs, then beginning to arrive in larger numbers, was made. The months served at Salazar with the Unit were the last as a black-boot and normal duties resumed;

but Salazar beckoned again in the future.

My career as a district policeman really started with my posting to the Salisbury Rural command. Police work is mainly about catching and convicting criminals. It was a thousand things beside that in the BSAP, but investigating crimes and convicting those committing them is the kernel of police work. Norton, a small rural village fifty kilometres out of Salisbury, was the first district station. It is in the middle of rich farming areas and many of the farms are irrigated by the Hunyani River and the nearby Lake MacIllwain. The wall of the lake is built in a narrow gorge in the Hunyani hills and downstream from the wall on the side of the hill under shady, thickly grown msasa trees are the remains of the Norton family homestead. Norton was a wealthy Englishman, who toured the area before the Pioneers and came up just after them to settle. He was granted thousands of acres to farm in the 1890s and he brought his family out from England with nurses and retainers; one a Texan cowboy employed to do bee-keeping. At the start of the first Shona rebellion, Norton and all of them were killed. Most were murdered by blacks with blows to the head with knobkerries while distracted and talking to someone else. The Texan and a nurse fought a battle against overwhelming odds. They were trapped in a bedroom, surrounded by gunmen but fought to the last round with a revolver each. The village was named after the Norton family.

Norton was a by-passed village. Once the main Salisbury to Bulawayo road had run through the small village, but a new road was built and the narrow strip of tar that was now the old road was used only by farmers. It ran along one side of the police station. The station was almost identical to all the other small police stations in rural districts of Rhodesia. It comprised a brick under tin roof single quarters building with a gauzed-in veranda, built in about 1930; a more modern house used by the station commander, an old English gentleman, and family. Then there was a collection of smaller brick buildings in a row on one side of the complex for native members. There was a long, low building under blue gum trees that was the charge office, a large room with a counter was at one end, and down a corridor on each side were offices, each with a desk and filing cabinet for the white staff. There was a lock-up inside a high fence, several cells with barred windows and doors where prisoners were kept. On the smaller stations, the police lock-up cells also served as a jail where minor offenders served their sentence. The cells were fenced and next to the cells were storerooms and an African police recreation room. That was a room with tables and chairs where tea breaks were taken.

The inspector raised and sold ducks as a sideline. There was vacant land over the fence from the single quarters and he used bandits from the lock-up to cultivate it and plant maize. In dry spells the several acres of maize was watered by a hose from a single quarters tap. Once the maize was mature it was harvested by the same convict labour and then friendly farmers husked the cobs and crushed the maize with machines. The crushed maize was fed to his young ducklings till they became eatable size. The ducks were then hawked to neighbours. The flock of ducks numbered about fifty birds and wandered all over camp in a solid mass scavenging for food, mainly snails and the like in the flower beds. They left behind a trail of duck manure, sticky and smelly.

At Norton and many other remote stations a magistrate arrived at regular intervals on a circuit to hear cases not sent to higher courts. Any suitable room was turned into a court for the day. The tea room at Norton was re-arranged for the court sitting, the best table reserved as the bench. The magistrate travelled with an interpreter, a native versed in most of the dialects of the land and who also acted as a clerk of court. The local public prosecutor was selected from one of the station policemen. The inspector handed the job of prosecuting over to me. Before leaving me to my own devices he let me sit in on one court session. That was nearly the first time the inside of a court or the workings of a court had been experienced. The district courts dealt with a wide variety of cases, except murder; the learning curve was steep. The law lectures in Depot had long been forgotten. I was pushed in at the deep end and left to swim or sink.

The first session was a case in point. But, like learning to swim, being thrown in at the deep end gets fast results.

'We are waiting Mr Prosecutor,' said the magistrate expectantly. 'You may begin.'

'You must call the first case,' the interpreter said as an aside. 'Shall I?'

'Please do.'

The accused was sent in from outside by the constable on court orderly duty. The interpreter indicated he must stand on the right side of the room behind a desk there. They all looked at the prosecutor.

'This would be the time to read the indictment and pass a copy to the bench', said the magistrate.

'Yes your worship.' Indictment? What was that? The charge sheet? Three copies were taken from the docket and two handed to the interpreter, who passed one on to the bench.

'May I put the charge?' The interpreter asked and went on to do so without waiting for an answer.

'Now he has pleaded not guilty, Mr Prosecutor, please make your case'. A long pause. 'Call your witnesses, Mr Prosecutor, and have them give evidence.'

It was a long day. At three when the court adjourned, we played a long set of squash and the magistrate assured me that it had not been too badly done and it would get easier. It did. But that red-faced day remains in memory. The sight of desks and chairs and the smell of furniture and floor polish always bring back the feeling of being a novice.

Being fingered as the prosecutor early on meant that every district station commander from then on designated me as station prosecutor. It was not a popular job as it was extra to normal police duties. For the rest of my service, dockets ready for the court ended up on my desk. In the end it was satisfying to be able to successfully argue the case against defence lawyers and see the magistrate struggle not to smile when a winning point was made. Most lawyers are not as versed in criminal law as police prosecutors are; they have less practise. They deal with a range of other civil law, while police and civilian public prosecutors in the lower courts deal only with criminal law. Normally a law degree is needed to be a public prosecutor, but the police members were placed in a special class. After leaving the police, my experience of those district courts enabled me to find employment as a full time prosecutor appointed by the attorney general by special exemption. It started in the tea room at Norton.

The public prosecutor at Norton was also appointed the official jail keeper. That made him officially responsible for the bandits' welfare and rations. However all matters relating to the prison and prisoners were already taken care of by other police as part of their routine duty, so it was merely a formality. With the appointment to jailer came the automatic designation as executioner. In those far off days, sentences could include the old English tradition of lashes. In cases where violence had been used and in minor cases involving juveniles who could not be jailed, up to twelve cuts with a heavy or light cane could be the total sentence or added to the sentence. The various hats worn led to not-so-perfect justice.

A sixteen-year-old boy, the son of a farm worker, had tried to steal from a house and had been disturbed by the housewife, stabbing her in the arm upon escaping. The investigation and docket was done by me as a police officer, the boy traced and arrested. He was released to his parent's custody and the docket was prepared for court. The police officer passed the docket to the prosecutor who summonsed the witnesses; one of those was the officer who recorded the confession. The prosecutor duly began the case in front of the circuit magistrate, and then called the policeman who crossed the room to the desk used as the witness stand. The officer gave evidence without interruption or being questioned and then returned to the prosecutor's desk. The case was concluded and the boy sentenced to six lashes with the light cane. After court ended, the jailer opened the store where the cane was stored and had the boy tied to the triangle with his hands over his head and kidneys protected. Then the executor administered the six cuts. At the end of the busy day my head was spinning.

# 3
# Feeling it out

Lake MacIllwain was a large body of water and during the teen years was an oft-visited fishing spot. An idyllic day on the water in a small rowing boat ended with a wood fire and fish on green sticks grilled before the two-hour cycle back home. The lake was about five kilometres long and a couple wide, and the shores heavily wooded with mature big trees. There were several boating and sailing clubs, and a handful of eating places. A large game park claimed an area of one bank. There were rhino and lions there. The National Park camp supplied thatch rondavels as in all the park land in the country; cheap and clean. The shores had prolific birdlife and the water made for good fishing. The Hunyani was one of the rivers with tiger fish. It had been a choice playground of childhood, two hours hard cycling from Salisbury. While stationed at Norton, the police often made use of one of the hotel resorts along the shore for a night out and dinner. All the spots along the shore held memories from schooldays.

Single quarters living was sometimes uninteresting. The mess was run almost as a commercial boarding house. A set of mess accounts was kept and checked monthly by a senior officer. The messing costs included food, groceries such as polish and soap, and the wages for a cook. The cook looked after meals and kept the communal areas such as the sitting room clean. Each officer also employed a personal servant, a batman, to do his washing and ironing and tidy his room. The batman was paid by the person he worked for. The share of the costs to be allocated to each mess member was worked out on the number of meals he was present for.

Breakfast was normally what is called a full English breakfast; sausage, bacon, kidney, liver, eggs, tomato and toast. In season at Norton, the park game rangers donated crates of mushrooms they picked in the game park one side of the lake to stop tourists getting out of cars to do so. The mushrooms were dinner plate size and then each meal had a pot of chopped mushroom in sauce added. Lunch was steak and vegetables, dinner a meat roast with potatoes and vegetables. That was the usual menu and varied little. In the 1960s, a meal worked out at two shillings at the most, so the monthly messing charge was about ten pounds. Rhodesians lived well.

At Norton, the wire gauzed-in veranda held a darts board and some easy chairs. Each afternoon at 4.30pm, after office hours, all the officers gathered to play darts and drink beer. This was a ritual repeated at most police messes all over the country. At Norton the dart games went on for hours, usually until the inspector's wife stuck her head in the door and summoned him to dinner. So it was a nice break from the mess to go off occasionally to a lakeside hotel for a night out to break the monotony of single quarters living.

Road accidents were one of the most frequent events needing the Norton police attention and there were no traffic police. People travelling a long distance to a big town tend to get careless near the town. Conversely, when leaving a big city and the dense traffic there, the car drivers stop concentrating as they reach open road. Both attitudes cause accidents outside big cities. The first fatal accident I attended in my police career was one in which the two cars met head-on in the main road to Bulawayo just outside the village. There was a family; a man, his wife and two teenage daughters in the one car. The impact jammed the doors of the family car and it ignited in a burst petrol tank fireball. The family were incinerated to human-shape cinders. A docket had to be prepared with detailed photographs and maps. The police investigation had to discover how the accident happened and who was at fault. Again, it was a steep learning curve staying objective while viewing the horror scene close up. By the time my tour of duty was up at Salisbury Rural, maybe a hundred serious accidents had been investigated, perhaps twenty of them fatal. The enforced learning led eventually to a magistrate's commendation in two separate cases. Man learns fast when he has to.

The accidents were only a small part of the duties. There was normal crime to deal with; some housebreakings, a lot of petty theft, drunken assaults and so on. In the farming area there was always stock theft, and that meant tracking on foot over long distances following the trail to recover the stock. Another regular duty on all stations was patrolling the entire police area at regular intervals. On a rural station that usually meant the P/O and a constable on a Matchless motorcycle visiting all the farms and stores in the area and talking to everyone. Sometimes it meant working out of a tented camp where fuel for the bike and food was dropped by the station Land Rover. All farm dogs hate motorbikes and a wise patrol officer bought a stock of balloons. Two or three were blown up before approaching the farmyard and handed to the constable on the pillion. The attacking dog was given a balloon to chew on and the explosion usually induced a tail-between-legs flight.

One of the Norton farmers was a young and very rich man; inherited money. His farmhouse was the centre of almost continual partying. The billiard room was vast with two full size tables and during the day that was where the guests gathered. At night the baronial dining room was full. He rallied off-road vehicles and ran a Renault Rally Team, often winning. One year he entered a Porsche in the off-road Total Rally. When that particular farm was visited on patrol, a waiter met the officer at the door with a tray of drinks and instructions that only draining a glass allowed entry. It was accepted that the visiting police would stay over-night, no matter what time the arrival. The car keys of all visitors had to be surrendered and were locked away till the next day. The parties were such as only the really wealthy can throw.

Having spent the Saturday night in revelry, a house servant arrived at dawn with a tray of tea and biscuits and instructions that everyone was required on the front veranda in half an hour. The guests met there and found waiting on the lawn two tractors, each towing two open trailers each and each trailer was loaded with six or so arm-chairs. Tin baths full of beer and champagne on ice stood near the chairs. Once guests were seated, shotguns and boxes of ammunition were distributed and the wagons were towed off down a farm track and along to old maize fields. Guinea fowl and francolin were put up at regular intervals and shot. Two farm workers rode on the tailgate and trotted off at intervals to collect the bag. The cavalcade returned before lunch; my police duties called and so the feast of wild fowl was missed.

The wild times always ask for payment. One weekend party was attended by racing and rally friends and the young bachelor and three others took off in his light plane from the strip behind the house to go and 'shoot up' more guests who were just then driving out from Salisbury to join the house party. The main electricity pylons to Salisbury ran along the Hunyani Hills. Each side of the Hunyani River, horizon to horizon, were green irrigated fields. The road cut through the fields parallel to the hills. The light plane dived on the car, swooping low over the road and peeling off to climb and turn and come back. The wing clipped the high-voltage cables and all on board died. Sometimes it is better to have lived well than have lived long.

Early on another bright morning a man walked up the corridor to the offices, passing the charge office counter. He came to my open door and knocked. 'Sorry to disturb you. Do you perhaps have a couple of plasters and some aspirin for me?'

'The first aid kit in the charge office should have that,' I said and stood up squinting at the man outlined by bright sun in the doorway. Then I saw dried streaks of blood down each side of his face on the cheeks. 'What happened to you?'

'Shot myself; last night next to the road in my car.' He laughed harshly. 'Can't even get that fucking right.'

'Shot yourself through the head? On purpose?'

'Yes. Wanted to die but can't fucking do it right.'

'You had better get to a doctor. Sit, I'll call one.' Having learnt from the hanged man at Marlborough the urge to suggest he try again was swallowed.

'Nay. Just a bit of a headache. Got some aspirin, please?'

The other officers had gathered and gawked. Arrangements were made to have relatives come fetch him and the car and he was taken away. The revolver in question was a Webley .38 calibre firing a metal jacketed military round. It made a neat hole each side of the temple and seemed to have damaged nothing. Only a small streak of blood each side. Suicide was not illegal and so no further action was needed. Since that incident it was hard to trust the efficiency of a Webley .38, which also happened to be standard issue to the police and other military units at the time.

Then one summer morning the fatherly inspector called me into his office. 'As you are well qualified, you have been nominated for the Police Anti-Terrorist Unit. Outdoor work should be enjoyable. Wish it was me. You are lucky to get the task. You are to report to Police Depot...'

There, in the beige painted office smelling of floor polish, is where the over twelve years' service in PATU began and it finished at the other end of the country, near the southern border in 1977.

The author. (© Ivan Smith)

Bruce Allen seen on a motorcycle in Matobo. (© Bruce Allen)

Dick Cotton – Villa Salazar 1968–70. (© Ted Ayers-Hunt)

(Left) Louis Fourie, (right) Chris Phillips – Villa Salazar
Support Unit camp 1968–9. (© Ted Ayers-Hunt)

Bruce Allen poses for the camera with his FN FAL –Support Unit, Makuti. (© Bruce Allen)

Elephant at a water hole behind the Chirundu police station. (© Bob Belder)

Elephant on shore – Lake Kariba. (© Ted Ayers-Hunt)

Land Rover modified to be an anti-mine vehicle used by the police. (© Bob Belder)

Short wheelbase police Land Rover – Zambezi Valley. (© Ted Ayers-Hunt)

The charge office at Chirundu. The iron structure behind is the single span bridge over the Zambezi into Zambia. (© Bob Belder)

Patrol in the tribal area. (© Bob Belder)

Makuti motel and swimming pool. Bar, dining room and reception behind veranda. Rooms to the side and behind. In the background hills of the Zambezi Escarpment. (© Bob Belder)

The Mana Pools tree house hotel in the early 1960s. Patrols from Chirundu and Makuti called there. The Chinese have built a lodge there recently. (© Bob Belder)

(Left) Dougie Napier, (middle) Louis Fourie, (right, foreground) Phil Kensett, range day – near Salisbury 1969. (© Ted Ayers-Hunt)

Bruce Allen with another white officer – Support Unit, Makuti. (© Bruce Allen)

Bruce Allen and 'C' Troop – Support Unit, Makuti. (© Bruce Allen)

Bruce Allen and Sgt Tarasawira – Support Unit, Makuti. (© Bruce Allen)

Bruce Allen on patrol – Support Unit, Makuti. (© Bruce Allen)

# 4
# Warming up now

The concept of the Police Anti-Terrorist Unit was a good one. But, like all concepts, the practice fell far short of the ideal. In all things, especially military matters, a small unit of men works best. It is said that the maximum number of men that can work as a basic unit is twelve. Throughout history and man's affairs, twelve is the number that is chosen as the uppermost number of men to easily keep under control and not turn into a mob. More men form a mob and that cannot be easily ordered. The Disciples are an example but there are many others. The army usually splits a company into sections of ten or so men under a corporal. In business also any committee of more than twelve becomes clumsy. The PATU unit was made up of five men. One of the members was a black policeman who was expected to act as the unit tracker and interpreter. He was usually from a remote tribe that still used hunting skills in everyday life. The four white police made up the rest of the unit. They all were supposed to train often and hard together. In small military units each man has to pull above his weight, and each man is responsible to the rest.

In Rhodesia it was possible to trace a black man to his home by knowing his father's name along with his headman and chief's names. The tribal society was arranged in a way that saw each family allocated their own land by a headman, who got that land from a chief. Each father allocated his children their own land on which to build their own kraal of huts. Till about 1980, there was no such thing as a Rhodesia native who came purely from a town. Those born in cities still called their fathers' tribal lands home. In recent years that has changed with the massive urbanization that has made many born in the cities landless. Having grown up with the Shona, their language was the second one I learnt. Having grown up bare foot and in the bush hunting, tracking was as easy as riding a bicycle. The constable in the stick and I checked on each other and helped each other. Normally the translating was left to him; it pays to pretend you don't understand what is being said at times. As I had grown up hunting the bush, I could reinforce the trackers work. The wild fruit, roots and edible plants we both knew supplemented ration packs at times.

The concept was that PATU would be a self-contained fighting unit able to deploy rapidly and stay in the field for extended periods. They would be highly trained in bush warfare and specialize in hunting down enemy gangs through the vast empty forests of the land, or in the heavily settled tribal lands. The units were to be skilled hunter-killers. When the enemy were known to be in an area in larger numbers, two or more units could be deployed to work alongside each other. Five well-trained men in thick bush-veldt can take on large concentrations of enemy. The units were supposed to constantly train together to reach the stage of required skill. And that is where the problems started. Five men fighting heavily outnumbered need to be well trained.

There was no rural station that had five men to spare. A few of the big urban stations might spare that many at a push. The insurgency affected the rural areas almost exclusively. That meant the urban commanding officers were almost remote from the problem and as a result it was rare that PATU sticks, which were supposed to be voluntary, were made up of members from urban areas. As rural stations did not have enough staff to make up complete sticks, it was normal for a rural PATU unit to consist of members from two or more stations from the same district. It was a rare thing to find the same men in a stick on two or more deployments. The norm was that on every deployment there were different members. Sometimes the same men came back for another later patrol. The constable tracker normally remained the core of the stick and in many later years, the tracker and I were the only two who went out time and again on deployment with the same stick. The fast cycling of PATU members meant that training had to be constantly repeated. For those like me who served for over a decade, that constant re-training became a tedious bore.

So the concept largely failed. Firstly, it failed because when an incursion happened a Joint Operational Command (JOC) was set up; army, police and air force, and the PATU reporting there came under police command. The senior police officer in charge would usually be unfamiliar with the area, having been recently transferred to the JOC. Instead of allocating an area to the stick, the officer would order it to move from one point to another, using a map to decide. Instead of ghosting through the bush as a hunting team, the patrol took a cross-country walk. Human prey in the bush is no different from hunted animals. Both eat and drink. Human beings cook their food and fire is alien and easy to detect in the forests. In dry seasons only the big rivers hold flowing water. All living things in the bush eventually have to find and use water holes. A hunter, like lions, knows to seek prey at water and feeding places.

The PATU stick needed to have free rein to hunt, but was not given it.

The second failing was that the small number of men in the stick made it essential that each man was highly trained and knew the bush well enough to feel at home. The constant changing of the stick members made a coherent unit impossible. The small number of African-born white men in the police force meant that most of the PATU members were city-born Europeans and the bush was an alien and frightening place for them until they had had a lot of experience. In the beginning, the original hunt and kill concept was put in place, but that rapidly fell away till in the end a PATU stick was just more men in the field working with a larger body of men. Over more than a decade with PATU my depression and irritation grew with each failed and faulty patrol forced upon me.

My military service began at the age of twelve as a school cadet; by then I was a competent hunter and had already shot lion and elephant. After school, Territorial Army training of six months followed. Then five or so years on TA call-ups and a contract as a mercenary in the Congo. This was followed by another six months training, almost repeating the previous army training, in Police Depot. Competitive shooting on the range had been part of my life since the school cadet days, and throughout my police career I shot for one police provincial team or the other in range contests. The BSAP also required all officers to do an annual musketry course; they still quaintly called weapons training that. Four days on a district range shooting shotguns, hand guns and rifles, with a minimum standard required, and then best shots were awarded a marksman's badge; small crossed rifles in gold braid worn on uniform sleeves. Looking back, it seems that the PATU training never stopped and that it was very repetitive. Sometimes the nominated instructors came up with something novel, and sometimes the enemy introduced a new tactic that had to be countered, but for the most part it was moving through the bush playing war games in a fashion the instructors imagined approximated actual combat. Few of them had actually been in combat.

That was an enduring flaw with the police counter-insurgency effort. The unbreakable tradition in the BSAP was that the senior officers did not "do", they delegated. Those who did the work were those too lowly in rank to be able to delegate downwards. There was a headman murdered; the terrorists killed those in authority in the area they wanted to subvert. The PATU stick would deploy to the area. The local station commander would have a large map on his wall with arrows, coloured pins and flags and annotations. These were placed on the map to mark information received second-hand by the commander; information he could not verify as he never went to the places marked. The PATU stick would be briefed that this was where the gang was. The gang were sure to head to there. The PATU stick must walk from here to there, which would mean crossing the gang's tracks and being able to locate and follow them. Another line on the map was drawn to indicate the PATU unit had patrolled that line. Things out there on the ground did not conform to neat lines and pins on maps.

During my police service of over fourteen years I was transferred over thirteen times. The one constant in each new posting was that I was a member of PATU at the new station, so within a short time of arriving, orders came to do a patrol. That required linking up with the local stick. Obviously, it also meant that the concept of a tight group of men who knew each other well went by the board. By the late sixties, the incoming gangs arrived at increasingly short intervals. Each gang was hunted down and accounted for by the police. Then more than one gang began arriving and soon the army was involved and the gangs coming in also grew in numbers. At first the gangs were less than ten men, but in time the numbers grew to fifty or more in one infiltration. From Norton, the next posting within Salisbury Rural was to Goromonzi, the area to the south and east of the city. Within days of arrival there, PATU was sent to Mount Darwin to work with a large contingent of South African Police (SAP).

There was a base camp in the African Purchase Area (APA), an area where black commercial farmers had been allowed to purchase large farms to own privately. In the Tribal Trust Lands, land was held communally. A tented base camp near a dam had been set up and each morning a large unit went out in vehicles to roam the area looking for information on terrorist gangs. Early one morning, informers came in to report that during the night two large gangs had visited various farms in the APA. The PATU stick, Special Branch (SB) and the SAP drove to the area and got off to look for tracks. One set of tracks was found and followed towards a nearby mountain range by the SAP. Another set led in another direction down a river valley. PATU and Special Branch followed that trail.

Within half an hour the SAP made contact with a large group on the side of the mountains who were entrenched with heavy machine guns and mortars. The battle raged and the rest of us could hear it going on some kilometres away. I took the PATU stick off towards the battle, hoping to cut off the gang when it ran. When we were some two hundred metres into the bush away from the river, Special Branch and the officers with them ran into the second gang. Our PATU stick was behind that gang which was trapped between SB and us, and we went at once to the aid of SB. The insurgents had gone to ground in ploughed fields, taken shelter in the furrows when caught in the open field by SB firing. The policemen had been in thick riverine bush and the insurgents had been seen in the open crossing the field.

My PATU stick climbed a big anthill at the verge of the forests overlooking the field and the gang was exposed to us as they fired at the concealed officers along the river. After three of them were shot dead by PATU, from behind, they realized their predicament and stuck up hands, throwing away weapons. The captured men turned out to be members of a gang that had abducted white agricultural advisors many months before, killing two of them and taking one to Mozambique; he was released some years later. One of the captors had his foot shot off in the contact. He had an artificial limb fitted and when he was healthy they were all tried for murder and hanged.

Goromonzi was an area where Tribal Trust Land (TTL) was bordered by a large area of small farms and plots held by whites. There were thriving small businesses all through the area. Many bred chinchilla rabbits for fur. There was a big onion farm. Several smallholders grew cucumbers and tomatoes in tunnels. One couple bred exotic birds and water fowl, some of fantastic colours. The same couple owned The Cossack Restaurant in the city and they bred a large pigeon that was used in the eatery as 'baby chicken'. There was a large 'horsey' fraternity and the Ruwa Country Club hosted gymkhanas. The police station was built in the 1920s and the single quarters was a T-shaped building with the spur the dining room and lounge in which there was a bar. The Goromonzi Country Club was almost next to the station and had tennis courts, a squash court, cricket field and swimming bath. The country club was a feature of every rural settlement. The tennis court was always an essential part of the rural community. Tennis every weekend and Wednesday afternoon. Squash every lunchtime. Swimming in the pool first thing in the summer mornings. An active yet in some ways lazy life.

Like Norton, Goromonzi was in the road accident zone, on the approaches to the capital. The road east to Umtali and the road north to Mtoko ran through its area of responsibility. The Arcturus Gold Mine was in that area and the hills of Borrowdale, the suburb of Salisbury, bordered the area. Fred, a local eccentric, was an architect who lived in a converted barn. The house was one vast open-plan room. A ladder led to an attic where the two teenage children lived with pet baboons. At night they went up with the baboons and drew the ladder up and closed the trap-door. The lighting was by paraffin lamps as Fred refused to have electricity. Apart from a vast dining table and chairs there were only Roman reclining couches scattered about, no other seating. Fred's wife cooked superb meals on an outside fire. The furnace of the wood-burning water boiler made an oven into which food on a flat spade was placed. While the guest reclined, eating and drinking, the wife played a large harp with professional skill. Fred had a full black beard and thick pebble glasses.

One morning while walking his dogs, Fred came across the dead body of a woman with a child still in her back sling, also dead. A cloth rope had been used to strangle her and the child probably died of asphyxiation. That case was the first murder I investigated on my own and was exceptional in that the perpetrator was identified, hunted down and arrested and the case docket was prepared for High Court. There, the evidence gathered was presented and the man convicted and eventually executed for the double murder. The woman had been at a nearby trading store with her baby, on a bicycle, when she was somehow lured to the field where Fred found her body. She had been raped and then strangled and left lying on her baby; the bicycle was stolen by the murderer, and that led to his arrest. Someone had seen him with it and recognised it. That person knew where he lived; he was a cook at one of the smallholdings. When we arrived he had left, but we managed to identify him. A photograph of the man was put in the Sunday papers and a housewife in Rusape, a hundred kilometres away, phoned to say she had him in her kitchen.

Not all murder cases are so neat. Another given to me involved a multi-killing. The bloated body of a ten year old girl was found in a river by herdsmen in the TTL. The autopsy revealed organs had been cut from the body. A long investigation found witnesses who had seen the girl with two men. Eventually they were arrested and said that they merely helped Zak, a local storekeeper, and that he had been the killer. Zak denied any involvement. His co-accused said that they had helped before and after the child had been killed by Zak, and he had taken the organs to bury beneath his newly built trading store. Nothing could be found to link Zak to the killing. A check on police records showed that Zak had been the accused in an identical case some years back when he was busy with his first trading store. In that case he had been seen with the dead child when she was still alive and he had been convicted of kidnapping only.

The two accomplices were tried separately and convicted as accessories before and after the fact, and given a death sentence. Zak was tried and his accomplices gave evidence. The judge acquitted Zak. There was a long and technical judgement, but the fact remained that men accused of being his accomplices were convicted and he was freed. So he got away with murder for the second time. His belief in the magical powers of body parts must have been mightily endorsed. At times the law is an ass. At the time of the conviction there was a political impasse on the hanging of convicted murderers. The government had sought a Supreme Court ruling to adjudicate if it was in fact the legitimate ruling party. That court ruling said the government was de facto in control of the country. A white man had been convicted of murdering a nurse on the overnight train to Bulawayo. To make sure there was no accusation of racial bias the multi-murderers and the nurse killer were hanged together.

The Depot training provided rudimentary lectures in the investigation of crime and once a P/O reached a station, he was presumed to be trained. There was no testing of the water; they were thrown in at the deep end. These two successful investigations gave confidence and satisfaction and showed me any police investigation is run along basic rules: who, how, where and what. A theft of a cycle or a double murder required the same technique; careful sniffing about, lots of knocking on doors. But it was the preparation of the actual dockets that differed. For minor cases in the magistrates' court, some papers such as the indictment had to be duplicated, but most were single. Murder was tried in the High Courts and all documents, photographs and plans had to be in twelve copies. Manual typewriters, most of them antique, could handle three duplicates with carbon paper. Some stations had a Roneo machine, but cutting the waxed sheet without a single mistake was hard work. Then a High Court case also required the investigating officer to attend the entire week-long sessions, in full dress uniform. If one case was unexpectedly stood down, the next was called and the judges did not want to be told witnesses were not present. In that way murder investigations were much more work than most other crimes.

Next to a rural road near Arcturus Mine in the long grass, stood a small cairn marking the grave of a man from pioneer days. The epitaph said he was a lion hunter and his middle name was 'Lion'. On rural patrol there were many old graves in places far from present habitation. Salisbury Rural stations had record books of old graves, mainly of deceased pioneers and ex-members. While on patrol the graves were visited and cleaned and the visits recorded in the book. In the Norton District there was an old fort made from stone walls built to fortify a large rocky kopje and used by British troops during the first Shona rebellion. There were a handful of graves at the base of the kopje. One of them was a sergeant's and the longhand annotation in the record book went something like: 'Fell to his death after stumbling on his way back to his billet from St Patricks Day dinner.' The grass and other debris were removed to keep the gravestones visible. There was a strange aura of forgotten things round the old graves, a feeling that there were still things unfinished lurking nearby.

Pensioned-off working police horses also had to be visited while on farm patrol. There were many on various farms around Salisbury and other towns in the 1960s. The horses were treated as police pensioners and if one died it took a mountain of paper work to finalise the matter. The owners of the farms were paid a monthly sum to take care of the horses and police rural patrols were required to physically inspect each horse and record the visit. It was not unknown for a dead horse to have another substituted so the pension payout went on; the sums were generous and more than covered stall feeding.

The smallholdings round Goromonzi had some magnificent houses on them. The bush here was mainly msasa trees, tall and leafy. Old, mature trees with wide umbrella crowns proliferated. There were also the endemic kopjes. Further north and east, the kopjes became thick and joined into rocky hill ranges. Here they were big isolated heaps of boulders. Many of the big houses were built on and into the kopje with the boulders forming walls and floors and trees used to prop up roofs, growing on through the thatch or tiles. Often a swimming pool had been carved out of solid granite and a nearby cave turned into the change room. The houses said loudly that this place is a man's castle. The biggest of them all belonged to one of the Meikles, the family who pioneered the retail business in Rhodesia, one of the first to open a store in the Salisbury of the 1890s. Meikles had a store in almost all the towns and owned the iconic Meikles Hotel across from Cecil Square in the centre of Salisbury.

The Meikle homestead was built on and over a small hill with a forest of mature tall trees including lofty palms. It really was a castle, with stone walls and balustrades along walkways winding over the hill, the garden a tangle of roses and bougainvillea creepers. It was presided over by the matriarch of the clan, then in her seventies. She ran a very successful horse racing stable and was often seen accepting the cup at major meetings. One of the neighbours was King Zog of Albania, then already in exile for some years. He was a slight, wiry man, and very reserved. He never attended any of the social get-togethers or played social tennis. Before black rule he left Rhodesia and went to South Africa, possibly now, with the fall of communism in Eastern Europe, back in his homeland.

I had another short spell at a station and then transferred to Beatrice, still a Salisbury Rural posting. The staff officers who arrange postings did not take into account the wants of the man posted. The police force was run on military lines and an order was never questioned. There was a staff chart and positions that fell vacant had to be filled. The posted man was only a rank, number and name. Not once during the years did I ever meet the shadowy headquarters men who initiated my transfers. Not once was I ever consulted by them. That was how things worked and it was not something that was queried or discussed. An order went out and was obeyed. Sometimes a request for transfer to a specified station was made but rarely granted, unless it was a request for transfer to a special unit like Dog Section or the Criminal Investigation Department.

Beatrice was a small village south of the capitol on the Bulawayo road. Once it had been a village each side of the main road, but the new wide, tarred road bypassed it. The old road ran in a loop through the village and then across a big, old iron latticework bridge over the Umfuli River where the Tobacco Road Hotel stood on the up-stream side and an Indian-owned general dealer's shop the other side. The river was deep and strong and was good for fishing. There were a dozen residential houses near the hotel. There was the police camp and the country club with a large hall, where dances were held and farmers meetings. The area was prime farming land and was predominantly Afrikaans speaking. There was a very active and well-supported shooting range. The rugby team were strong contenders in the rural league and in the evenings they trained inside the sports club hall.

The Tobacco Road Hotel always had nubile young women as barmaids and there was a large mural of the Battle of Blood River on the wall above the bar. That battle was an iconic one for the South African Afrikaners. They made a covenant with God to uphold that day as sacred if He allowed them to defeat the Zulu Impis then besieging the wagon laager. It was a long fight in which the river on whose banks the wagons stood ran red with blood. The Day of the Covenant was kept till the advent of the black government in South Africa, when the holiday was renamed Conciliation Day. It was not advisable to discuss Afrikaans politics in the Tobacco Road Hotel bar near closing time when sentiment got heated. There was a strong following of the game jik-skaai, called horseshoes in America and played by tossing batons at a stick stuck upright in a sand pit, the scoring similar to bowls. And there was hunting to be had, especially of wild pigs that thrived and played havoc with the large mealie fields stretching over the farmland.

The member i/c, a married man, brewed beer at home. Every evening the police gathered at the single quarters to play darts. The veranda was the normal gauzed-in type with the darts board on one wall and chairs for spectators. The beer was made in quantities that regularly used up all the available bottles and the surplus was brought over to the mess in a deep basin containing many gallons of brew. The darts games went on into the midnight hours. The 6am 'stable parade' took a lot of willpower and years of practise to attend on some of those Beatrice beery early mornings. At times there was police work to do. The station was also in the prime accident zone and also a main route for passenger buses heading to the tribal lands, usually overloaded and un-roadworthy. So the inevitable fatal accidents produced multiple bodies and a ferry of body-boxes carried the carnage to the mortuary.

Typical accidents were like one I dealt with on the Mtoko road in the Goromonzi District during my previous posting. My week of standby duty had begun with an almost all Friday night session of call-outs. Saturday midday while trying to get some sleep the phone from the charge office again demanded attention and a serious fatal accident had been reported. The duty constable had already loaded the body-box on the roof of the Land Rover so all that was needed was to grab the briefcase with all the necessary stuff like accident report forms, tape measure and camera.

Two buses had been racing each other on the way to Salisbury, vying to be the first to the next bus stop and add a few more passengers to the already overfull vehicles. It was the dry season and the road was lined by chest high spear grass, endemic to Mashonaland and used as thatching material. It was also fire season and the grass one side of the road was alight and thick blue smoke, driven by a breeze, cloaked the road. The sole surviving driver said that the smoke was making it difficult to see the road so they used the centre white paint line as a guide. Going the other way was a thirty-ton truck carrying bagged maize headed to Malawi. The leading bus and the freight truck hit head-on without a sign of braking, no tyre marks on the tar. The second bus slammed into the back of the first. Fuel tanks burst and the grass fire set all the vehicles alight. There was one small fire extinguisher in the station truck.

The rest of the afternoon was spent calling for help from the Salisbury Traffic Department, arranging a fleet of ambulances, getting mortuary staff and vehicles to the scene and having a commercial heavy-towing concern called to help with hydraulic cutting tools to remove trapped passengers. Then when the fire brigade had put out the flames and while the dead and dying were being moved, the constable and I frantically tried to document everyone. Once we were left with only the wrecked vehicles, the to-scale sketches of the accident and comprehensive photographs were done and the big tow trucks dragged and lifted the wrecks away to the government vehicle inspector's yard on the Umtali road on the outskirts of the city.

These accidents happened often enough to make me a bit of an expert at unravelling the scene and deciding which driver was at fault. Plenty of practice and a close oversight of the dockets by seniors made sure the public prosecutors had all the ammunition needed to convict. Another spur to good investigation was the fact that that prosecutor was sometimes me, the investigating officer. It was not only my own opinion that led me to believe I was expert but also twice receiving a magistrate's commendation for good work as previously mentioned. Practise makes perfect and on the stations on the edge of Salisbury there was plenty of that. There was also play.

The Beatrice farmers had problems with wild pigs and one day I offered to show a farmer's crop guard how to go about shooting them. Wild pig are wily, hard to hunt and can be very dangerous. Most farmers had a hunter as crop guard, tasked to reduce baboons and pigs and also predators that attacked the domestic stock. Wild pigs are the most tenacious and cunning crop raiders and thrive in peri-urban areas where there is food, especially maize fields. All Shona people plant maize, even those who are today living in the once lush suburbs of Salisbury, where once-green lawns are now fields of maize. As a boy-hunter on my grandfather's farm, wild pig had been a great pest and we learnt early how to kill them successfully. Once the maize was head high and lush, founders of pigs moved in to the heart of the lands. As the maize stalks grow close it is impossible for a man to walk through the rows without moving the stalks, no approach can be made without making a noise and the pigs know that. So when feeding, the entire founder, on a cue, stops feeding and stands absolutely still and quiet, listening. Then, again on cue, they go back to the business on hand, eating with gusto.

The trick was to pick a windy day, in fact preferably a windy and rainy day. Then pigs could not distinguish between the noise of the wind and rain on the stalks and the noise of a man walking through the lands. A hunter also takes advantage of the wind by walking into it to keep scent from the prey. The game guard had a Mossberg bolt action shotgun, and my 7.62 FN with two magazines of twenty rounds each and a .45 Webley revolver for insurance went along. The tusks of a wild pig are sharp and dangerous, and they are fierce fighters when pushed. The guard was shaking with fear, mainly because he did not know what to expect and it was dark and close in the tall maize. When we got in range, the breaking of the stalks and the grunting of the pigs and the chomping of teeth on the maize was clearly heard. Then all fell suddenly quiet and we hunters stopped dead still, miming statues. The wind and the rain rustled the maize. The feeding sounds came again.

Then, when very close, we lay down in the furrow between rows and wriggled forward. Suddenly the sound of wild pigs was all around us, but none of them were aware of us. For half a minute it was chaos as both guns opened rapid fire. At the end of the storm five bush pigs, including a massive two hundred kilogram boar, were dead. The guard was dancing with delight, having broken his taboo. The farmer was delighted and fame touched me briefly in the Tobacco Road Hotel that night. Everyone knew bush pigs were hard to hunt and usually only one at a time is shot if the hunter is very lucky. Five was something of a record.

Old Man sat in his corner, back against the wall and his own sherry glass always kept full. His oiled moustache curled up each end in a double circle. No-one knew how long he had been sitting in the corner all the hours the bar was open. He had seen a lot of life and there was a sardonic slant to all his dry jokes; always there and never offending just observing.

'Ivan, I hear on the TV the Yanks call cops pig?' There was an ironic drunken cheer from the drinkers.

There had been a lot on TV about student riots in America and the newsreels showed them shouting 'pig' at the riot police and carrying posters with 'kill the pigs' on them.

'Well, Old Man, I'd say to them "your mother sucks bacon".' Again the drunken cheering and laughter.

'Guess we had not better call you that then. How 'bouts bush pig? What you guys say? Bush pig the rural policeman. The great hunter of bush pigs.'

The name stuck for a while but not past the next transfer. The Rhodesia lottery required a nom de plume on each ticket and for years 'bush pig' was used by me when buying for the monthly draw. It never brought any luck at the draws. I thought it was a good nickname anyway.

New recruits were being brought in from England as fast as they could be signed up. They were needed to boost the number of police as the insurgency needed more and more men in the field fighting as soldiers. That was a role the BSA Police had played since the earliest days of its existence. As England was in the van of sanctions on Rhodesia it also made sense to lure their citizens to the country. Three raw Englishmen were posted to Beatrice. They went through a shortened course in Depot and were shipped to the station to relieve more experienced men for the fight in the remoter areas. They were all milk-white, almost pink, not yet touched by the tropical sun since they had arrived in Africa only a few weeks ago. The police mess diet of meat and vegetables did not suit them. Over the lunch break, while playing a never-ending game of cribbage, they complained that the food was not what they were used to. The running of the mess was gladly handed over to one of them as it was an onerous duty no-one wanted, and at once the midday meal changed to meat pies and milk, and they did a deal with a neighbour to buy in his meat rabbits. Rabbit stew replaced roast joint of sirloin. They were not used to beef being very cheap. One of them fell under the spell of an Afrikaans girl whose father had recently retreated from Kenya and bought a farm in Beatrice. They married, but soon afterwards the father again saw the writing on the wall, sold up and moved south. The new recruit bought himself out and went with.

The other two showed great interest in hunting and wanted to try their hand on bush pigs. Wild pigs are a very dangerous quarry for rookies and they were put off, but one evening a dead boar was brought back to the mess from a hunt by me and strung up by the back legs from a branch of a tree in the backyard. The next morning, one pink one asked if he could help in butchering the animal. The pig had purposefully not yet been bled. All the blood had been gathering in the front of the body, mainly in the neck, while hanging. There is more blood in a pig than any other animal; the blood in the carcass hanging there was causing the throat area to bloat like a tight balloon. The pink one was all eager to start his career as an African hunter so the hunting knife was handed over and I casually moved out of range while telling him where to cut. The old and well-used knife was razor sharp and it cut deep into the neck. The pig's blood spouted out like water from a burst hose. The scream of fright and disgust ended in a long session of barking at the ants. For some strange reason, he did not want to try the roast leg of ham from a bush pig that night, but stuck to a Cornish pasty.

All district sport clubs had a tennis court. There were almost always a cricket field where the farmers played in winter when the farms need less attention. Some had squash courts and rugby fields. Swimming pools were a part of everyday life. Friday nights saw the single officers head for Salisbury and the nightlife there. It was a regular thing to end up with a woman in the mess bedroom for the weekend. Come Saturday and Sunday these women usually came to the cricket or rugby or tennis. For some months, my favourite was a voluptuous New Zealand girl who worked as a barmaid at Coq d'Or nightclub. She would spread her tanned body on a canvas deck chair on the side line of the cricket field and drink beer, dozing in the winter sun. It was a sight that caused many young farm assistants to make idiots of themselves on the field in an attempt to impress her. Apart from the Salisbury women there were willing girls at each small settlement, usually farmer's daughters or teachers. My happy excess in the fleshpots of the big city continued. But then things changed. Orders came of a transfer to Chiredzi, a place remote from any big town or city.

# 5

# Sweating now

Chiredzi came into existence and is still there because of dam water. The south-east low veldt of Rhodesia had always repelled any attempt at commercial farming because of the lack of water. Even the big rivers such as the Sabi dried to a trickle in the middle of a sea of sand after the rains. The entire area along the Mozambique and South African border is a vast ocean of scrub mopani; small hardy trees of about two metres that fed an assortment of game on their leaves. It took ranchers fifty years to bring stock to the land, as they had to dig wells and bore holes and lay pipes and build tanks. They also had to build every metre of road and build bridges and culverts before bringing in cattle. It was unoccupied land, hard for human beings to live in. Then they had to fence and protect the stock from lions, leopards, hyena, lynx and jackal. There had been dream of building dams higher up the central plateau and piping water to the low veldt where the climate and soil was perfect for crop and stock farming. In the 1960s the dams were finally built and river-size concrete canals carried fast flowing streams to the low-lying areas.

Vast areas round the small village of Chiredzi were cleared of vegetation by bulldozers linked by ship's chains and then levelled by graders. Tens of thousands of hectares of scrub trees were piled in heaps and burnt, and the land from horizon to horizon was levelled, leaving only the odd baobab tree dotting the flat landscape. The main canals took the water to the vast estates and then a network of smaller canals took the water to the crops. Where there had been endless mopani scrub, suddenly there were lush green and yellow fields of sugar cane. Then another massive operation cleared thousands more hectares and just as suddenly there were vast fields of wheat. It was like the waving of a magician's wand, feeding that water to the bush scrub. Men rejoiced, but the wildlife paid a heavy price. My posting in the late 1960s to the sugar cane fields coincided with the apex of the war over the land between man and beast. And as always in Rhodesia, the police were in the front line. The police tried hard to balance the interests of man and beast.

Every day there were reports of poaching by tribesmen on the local cattle ranches, interspersed with theft of stock. Each day a rural bus driver was reported as having deliberately run down impala or other buck on the road. There was an Austrian rancher who called his land the Impala Ranching and Canning Company. The wildlife on his land was hunted to supply the pet food factory. At 2am one morning a report came in that the Austrian was poaching elephant on his neighbour's land. The neighbour had his own company of game guards. On arrival at the place where the game guards were waiting, it was found the Austrian's Land Rover and seven ton truck were parked on the border of the two ranches, and tracks of a party of men led from the parked vehicles across the neighbour's game fence.

While waiting in concealment near the vehicles, heavy rifles were heard firing in the distance and soon a hunting party showed through the trees returning to the trucks. They paused to cut the fence and then headed for the truck that had a crane on the back. As arranged, the sergeant took aside the half dozen black staff as we sprang the ambush and I took the Austrian and his white manager to another place; both carried heavy, expensive double rifles. He flatly denied hunting elephant. They had been looking for a kudu wounded the previous day on his own ranch. The sergeant soon called to me; two elephant had been shot nearby and the party had returned to fetch the truck with which to load the animals. The Austrian took to threatening bluster. The final up-shot was that a heavy fine was paid when the magistrate convicted both men; the vehicles and both rifles were forfeit to the state.

The local Shangaan tribe lived by hunting and saw no reason to change, their way of life so often fell foul of the law. The men often hunted buffalo with home-made longbows that fired arrows tipped by a spear point type arrowhead that was a trade item at any store on the Mozambique side of the border. The bow and the arrows were made from an extremely hard wood and the string from plaited hide. The arrow was a metre long and fletched. When fired from a bow at full stretch, the arrow flew for about two hundred metres. Given the hefty weight of the arrow, the energy was more than enough to drive the arrow fletch deep into a buffalo shoulder, piercing the heart. They stoically accepted the short sentences they received for poaching, if arrested; white law was baffling.

Another round in the battle I dealt with was when a drunk stopped to defecate off the side of a low level bridge one evening and was bitten nearly in half by an offended hippo. There were no witnesses, but I often wondered at how that came about. A day later, a buffalo bull pursued a worker riding a bicycle on a track through a freshly planted cane field. The man tried to climb a tree just as the bull caught up with him and he was crushed between the animal's boss and the tree trunk. As the game rangers were not available, I was tasked to shoot the bull. The member i/c arrived at the death scene and handed me a rifle that fired .600 Nitro Express ammunition, the biggest and hardest-kicking bullets ever made commercially. Having had many years of hunting and being young, fearless and foolhardy, I followed the bull into the chest high cane.

The bull looked up with a mouth full of cane stalks; it took a second to aim and fire. The booming of the massive rifle totally stunned me. I could not see, hear or think for some seconds. Luckily, the shot from the powerful round was true and did its work. There is a hunting principle that insists that any hunting must be done with a rifle that the hunter knows well. That lesson was driven home to me very forcefully that day. The bull had already killed a man for no known reason and there is no hardier animal than a wounded buffalo bull. My life had been staked on that one shot. If the animal had come at a charge it would have reached me before my senses recovered. A lesson learnt. For weeks it haunted me, that moment of bravado and stupidity. Can man ever live at peace with wildlife? It seemed not at that time and in that area.

The corpses of people who died unnatural deaths were taken by the police investigators to the government mortuary at a hospital at Ndanga, which was a hundred kilometres away on heavily corrugated dirt roads. There the forensic autopsy was carried out and the results formed part of the police docket. Usually the body was carried on the special roof rack in the fitted stainless steel box with the insulated clip-down lid. On one famous day there was no Land Rover available and it was necessary for a murder investigation to have the post-mortem results quickly. The investigating P/O used the station Matchless motorcycle. The duty constable was roped in. The corpse was placed on the pillion and the police details sat in front and behind it on the same seat. Then straps were wound round all three and the body driven off to the mortuary. There was a series of photographs on a board in the charge office documenting the trip. It happened at Hippo Valley which was a sub-post of Chiredzi and so had few resources. Another day at the office.

The cane and wheat farmers were fairly well-off when compared with the stock farmers in the dry land. Many of the sugar cane growers were French-speaking and from Mauritius. The block of farms allocated to them was known as the Settler Farms. There were also many people working for the massive sugar mills and others in the thriving commercial section of the small town. All the small towns of Rhodesia had a country club. Chiredzi and Triangle were two small towns half an hour apart and they shared one golf club. There came a time when the old golf clubhouse was no longer big enough or fancy enough for the increased numbers of members. A demolition party was arranged to get rid of the old clubhouse; a new one had already been built and the party would be a fun way to remove the old one.

It was a sultry summer's night with the temperature around forty degrees with heavy humidity so the clear stars shimmered through the haze. The music was loud and there were plenty of girls so the dancing was frantic and men's shirts were soaked with sweat. Sledgehammers had been handed out and walls began to crumble; as the stock of liquor went down things became hectic. By 1am just a few stumps of the walls remained and the roof sheets had been stacked for later removal. The floor of the old club was full of broken glass from the windows and all the revellers were covered in dust, the sweat turning it into dark streaks like face paint.

The liquor ran out and a general gloom descended. Someone discovered a case of cane spirit partly covered with rubble. Cane spirit was a drink unknown then in Rhodesia and that case must have been one of the first ever imported from South Africa. Because no-one knew about it, none of the bottles had been opened. No-one had ordered any from the voluntary barman.

'What the hell is this stuff? It says Cane Spirit; is that fuel for a car?'

'Who cares? Open it, let's drink the petrol. I need a drink, man.'

'How does a man drink this stuff? Agggh. Tastes shit. Needs a mixer. Any coke left? None, you sure?'

'Tell you what guys, there's a whole dam full of water just there outside of the door.' There was a small dam as a hazard alongside the green near the demolished clubhouse. 'I'll go get some in this jug. Ice finished though.' A minute later he came back from outside carrying a full glass water jug. 'That should do it. Who wants? OK, OK one at a time.'

'Fuck me, look at that' He held his glass to the guttering lamp. In the mix of cane and dam water were several tadpoles. The water was also a tea colour. 'Well then, hey, tadpoles and cane. Why not? Cheers.'

'Give me a treble, easy on the water and frogs.'

'Make mine the same.'

'Me too. Bet I can sluk more tadpoles than you guys.'

'Oh, yeah? Go get some more from the dam, you're on.'

The mess at the single quarters had a swimming pool that came within a step of the dining room sliding door. It was possible to dive from the dining room into the pool. It was a big pool, and the filter was a concrete tank filled with sand on the edge of the pool at the deep end. Water pumped through the sand, cascaded out in a small waterfall back into the pool and over a ledge at the side. The pool was a very welcome refresher in the steamy heat of the summer days; at night the water felt lukewarm. That season there had been a glut of citrus and the citrus section of the sugar estate had donated trucks full to the mess. Each morning, several jugs of fresh ruby grapefruit juice were put on the breakfast table. The morning after the tadpole and cane drinking contest both the pool and the cold grapefruit juice was put to good use. What doesn't kill makes one tough.

Outside the graded fields the mopani scrub was endless. In the 1950s as a schoolboy, my uncle, who was then a clerk in the Native Department and later the chief magistrate of Rhodesia, undertook a tax collection tour from Nuanetsi. There were no roads and native messengers had walked the trail beforehand, blazing trees with axes to mark the way for the vehicle drivers. The convoy travelled at about ten miles an hour and only a few tribesmen lived there, scattered widely in small kraals. The area then covered by the Nuanetsi government area was broken down to three police areas some years on. That tax patrol ended at Chipinde Pools, near Chiredzi. The river widened there to a large reed and vegetation fringed lake full of crocodile and hippopotamus. That long-ago trip arrived at the pools the morning after a lion had attacked the resident game ranger while he was ironing his uniform with a coal iron. The lion released his arm when the iron was stuck in its face. We stayed then for a night in the thatched rondavels next to the pools. Neither the bush nor the pools had changed much when I was posted to Chiredzi and on odd weekends fishing trips were undertaken to the pools.

# 6
# Staying in the ring

My doubts were getting stronger. There had long been a vague feeling that the war on the nationalists was being fought with one hand tied behind one's back. There was no senior officer who was prepared to give orders to intensify the response to terrorism. Weekly reports told of atrocities; headmen and chiefs executed, informer's lips and tongues cut off, rural government officials abducted and tortured to death. Police in the form of the Support Unit and the Anti-Terrorist Unit chased after the perpetrators, sometimes with success, but it was all too little and bit by bit the insurgency intensified.

The usual call came to form the PATU stick for a two-week patrol. The stick would come under orders of Chiredzi and three of the members were coming from other stations, while I and the tracker were, as usual, the only two who had worked together. Of the three P/Os, one had come down from Salisbury and the other two were local men. It was the middle of the hot season. Forty degree heat with high humidity ruled night and day. The locals were acclimatised but the Salisbury man came down from the high plateau where things were much more comfortable. This constant changing of men gnawed away at my confidence of not losing my country.

There was a set of maps stuck to the wall of the office, overlaid with plastic film. They were detailed and showed hills, valleys and rivers. Lines of assorted colours criss-crossed the maps and linked stick-pins with red, green and black heads. The inspector had marked the maps over a long period. Only he knew what it all meant.

'Ah, P/O Smith is it? Your stick ready?'

'Yes, sir.'

'Good man. Now look here, I am unable to say if there is a presence in the area but am engaging in clearing all likely areas. You are to patrol from here to here.' A green line was drawn on the map using a ruler. 'Take a look.'

'That is across ranch land?'

'Yes, well, no-one has been there for a while. Can you manage – how far is that, about twenty miles – in the two weeks?'

'Just patrol from that point in a straight line to that point?' Twenty miles was one day's patrol but it would not be me who told him that. Another waste of time and energy wandering through uninhabited thick mopani bush, where only wild animals and the odd herd of cattle roamed. Terrorists had to make contact with locals. Orders were to be carried out.

So the PATU stick dropped in the late afternoon on a road on the ranch near the start point marked on the map in the office. The next morning at dawn the patrol started at the designated map reference. By five in the afternoon it had arrived at the end point. Between the two points had been thick mopani forest, the odd pan where animals dug seep holes for water, some cattle that were as wild as the scattered game and groups of big, black ground hornbills hunting along the scrub. For six days the stick relaxed next to a water hole fed by the ranch windmill, camping out and then went back to the inspector's office and maps.

'No sign at all? Well done. We can call that area clear then.'

'Nothing, sir.' Did he think that the terrorists were static in one place?

'Now look here. There is a fairly large island here on the Chiredzi River. That would be a perfect place for a terrorist camp. What do you think?'

'Any reports of activity in the area?'

'Nothing at all. But they could be establishing a safe camp there on that island.'

'That is on the edge of a sugar estate.'

'Yes. Take your stick and check it out, there's a good chap.'

So the stick crossed the river on the girders of the railway bridge and walked down the hill range that ran along the river and then down the two hundred metre steep slope to the river edge. In the thick riverine forest at the edge of the fast flowing water an observation post was put up. The sun beat down and sweat flowed even in the shade of the evergreens. There was lots of available water though. The island was fifty metres off, maybe a hundred metres long and that wide as well, the river dividing round it. There was vegetation on the island but not enough to hide men. The banks of the island carried crocs, and hippo lurked in pods upstream and down.

'See those red berries on vines on the island?' the tracker asked me, speaking in Shona.

'Yes?'

'Very good eating. Make a man strong for many women.'

'You think?'

'I'm sure. At my home always eat them.'

'We go in the morning. And the crocs?'

'Water too shallow and also we walk together, no problems. Good fruit, very good.'

After eating breakfast in the warm dawn, each man sipped slowly at a mug of coffee and then we cocked the rifles and stepped into the swift water. It came up waist high and the stick bunched together for balance, the riverbed being pebbles and sand. The bed was visible and a sharp lookout was kept with rifles at the ready for any of the reptiles that were hungry enough to attack. As we were bunched, that was unlikely; crocs select un-alert prey. The berries were large purple grapes growing on thin vines that clung to and climbed trees. They were sweet and tart and extremely refreshing in the cloying heat of the mid-morning sun. There was an abundance of fruit and all the men were eventually surfeited. The wade back through the pushing current took us under the black shade of the evergreen trees on the bank.

My patience finally broke by the fourth day and so we packed the stoves and mess tins and made ready to climb out of the river gorge and finish the patrol. Half way up the steep slope, the Salisbury man went down with heat stroke. The only thing possible was to take him back to the river quickly and immerse him. His condition was serious and he moved in and out of consciousness. The helicopter called to evacuate him could not land on the slope near the river because of the steep angle and the tree cover. The stricken man was wrapped in a wet ground sheet, put on a stretcher made from cut down branches and carried up the slope to the medics at the chopper at the top. He recovered the same day. The rest of the stick sat for some hours, exhausted and sweating heavily in the heat, waiting for sundown. Next day, in the cool of the predawn, we went back to the police camp. The emergency gave me an excuse to cut the patrol short. Yet again a waste of time and resources had taken place. When would it come right? When would those giving the orders get to know the situation?

There was a party in the single quarters that Friday. The dining room was the dance floor and the lights had been dimmed. Liquor flowed and the sliding doors were open to allow dancers to cool in the swimming pool. She was very attractive but had a missing hand which she draped with a scarf so it was hardly noticeable. She slow-danced me down the corridor to the bedroom, and she was very happy to catch me. She was sensitive to the missing limb and that undermined her self-confidence. She was an attractive young woman and very lusty. In the dark of the room, in a very inappropriate moment, the sickening thought that my home, my country, might be slipping away came and slammed my head. Would it all be lost? Would the incompetence of others make me a refugee? It was like falling into icy water.

She was suddenly crying and the tears dropped on my bare chest. My distance, my withdrawal from the moment had at once registered on her and she mistook it. She had no self-confidence.

'You don't really like me do you? You are not even here with me. Oh, I hate you!'

'Wait, I was just...'

She dismounted in a rush and snatched up her clothes and ran sobbing down the corridor, pushed naked through the dancers and ran to her car and drove off. It was a disaster of misunderstanding. She was sexy and likable and the last thing on my mind was to be indifferent to her, but the frightening thoughts of losing everything had grabbed hard and took me away for a moment, made me seem uninterested and led her to the wrong conclusion. As badly as I needed to explain to her, there was never a chance to do it. She flatly refused to speak to me again. I wish I could have made it right.

There was rugby and the team played in other towns with much travelling and gallons of beer after the game. There was the weekly film screened in the hall near the hotel and when the reel was being changed, the crowd mingled and friends were made. There was the heat, always the heat, and at noon there was a baobab with wide branches and it was much cooler up there, lying like a leopard in the shade on a branch. There was police work, mostly about wildlife and illegal hunting; only the white man saw taking wild animals off the land as breaking the law. It was a losing battle and today, in Mugabe's Zimbabwe, the wild animals have all become bush-meat. Then in the morning after stable parade, the morning run and a swim, after a big fried breakfast and several glasses of fresh ruby grapefruit juice, I went to my office at the Charge Office, and the transfer order was handed to me out of the blue again.

Report to Nuanetsi the next day, said the order. The transfers were always the same, sudden and without discussion or explanation. Sometimes the transfers were resented, as moving house is a bit of a chore even if all worldly goods fit into two iron trunks. There were usually goodbyes to be said and regrets. But going to Nuanetsi was exciting news. Two uncles had been there in the 1950s, one a Native Commissioner and the other a clerk in the same department. As high school pupils, my brother and I often visited in the school holidays. The small government village was off the Ft Victoria to Beit Bridge road, near where the road crossed the Nuanetsi River. The few houses were set in a clearing in the endless sea of mopani bush and it was a prime game area. The police area included cattle ranches and tribal areas. It was the dry country and the ranches were very big, most of them a hundred thousand acres or more. Nuanetsi Ranch was once over a million acres but was reduced to about five hundred thousand in later years. Many of the ranches also utilized the game by allowing hunters on the property or by culling game for meat, hide and other useful goods.

In the school days of the 1950s, the railway bus had a small compartment of about six seats for first class passengers, a bigger compartment for third class and it carried many tons of cargo behind in a large trailer, delivering goods to farmers all along the road. It left Salisbury at 8am and at 6pm arrived at Ft Victoria. The fare of ten shillings return included over-nighting in the Ft Victoria Hotel and meals. Ft Victoria was where I was born and it was the town from where farm supplies were fetched or farmers' meetings held. When I was a boy, it was the home town. At 8am the next morning the bus went on south and finally arrived at Nuanetsi at 3pm. That was in the fifties. Today that trip is half a day's drive. The excitement always rose during those school days after the hilly country south of Ft Victoria was left behind. Going down to the low veldt meant a change of vegetation. Going down from the high ground the narrow road became flanked by tall mopani trees, and the odd baobab, the trees slowly becoming smaller as the country got drier and then impala and kudu and wildebeest could be seen. The game seen in the school days meant soon we would be out on foot, deep in the forests with gun in hand. The last hours on that dusty, bumpy bus ride were always filled with impatience.

Another playground of my younger years was this game-filled vastness and few could have been better. The old village had three Native Affair houses: solid old brick houses under silver tin roofs with wire gauze closing in the wide veranda that ran all the way round the outside of the house. Across from the houses was the sprawling building of the office block with attendant outbuildings butting into the encroaching bush. To one side were the clay tennis court and the thatched hut, open at the sides, with chairs for the off-court players. A little way off stood the police station, in those days only a single quarter of the same construction as the other houses, but with an added outside kitchen. The black police lines were a few round brick huts with thatched roofs. Over the road from the mess was the charge office, a large oval hut, also thatched, with a massive hardwood counter down the middle and two desks with chairs for the two white police officers behind it. At each corner of the houses were rainwater tanks. In the long dry season, the collected roof rainwater was the only water. In later years, a new house for the married member in charge of the station was built, and a new multi-roomed charge office. The water problem was solved by the government works department driving long perforated pipes into the riverbed through the sand to the water under it. A diesel pump drew the water up and to raised tanks at the village.

There was also a jail. That was another very large oval hut divided into three cells, with sun baked brick walls and thatched roof. The jail had a two metre high diamond mesh fence round it and a rickety gate. The inmates were all low risk convicts; most of them were there for wildlife offences or for beating their wives. They wore white shorts and shirts with red arrows on them. They were required to do hard labour. All day they moved slowly round the government houses, sweeping the ground with grass brooms. At other times they were taken into the forests to collect firewood with a large two wheeled hand cart. The warden did not bother to go on the wood collection as no-one would escape. Each prisoner was a local tribesman and it was a simple matter to fetch from their home kraals anyone who ran away. The food in jail was a lot better than the convicts had at home, most being subsistence farmers who supplemented with poached animals. In the evening, the warder gave one prisoner the gate keys and told him to lock the gate and cells and throw the keys out.

As a schoolboy, my first hunting with a rifle bigger than .22 calibre was done with the bandits from the Nuanetsi jail. Impala or similar size buck were shot for the village and jail inmate's weekly meat rations. One evening, my uncle handed me the 7mm with the scope and told me to go out early next morning and fill the hand cart with impala. At dawn, a dozen bandits joined the hunt and we headed for the river about two hundred metres off. There were still pools of water in the riverbed, and big herds gathered there to drink morning and evening. Impala were in vast numbers all over the low veldt; great big herds of russet red and black strips that looked like a flowing liquid when they ran leaping over grass and logs. In the early morning, both banks of the river were infested with wild animals but impala were in the greatest numbers. The bandits pulled the hand cart over the sandy ground and nearer the riverine vegetation. They stopped in the shade of a baobab and only two moved on with me. In an hour I had shot ten or so impala. At each shot the herd milled, stopping and starting before heading in one direction and then another and it was easy to zero in with the scope.

The bandits made a fire and a buck was butchered and roasted. The skin and bones were left for the hyena and jackal that had already arrived, smelling the blood. On the way back to camp, the bandits made up a praise song for the young hunter and chanted all the way to the police camp. It was but one of the magic days for me at Nuanetsi. There were many others as each morning of the school holidays we left the village to roam and hunt the forest and riverbanks.

There were a few milk cows kept nearby and each dawn a young boy of our age arrived with two cordial bottles filled with fresh milk, corked with inner bark, and sold them for a few pennies. Then a few more boys arrived and my brother and I would pocket the five bullets we were rationed to for the day and snatch a slice of bread and join the waiting boys. It was permitted to shoot buck up to impala size, but usually only guinea fowl or francolin were taken and cooked over a fire. Interspersed with the evergreen trees along the riverbanks were a variety of wild fruit trees. There was enough fruit for us and the monkeys and baboons. At sundown we returned to the village, tired and happy and dirty. Once we found a giraffe that allowed us to take turns clinging to its front leg, a swinging slow ride as it browsed unconcerned. Another day we were treed for a couple of hours by a curious pack of wild dogs that chattered and scampered about under us, smelling our scent and lifting legs to pee on the trees we were in. It was also from Nuanetsi that I had travelled to a school friend serving in Customs at Villa Salazar and had hunted an elephant bull alone; one unforgettable, unrepeatable hunt.

Now as my Chevrolet Biscayne rocked gently on the dirt road leading from the tar strip to the Nuanetsi village, those happy memories filled me with anticipation. It would be a wonderful world if childhood could be re-lived at will. Ten years on and the memories were distant but still strong. Then I found soon enough the grip of mankind had become a lot stronger in the area and the vast ranches were now fenced and the game jealously guarded as personal property. Water for stock came out of boreholes and dams and was pumped great distances to open up grazing far from natural water so there were many more cattle. Through the open windows of the car the hot air still smelt of wild things. The yellow and green mopani leaves were herbal and the animal dung earthy and the dust clinging. The hooting of hornbills and calls of various birds was constant. The village itself had hardly changed; but there was now a small square one-room building with a Post Office sign on the front wall. The small tin-roof store had expanded and was now a larger general dealer with a liquor section to one side. The old internal affairs houses had not changed and the clay tennis court lines were newly painted and the surface rolled.

There was also a new system of game use operating on the commercial land. All the ranchers had game cropping permits. In the beginning, the national parks rangers had done a survey on each ranch and the owners were issued permits to crop game on a sustainable basis. The game taken was to be recorded and each year new permits were issued, taking into account the numbers shot the previous year and new surveys done. The system did not work. There were never any accurate counts done. The ranchers, who abused the system, did so with no fear of any retribution. Luckily, most of the landowners did not want to destroy the game and only one or two saw high profits to be made. In the one case, a motor-driven searchlight was set up at one of the scarce waterholes and day and night culling was carried out when the animals became desperate for water. The excess of those few did not impact on my own hunting. Many of the landowners gave permission for members of the police to hunt on their ranches. The police had permission to hunt on well over three hundred thousand acres of game-rich country. As a token gesture to the law, a General Game Licence was bought from the small post office. Like the cropping permits, the licence permitted the taking of a limited number of animals and, as with the permits, there was no agency that could ensure the number was not surpassed. Except the police. Who guards the guardians?

The old thatched gaol was still there and the bandits roamed the village with brooms, watched from a distance by one warder sitting in the shade. As the appointed police prosecutor, many of the same would later be convicted at the conclusion of my case. Almost without exception the bandits were serving sentences for poaching wildlife in one form or another. The bandits still went off daily into the bush to fetch firewood for the government houses. There was no electricity. The only modern amenity was a phone, a party line on which each subscriber had a call made up of different combinations of long and short turns of the crank, and sometimes there was radio reception. All cooking was done on iron wood-burning stoves. The charge office radio and security lights at night were run from a diesel generator. There were two in the generator room, used turn-about. Pressure lamps were hung in the mess dining and sitting rooms at night and paraffin storm lanterns did service in individual bedrooms.

One morning during that tour of duty, there was a commotion and on investigation it became clear that the convicts had run off. There were a dozen missing when the hand-cart had returned with half a load of wood. There was a great deal of shouting and running about. The prison warders were extremely agitated as they would be held at fault. A pursuit party of the two wardens and a handful of police gathered. As they were about to set off there was a shouting from the nearby bush and the missing bandits arrived with the main miscreant pushed along in front of them, his hands tied with bark rope. The intended escapee was missing the comforts of his wife's arms. His companions did not want the easy life compromised so had at once chased after, caught and returned him. Order was restored and the man was brought in front of me. The prosecutor was as good as the magistrate in some minds. He promised to serve out his remaining three weeks sentence and was warned that further escapes would mean longer sentence. Case closed.

Nearly every Sunday I went hunting. For most of the day I wandered in the bush, watching the birds and the animals. Just being out in the fragrant-smelling bush was enough. At the last hour I sometimes took an impala or warthog for the mess. When a new batch of biltong needed to be made a young kudu bull was shot and slaughtered. The mess, like all the old police single quarters from forty or more years back, was a low rectangular building with a gauzed-in veranda that ran all the way round. There was a dining and living room at one end, four bedrooms and then a bathroom and toilet and a biltong room at the end of the building, with gauze walls on three sides. Mess hot water was supplied by twin steel drums set in a brick wood furnace outside. The biltong room always had meat hanging to dry in the cooler months of the year. All the ranchers also made large quantities of biltong and on every farm-patrol police officers brought back quantities of good quality biltong. Nuanetsi was a meat eater's paradise.

There was a quaint hotel nearby built on the high north bank of the Bubi River, thirty kilometres south, under the massive evergreen trees. The Lion and Elephant hotel was owned by a local rancher. It had the only commercial bar in the area and it was two hour's drive from the border at Beit Bridge. There was also a tennis court under the trees overlooking the sandy bed of the river and on weekends many locals gathered to play social tennis. A pet full-grown black mane lion roamed freely and had a habit of coming in to the bar at night, snuffling for fallen scraps of potato chips or waiting to be fed a titbit of biltong by one of the drinkers. The lion was big and had yellow eyes and was missing a front leg lost in a snare as a cub. He was raised as a household pet. The locals were uncomfortable when the lion came in. Visitors froze in fright. There was also a pet giraffe that had a taste for beer. At one end of the bar counter was a window and the giraffe watched carefully for a beer left in a glass near the window. The long neck would come through the open window and the long tongue slurp beer rapidly from the glass. Again, frightening for tourists.

One late Saturday afternoon after eating steak and eggs served on the hotel lawn, the time to go back to the station was approaching. Just then a young man came over to the table under the trees with his glass of beer, looking for company.

'I'm Splinter. Live further down the river in a caravan. Mossy control spraying. Can I join you?' He called the waiter for more beers.

'Have to go back to Nuanetsi soon. But thanks.' It was half an hour's drive north.

'Nuanetsi? Do you know the manager there? And the cattle assistant? Met them last week. Plenty game around here hey?'

'Thanks. Cheers. Will buy you one next time. Come here most weekends, see you then.'

'Tell you what. I got a rifle in the car and there are plenty of buck on the road. Let's take a drive and shoot a couple of impala. One each. What you say?'

'Have you done it before?'

'All the time. No-one around to catch you. Good eating impala. Often go out with a headlamp at night too.'

'Poaching?'

'Well hell yes. No cops around ever.'

'By the way I am Patrol Officer Smith. Nuanetsi Police not Nuanetsi Ranch.'

'Oh... I knew that... I was only joking... testing you...'

On a clear hot day the station inspector called me to his office and closed the door after glancing up and down the corridor. He was one of the many men recruited over the years directly from England. His only loyalty was to the police, but when his twenty-year service was up he would weigh the options. If higher rank looked likely, he would stay on for a few more years for bigger pension, if not he would go 'back home'. On Friday nights his wife cooked a dinner for the single members and after the meal everyone sat in the lounge and listened to records of Peter Sellers telling jokes, while outside the window was the surf roar of a tropical night and wild animal eyes reflected the lamp light. The inspector was exceptionally paranoid about secrecy in terrorist matters. That was about to be drummed home to me.

'Please keep this in this room. Some tribesmen have been seen here,' he tapped a finger on the map on the wall of his office, 'and they are probably illegal hunters with muzzle loaders, poaching.'

'Yes sir. But most poachers today use modern, stolen rifles.'

'Ah, yes. Maybe. Anyway please take a constable and go and see. You can meet officers from Chiredzi at the DC's camp here on the border of the Gonarezhou game reserve.'

'Sir. Why Chiredzi members?'

'Um, yes. Look old chap just go and meet them. That's the spirit. And, oh, by the way take your webbing and rifle just in case.'

Three hour's drive on dirt tracks through the bush with francolin, ground hornbill and flocks of doves flying up in front of the truck took us to the spot. Driving into the clearing at the camp, it became apparent that there was more than a hunt for poachers on the go. There were tents pitched in addition to the normal building of the DC's camp. The biggest surprise was the number of men in camouflage uniform that was not Rhodesian police issue. They turned out to be South Africa Police. The place had a small Joint Operation Command established in the mopani forest, complete with water bowsers and mobile workshops on the back of big trucks. There was a caravan in use as the control room. On reporting there, the police superintendent in charge looked me over in surprise.

'And you are the PATU stick from Nuanetsi?'

'No sir. Me and a constable.'

'And the rest?'

'My member i/c sent me to investigate a suspected gang of poachers.'

'Hey? Were you not told an operation is on the go?'

'No, sir.'

'Well bugger me. Can you deploy to chase down the remnants of a South Africa National Congress gang? Good man. Look, there were six of them walking on the Mozambique side and they were bumped by the Portuguese police. Two police shot dead in the contact and the gang crossed to our side. All but two accounted for by us and the SAP. They have split up and are heading south still. We need as many men on the ground as possible as they are a small target. I want you to move to there,' he pointed to another camp further south where there was a cattle sale pen and another DC's rest camp, 'and you can then track south looking for boot marks. OK?'

'Fine.'

'This call sign is JOC One. Contact us if you find anything.'

That evening we stayed at the ranger's house in Gonarezhou near Tstorapasi. In the early morning coolness, just outside the game reserve and in the Tribal Trust Lands I shot an impala and butchered it for meat. From there the hunt was by vehicle not on foot. At the isolated kraals the constable and I got out, looked around and talked to the tribesman asking for information; no-one had seen strangers. By midday we were at the sale pens and the substantial DC's rest house, with running water and flush toilet. A haunch of impala went into the oven of the fired-up wood stove. Food first and then an extended walk looking for tracks would be done. The sun was overhead, the heat high and the land parched. Having not eaten that day yet, the smell of roasting meat set saliva flowing.

'Excuse me, sir.' The constable came into the sitting room where I was reading a year old magazine. 'A cattle guard wants to see you.' There was a foot and mouth cordon fence nearby and the guards were there to ensure no cattle crossed it.

'Good morning, sah. The very man you want. I have handcuffed him.'

'Hey? What?'

'The Xhosa the mapolice asked about. He wears my handcuffs at the store near here.'

Webbing and guns were dragged on at the run and we drove the hundred meters down the track to the roadside store. The sign on the wall read 'General Dealer. Hotel. Fine Food.' There was a dark eating area with several tables and chairs just inside the front door. There was a man in camouflage sitting at a table, bent forward and hands cuffed behind his back. A man, who turned out to be the store owner, stood nearby with a hunting spear, on guard. The sitting man had a bulging lump on his temple.

'I use my truncheon stick when he was eating.' The cattle guard said proudly.

'Where's you rifle?'

'There is no rifle, murungu.'

'I will not ask again,' and I stepped closer and jabbed my FN barrel in his face. He jerked back but my push was heavier than meant and the round barrel broke a circle of teeth, splintering them.

'No, please murungu, there is no rifle only a Tokarev, a Tokarev revolver.'

'Where is it?' Feeling remorse as tooth chips were spat out.

'With my pack. Hidden behind the store, murungu.'

'Take the cuffs off. OK, now walk ahead of me. If you run or try to shoot me I will kill you.'

'No please murungu.'

'Pull the pack by the straps back to me.' It was hidden fifty metres from the store next to a red anthill. 'Now sit down there. Constable, cover him.'

The tatty canvas pack contained dirty clothing, ammunition, a pistol and several hand grenades. In a side pocket was a twenty pound note. That quickly went in my shirt pocket. There were also a number of hand-written books that looked like diaries. The SAP would have it all except the money. Back at the rest camp, the roast leg of impala was taken out of the oven perfectly brown and moist. Radio contact was made with the JOC. The other gang member had been killed earlier by a platoon of SAP. They were unbelieving when I reported no shots were fired, even more incredulous when I reported the cattle guard had made the capture with baton and handcuffs. The SAP later duly rewarded the guard. The order was to drive at once and urgently to Vila Salazar with the capture. It was a six hour drive. The constable broke open a ration pack and we shared the bully beef and beans while on the road.

'Please murungu,' the remains of a liberation army pleaded, 'I have not eaten for four days. That is why I went in the shop, murungu, I was dying of hunger. Please something to eat and water, murungu.'

'Give him the impala, constable. Don't worry, we will shoot more tonight. And my spare water bottle.'

My vague feeling of guilt for smashing his teeth almost vanished as I watched him attack the haunch like a wild beast. It was not long before most of the four or five kilograms of meat had been reduced to a bone. As we neared the Salazar police station more and more SAP vehicles pulled in behind the truck, all the men in them bristling with weapons. The capture began to look worried.

'What were you going to do when you got to South Africa?'

'We were going to fight the Boer army.'

'Six of you?' But he looked nervously back at the following convoy and did not answer.

The man was whisked away as soon as the truck stopped at the Vila Salazar police camp. Special Branch of both countries barked questions which the constable and I could not answer. The SAP slipped us both twenty pounds as a reward; not a word was said about the note already in my pocket. Forty pounds was a month's pay. A long, hard day but worth it; certainly one of the best PATU patrols done so far. That night was spent sleeping on the floor of the mess in a borrowed sleeping bag and at dawn we drove through the fragrant bush back to Nuanetsi.

The previous night a red plastic-covered file had been handed to me by South Africa Police Special Branch. It was marked Top Secret in English and Afrikaans. On each page was a photograph and complete history of every member of the African National Congress hierarchy, maybe a hundred of the top leaders. Instructions were to hand it to the member i/c at the station, who, in turn, had orders for its onward transmission. It was a very secret document and had to be carefully guarded. It was duly handed over to the very man who had considered the operation to which he sent me too secret to tell me about. Two weeks later, a delegation of senior officers arrived from Provincial Headquarters in Ft Victoria and for a full day I was interrogated about the book. It had gone missing and I was one of the suspects. A volley of reports had to be put in. Then the officers left and I heard nothing more of the missing top secret document. The answer to that mystery would be revealed at the end of my police career.

The long hot days and the hot moist nights were broken often by hunting, day trips to a nearby ranch and days of wandering through the bush, and also by patrols. As usual, at regular intervals, patrol officers were required to visit the far scattered ranches. In the end, two homesteads could be done in any one day. The first was reached in the morning and the owner and family insisted the P/O stay for lunch. After a gigantic meal he was sent off with cookies and biltong 'for the road'. The next homestead insisted on putting the police patrol up for the night and more extravagant hospitality. By the time the patrol finished after a week or so the truck was filled with cakes, biscuits and biltong of the highest quality. The purpose of the patrols was to assure the isolated homes the police were around and to give the ranchers a chance to bring any problems to the notice of the police.

It was when working in such an isolated place as Nuanetsi that one saw the reason behind the early prohibition on junior police details marrying. Life would have been hard for young women left at the station in total isolation while husbands went away for weeks at a time. It was hard enough at times for single men to bear. The single quarters dated from the earlier pioneering days. The bedrooms still had saddle racks on the walls. In the storeroom was still the five gallon glass jar full of cold tea. Until the 1950s, that bottle had been issued filled with brandy 'malaria, medicine, for the use of' and the district quartermaster came round the stations every six months to check and renew stores. As soon as he left the bandy was drunk and if no-one got malaria cold tea replaced the liquor for the next inspection. It was an excellent, if temporary, antidote for isolation. If an officer got malaria then it was presented empty, the sick man fortuitously having used all the medicine. There were other deceptions.

The district stations once had donkeys which were used as pack animals in the days of horse patrols. At Nuanetsi in the late 1960s there was a donkey nearly seventy years old. The station donkeys were identified with a number branded on a front hoof. Like the police horses, the donkeys were members of the force and entitled to pension and medical treatment. When a donkey was lost to lion or disease there was as much paper work to be done as when a police officer was killed on duty. Donkeys could be bought locally for two shillings and six pence. The easy option ensured the extremely long life of the station donkey and avoidance of reams of paper work.

The mantel of public prosecutor was still round my shoulders. At least those of jailer and executor fell on others. A senior magistrate called at Nuanetsi at two-monthly intervals, putting up at the Lion and Elephant. The courtroom was a small one at the district commissioner's office block and it was a miniature of big city courtrooms with the massive, high magisterial bench at one end of the room and a wooden rail dock, and wooden benches for the prosecutor and others to the rear for the public. The district commissioner had until recent years been the magistrate presiding over all matters involving natives. The old courtroom was still put to use by the circuit magistrate. The present magistrate had been a swimming coach at my high school and for years was the coach of the national water polo team. He was an unconventional man.

He made a habit of arriving at the police station the evening before the court day and called in to see me. After a hard handshake and hearty greeting he would ask to see the next day's dockets and indictments. Then he would go over the state evidence; all strictly taboo in normal times. Almost always the court case roster consisted of wildlife offences. Sometimes there was an assault case, inevitably concerning a man returning to his hut drunk and beating his wife. He would make notes and if there was a weak case he would put that docket to one side. That was a cue to the prosecutor that the case was weak and would have to go to full trial. Then the two white members of the court would adjourn to the Lion and Elephant for an evening of beer and talk. He was not your average aloof magistrate. At 9.30am the court was in session.

'Good morning, your worship. May I call the first case? Orderly! Number one on the roll please.'

'Ah, yes,' says the beak, as the miscreant enters cap in hand, 'So you are the man who hunted impala on Ingwe Ranch with dogs. Is that correct?'

'Yebo, eshe.' Then a crafty glance. 'But, eshe, the farmer shot my dogs.'

'One impala, illegal dog hunting. One month hard labour or thirty dollars. And it is ordered the dogs be destroyed. Next case.'

'Orderly! Number two.'

'Ah, Mutt and Jeff I take it. Don't translate that,' he orders the translator come clerk of court, 'eh, Simon and John. Is that your names? Yes. You took a wire from the farmer's fence and caught a kudu. You were caught skinning it?'

'Yebo, eshe,' they chorused. 'We were hungry.'

'There's plenty of work on the farms. There is also work on the mines at Mashaba and Shabani. The fence must be mended and cattle straying collected. The tribal land has no kudu because of wire snares. Three months or thirty dollars. Each.'

'Orderly! Number three on the role.'

'Mr Prosecutor, it is nearly time for the tea recess. After this case?'

'Yes, your worship.'

'So? What is this? A man who hits his wife?'

'Eshe, I was drunk and she laughed at me.'

'Have you sent her back to her family?'

'No. Eshe, she is here. She came here with me. To pay a fine.'

'A very serious offence. You are sentenced to death. Court will adjourn.' And he rises, bows and strides out the side door.

In the court, the accused sits down suddenly stunned with disbelief and horror. The interpreter can hardly speak as he suppresses his giggles, and the court orderly constable pretends to sneeze, covering his face with both hands. The beak and PP drink sweet coffee and eat sandwiches from the basket the hotel packed earlier. A game of tennis is arranged for later. It is agreed that the remaining case, another poacher, is scant on evidence and will be formally withdrawn to save time. The court re-convenes.

'Orderly! Bring back the last accused.' A short pause and the worried wife beater creeps in. 'Now look here my man, the court has reconsidered sentence. Your sentence is altered to six months hard labour or sixty dollars and twelve lashes with a heavy cane.' The beginnings of a smile on the accused face turns to a scowl again. 'As I said, hitting a woman is very serious.' A long pause while the beak's pen busily scribbles on the record. 'All suspended for three years on condition the accused is not again convicted during that time of any case involving violence.'

'Orderly, number four. That will conclude the role, your worship.' The tribesman comes in fearfully. He stands before one who passed the death sentence on the last accused. 'The State wishes to withdraw the case, your worship.'

'This is your lucky day. You are free to go. But I know what you look like now, and next time it will not go well.'

'Yebo, eshe. Thank you, thank you, eshe.'

'That concludes today's court roll, your worship. All rise.' It is just after 11am.

By midday, the game of tennis is over and the district court officers sit sweating heavily in the black shade of the evergreen trees growing on the high banks of the Bubi River. A waiter comes across the deep green lawn carrying a big tray with two cold beers and two kudu fillet steak and vegetables. Another hard day of legal battling is over and justice has been royally served.

The slow, old-time life was of hunting on weekends when off duty and sitting on the gauzed-in veranda at night drinking beer and talking with the other exiles, the pressure lamps hissing. Also there were early nights and rising before sun-up for a run along a bush footpath along the riverbank and the old-time police life of socializing and mixing with the locals as respected members of the community at the weekend tennis social, followed by dancing in the open-sided thatched roof hut. The once-a-month film was projected on to a wall in a rancher's house in a room with rows of chairs, and during reel- changes there were hot drinks and cake. The massive bougainvillea creepers grew next to the mess, the stems tree-thick with age, and the rows of pomegranate trees were the only hardy plants that withstood the heat. All comprised a pleasant and different experience of life but one that pales quickly. The fleshpots of town called loudly to most young men.

The transfer came, again without warning. Arriving back after another fruitless week chasing shadows of insurgents through waterless bush where no-one lived, the member i/c called me to his office and said Provincial Headquarters had sent orders to report to Kariba with immediate effect. Kariba was on the northern border of the country, Nuanetsi almost on the southern one; only one longer transfer was possible; from Beit Bridge to Kariba. The isolated bush-life meant there had been many months of sexual abstinence. Kariba was a prime holiday destination and had casinos and hotels and tourists. There would be women again. So instead of asking 'why me?' a sense of excitement and adventure stopped any query of the transfer to another police province and a far one. The many transfers already over the few years of service led me to accept that postings were temporary and short. It was not unusual to be transferred within a police district, but transfer to another district did not happen all that often. Or so it seemed at the time.

It was a drive of a thousand kilometres and took all day. Kariba was another remote area of thick bush teaming with wild animals, so the bush was familiar and the scent of the wild places that came through the window in the technicolour sunset well known. I took the road from Nuanetsi to Salisbury and then on north along the road that was once called the Great North Road and was to have been the road linking the Cape to Cairo in Rhodes's dream. There were several small farm towns along the way and the last was Karoi, and that small place stood in thickly forested rolling hills and the road a gentle roller coaster through tobacco and mealie fields and the odd isolated farmhouse and then up into the mountain ranges that made up the Zambezi Escarpment, up through hill ranges in twists and turns and through steep sided cuttings, with herds of game now visible on the far slopes. Often the grey boulders of elephant herds watched, partly hidden in the trees, or stately kudu bulls looked down their noses from the hills with massive curling horns lifted back.

Then Makuti, through the fly chamber and on up the hill to where the police station, now no longer tents but brick buildings, stood just off the road in the trees, and then down the hill to where the road to Kariba branched to the left and northwards, just before the Makuti Motel. Memories of Support Unit days, but no time to stop; fatigue was setting in and there was only an hour's drive left. So on down and down, twisting and turning through the mountains and more cuttings till the heat of the lower land made the inside of the car hot enough to bring sweat. The feral smell of the mopani bush and large herds of wildlife, cat fur and strong herbs filled the car. Then the road straightened and ran flat past the small airstrip, and the smell of the lake water also in the car, the lake just beyond sight to the left. The scattered lights of the hotels along the lake shore and houses up there in the sky at Kariba Town on the mountains.

# 7

# The sweat begins to flow

Kariba is a holiday destination to rival the very best in the world. A massive inland sea stretches nearly three hundred kilometres long and fifty wide, a sea ringed by pristine bush and mountains with dozens of small islands. When a storm blows in, the waves are three metres high and boats are in peril. Scattered along the shore are luxury resort hotels, and two casinos. A visitor can fish in some of the best fishing water in Africa, while watching rhino, elephant and buffalo feed along the shores where waves break, and crocodiles and hippopotamus share the boat space. They can have lunch in air-conditioned rooms and swim the afternoon away in blue pools, and in the evening call at the casino and indulge in nightclub life till the early hours. The lake and pool water is warm enough to swim in even in the pre-dawn hours. And there will be lions flopped down getting the last of the sun's heat from the tar road on the drive home, and animal eyes both sides of the road reflecting the car headlights.

For a tourist it was an ideal place, except for the ever-present heat that seldom dropped below thirty-five degrees day or night. In winter sometimes it was cooler, but in winter the sky was cloudless and the wind never blew. For the police officers and other workers living there, things were different than for the tourist. Police pay did not stretch very far, and resort life was expensive. A boat was necessary to savour the magic of the lake. Boats are expensive and boat motors burn fuel at a terrifying rate. The village people had a simpler life than visitors. The town sprawled round the mountain tops of the range that formed the gorge where the massive wall was built. Houses were built on many flat places in the mountains and at the very top of the winding road were a hotel, bank, shops and a country club. Near the club was the open-air cinema with a curved bank of brick seats much like old Roman theatres, and a whitewashed wall on which the film was projected. The bright projector attracted swarms of insects and flitting shadows joined the flickering film on the whitewash backdrop. When the casinos first opened, local residents were banned by law from gambling; apparently only tourists did not become addicted to gambling.

Of usual police work there was none. On each police station the crime register was the bible. The register was a massive leather bound book with hinges that opened and closed with a crank so that pages could be added or taken out of the throngs that held the covers together. The book normally stood on its own plinth in the charge office. Every report made of any sort of crime was entered in the crime register. The progress and final conclusion of the crime was added as the investigation progressed. The cardinal sin was to make a false entry or delete any entry already made. It was the record that tracked all crime and investigations in a BSA Police station. At Kariba it was not even open, and in all the months that I was stationed there no crime was recorded in the crime register. With no crime to investigate, the member i/c found ways to occupy the junior ranks. That meant patrolling in various forms. Boat patrols covered a vast area of the lake and shore that fell under the station, reaching a hundred kilometres to the west to Binga Police in the Matabeleland area. Foot patrols went out into the dense game-filled bush, foot patrols in an area full of hills and mountains which were away from the lake or feeder rivers, where the land was dry as a bone except in the rain season.

Each police station was connected to District Headquarters by a radio network. Every morning at 8am, a radio operator in headquarters conducted a district broadcast. Firstly, messages for all stations were sent out; stolen cars, missing persons, and new orders from the district commander or other officers. Then each station was called in numerical order and messages for other stations were dictated. The duty P/O taking the messages had to type them on a Radio Message Form, in duplicate with carbon paper making the copy. The typewriters were all very old and battered by constant use as all BSAP paper work was typed. The messages were dictated at a fairly fast rate and it required a bit of skill and alertness to keep up. The rest of the district was listening in and each duty officer anxious to get done with the broadcast and get on with his day, so any slowness called in acid comments.

It was on these morning broadcasts that a daily situation report put out by Joint Operational Command listed all terrorist activity. JOC was a command post set up to deal with the insurgent situation, made up of army, police and air force. At first JOC was temporary and once a gang had been accounted for, dissolved. In later years it became permanent and in the end there was one central JOC and a number of regional ones. More and more insurgents were entering the country and nearly every day there were reports of murders and atrocities. Anyone seen as being government authority, like chiefs and headmen, were shot along with their families. People suspected of being informers were mutilated, tongues and noses cut off, legs and arms chopped off. Terrorism relies on terrifying the local population to enable the terrorist to move around without fear of reports being made to the government forces. Initially almost all incursions were from Zambia, but with the demise of Portuguese control of Mozambique, the focus moved to that much longer border.

Kariba was on the Zambian border and during that posting insurgents still came over the river and lake. So foot patrols were sent out to see if any gang could be located. The border was hundreds of kilometres long. The lake was also a vast stretch and the government boats a handful in number. The terrorists crossed the water in the black of night in 'banana boats', canoe shaped craft with small motors that were almost silent. The boats returned to the Zambian shore after dropping their cargo.

So the patrol officers and constables of Kariba were required to walk long distances in searing heat in the proximity of dangerous animals looking for boot spoor. The water of the lake bred large numbers of insect pests. The low veldt was tsetse fly country. The fly landed unfelt and the proboscis entering stung like a bee. Swatting a fly did not kill it. The insect had to be ground between palms or nipped between fingers to kill it. Then there was the minute mopani bee, a shiny, hard-shelled winged insect that gathered in clouds round the head of any man or animal. They crawled up noses and into ears and eyes, seeking moisture and wax for hives. It was almost impossible to wave them off, the only relief coming from head scarves carried for camouflage. The net scarves were pulled over the head as fly protection. The tsetse and mopani bee vanished at night. Sundown called out millions of mosquitoes. Anti-malaria prophylactics were the order of the day, but a good mosquito net was the only thing that allowed a man to sleep at night. On patrols, the nets were often rigged in the day when a tea or food break was taken and men sat inside them while eating or drinking, out of reach of the tsetse and mopani fly.

As ever, the patrols at Kariba were plotted on a map on the wall in the officer of the member i/c. The route chosen for one of my patrols was from the Eastern Basin where the Nyaodza River fed the lake, upstream to the top of the escarpment where there was a small mine called Jack's Luck. It was a thirty-kilometre climb up steep mountains and it was September, six months since the last rain and one of the hottest months of the year. The map was marked 'permanent spring' at a point about half way up the mountains. When it was pointed out that it was highly unlikely, the member i/c promised that a helicopter carrying blocks of ice would be dispatched if there was no water.

Dropping ice blocks in sacks was the option if there was no landing ground.

Early on a hot dry morning, the station Land Rover dropped Dusty, two constables and I at the concrete culvert over the Nyaodza River. Dusty had been in my squad in Depot and a couple of years back had been a fresh-faced eighteen-year-old English recruit who enjoyed running cross-country. The green fields of the high veldt were a world apart from the dusty, dry brown and grey mopani and baobab bush creaking in the heat of the white-hot sun. So the packs were shouldered and the trail led upstream along the river, an ancient elephant path that all game used when moving through the bush. The stream came down out of the hills over a series of giant boulders, a cascade of small waterfalls. The only sign of water at that time of the year was the eroded rock of the riverbed. Each man carried extra water; the sun sucked up sweat fast, and sweat was all that kept the body from overheating. Sweat had to be replaced by water. Before beginning the climb each man drank as much as he could and then the bottles were refilled at a seep dug in the sand bed of the river by elephant.

The elephant path followed the easiest contour upwards. The big animals were heavy and needed to find the best way up. The track they used was clear of vegetation and the ground hard packed. The patrol laboured upwards with only heavy breathing breaking the hot stillness. Clothing was soon soaked in sweat. Every forty minutes a halt was called for ten minutes rest. The men sat together and each had cut a switch of a leafy stick and swatted the tsetse and mopani bees on the man next to him, so the short rest was disturbed. And then upwards and onwards, labouring hard to reach the mine marked with a red-topped pin in the office down far below. Midday came and went and the promised 'permanent spring' was near. Just two more hill ranges to go. Then a watercourse showed and, following that uphill, the spot marked on the map was reached. 'Permanent spring' had become an intermittent spring, flowing only in the rains. With still ten kilometres to climb uphill all the way and little water, the situation was bad.

The radio had to be carried up a nearby rock peak and then the spider aerial pulled up a dry tree before Kariba was raised.

'Please have the chopper sent with the ice blocks. Copy?'

'Roger. Stand by. Over.' A long pause and then the member i/c, concern in his voice.

'Sunray Kariba here. The chopper was dispatched to an emergency in Mashonaland. Regret no re-supply. Repeat no re-supply. Copy that?'

'Roger. Situation here serious. Suggest remedy. Over.'

'Make do somehow. Copy?'

'Roger. Wilco. Out.'

It was a rueful and tired patrol that hitched up packs and laboured on upwards. A dry eternity later, a plateau was reached and the path was now level, but there was still six kilometres along the high ground to walk to the mine. First the mouth gets sticky and then dries and then lips have a dried crust on them and it is hard to swallow. A porcupine crossed some open grass and I shot it for dinner. Very like a young pig to eat. Dinner would be eaten at the mine soon. A mine and workers most importantly at that moment meant water. The track went down the side of a gorge and below some thatched huts showed and a big building with a tin roof. The patrol rolled floppy-legged down the path. Before reaching huts some youngsters were seen gathered round a seep hole dug in the bed of a dry stream against one bank. Without taking off the backpacks, the patrol fell onto the white sand at the edge of the small pool, face down and drank and drank. Jack's Luck had a water hole and the condition of that water meant nothing to thirsty men.

Jack Fynn was an old time prospector who, in the first half of the 20th century, wandered the vast Zambezi Escarpment region looking for the elusive Eldorado. There were small workings scattered throughout the empty game country that he had scratched a living from; mica here, a bit of copper there, and so on. One night at the Kariba police pub, The Jam Jar, when there was still a two-pound bounty on wild dogs, he sold two skins to the DC who was drinking there. During the evening he sold two skins twice more to the DC. Then he vanished and later the DC admitted, to our great amusement, that Jack had sold him the same two skins three times, fetching the skins from the DC's truck in the dark night and re-selling them. Lost Horizon, another remote mine in the Chiwore Wilderness, where the Support Unit was sometimes based, was another of Jack's. Jack's sons sent him to an old age home in Salisbury when he became frail and one morning he walked out the door and was never seen again. I like to think he found his way back to his remote bush home and died a natural death at the hand of predators.

Dusty had started the patrol full of the bounce of youth; he was five years younger than me and had lived a far more healthy life. At the bottom of the climb, he had walked ahead and made small detours to examine things in the bush that attracted his attention. As the day got hotter, the water in shorter supply and the path upwards endless, he lost some of that bounce. By the time the 'permanent spring' was reached, his face was showing tension. He did volunteer to climb higher with the radio aerial but was beginning to slow down, as we all were. The last half hour descending down the edge of the gorge to the waterhole his breathing was just as loud as the other three men. There was a secret satisfaction for me in that. A slight distaste for Englishmen was something that grew over the years, and got stronger as the ducking and diving over black rule continued. Today fifty years on that distaste is as strong as ever. Dusty was English but also he was fit and brash; it was satisfying to see him worn out.

The manager of Jack's Luck was an Englishman with a cultured accent, married to a local woman, and he asked her to cook the porcupine and do dinner for the four of us. Then he produced a battery run record player and put on some classic piano music very loudly while waiting for food. The soothing music fitted very well with the purple, orange and green sunset. The meal was a feast, the porcupine succulent and there was plenty of coffee; most of us were still in need of liquid to replace that lost on the climb. It occurred to me then, in one of those moments of clarity that were often followed by despair, that a radio at this mine would do a lot more good than sending out patrols. Any terrorist activity would be easy to spot and certainly the news would spread fast here in this remote place and a simple radio call would help locate the terrorist gang. The flood of despair at the lack of foresight and action by the senior officers hit me. How many more hard miles of fruitless seeking?

In the early evening, the patrol shook out bedrolls under the tree near the mine huts and rigged mosquito nets. An early night would rest us all and there was still some way to walk, a lot of it still in the mountains, before we reached a dirt road where we were scheduled to be collected by the station transport. Shortly after rolling under the net, a grumbling from my stomach announced severe stomach problems. The rest of the night was spent either on my haunches evacuating my bowels or bent over double emptying my stomach the other way. Dusty and the other two were not affected so it must have been in the water hole on the side where I fell down to drink. As the senior member of the patrol my decision was to terminate the patrol and the station transport was called for. It was a long walk on shaky legs for me to the dirt road and by the time Kariba came into sight, a doctor was urgently needed. The medicine prescribed worked a miracle and almost instantly after downing the pills my stomach cleared, so fast the member i/c became suspicious and suspected 'lead swinging'.

The other job allocated to me at Kariba was keeping records of the bar stock. The Jam Jar was very popular and had a high turnover. All the locals used it as the prices were very low and no hours were kept. The hotel bars closed at 10.30pm and then a crowd arrived at the Jam Jar. The barman was whoever wanted to do the job, but in later years an ex-member of the Rhodesian African Rifles ran the bar. He had been wounded and had a gammy leg, but was very fast and alert with the orders.

The bar had latticework doors in black iron and on the wall was an old armour breastplate, several cannon balls and an ornate and slightly rusted sword. In the 1600s the Portuguese sent an expedition up the Zambezi from the coast; hundreds of men in full armour and with cannons on carriages. The tsetse fly soon killed the horses and the men had to drag the guns. It is hard to imagine the hardship of men in the deadly heat of the Zambezi Valley, hauling cannons through the thick bush in full body armour. The expedition reached the Kariba Gorge, but then was a spent force and could not go further. Only a handful returned to the coast, the mosquito was more deadly than any native army. The bits of antique on the wall of the Jam Jar were found when the wall was being built across the gorge.

There was a wide green lawn shaded by big trees outside the bar. One afternoon, the barman looked up to see a pride of lions slinking over the lawn, bellies down, in stalking mode. He was the target and was lucky he had looked up when he did. He managed to slam the iron gates in the charging lions' faces. One big male stuck a massive clawed paw through the gates and tried to hook him. He took the old sword from the wall and chopped at the leg, causing the offended beast to give voice to a thunderous roar of anger. That brought an armed posse, spilling out of the charge office buildings nearby. They arrived to see the last of the pride vanish over the lip of the gorge on which the bar stood, over the edge and down through the dense forest.

Checking the bar stock meant measuring each liquor bottle with a ruler made especially for that shape of bottle, and counting each beer and cold drink. Sales for the previous night were then worked out. The cash taken was counted and then a storeroom opened and the bar restocked as required. All the numbers were recorded in a large ledger. The job took a couple of hours. The bar takings were seldom out. There was not much work really. The ex-soldier barman did most of it.

The Jam Jar got its name from the litter of food cans that once covered the steep slope running down from the police station to the gorge below where the river flowed black, silent, deep and fast. Italian workmen had been the major workforce when the dam wall and hydroelectric power station had been built, as the main contractor was an Italian firm. The village of Kariba was largely made up of workers houses scattered at random each side of the winding road going to the top of the hills, where a multi-story hotel stood overlooking the vast inland sea. The police station and quarters were also ex-builders accommodation. In the earliest days of the station, the bar was in one of the prefab buildings and the old tin cans from the littered slope were used as beer mugs. In later years, a thatched roofed brick building was built, the logs supporting the thatch open with no ceiling. When sunbeams slanted across the room in the afternoon they picked up a thin, drifting dust. Woodborers were always busy with the logs overhead.

The Italian workers had also built a small jewel of a church up on the heights. It has stained glass windows and has become something of a tourist attraction. There was also a squash court on the side of the hill on the opposite side of the road to the police station. It was a court where only keen and fit players could play. There was no roof so it was open to the red-hot sun. The floor was un-plastered rough concrete and the sun and rain had buckled and worn it so that the ball did not ever bounce true. There were a few other men who, like me, were addicted to the game and the same handicap was on each player. The one other official activity involved boats.

A vast area of the station responsibility was the lake shore. Along the shore were a number of resorts and also native fishing villages. When the lake first filled some tribesmen had to move and they now lived along the shore. Special permission had been given to them to use gill nets and sell fish commercially. A large boat from a commercial company with cold holds did the rounds. Apart from fresh fish a lot of the catch was salted and dried. There were also commercial holiday resorts along the lake shore and on islands. Numerous old hill and mountain tops made islands all along the length of the lake. Before the lake filled, the Zambezi had run along a long valley and now in many places the high ground is islands. At Bumi, across the lake and about seventy kilometres from Kariba, where the Bumi River joins the lake through a gorge, a hotel sits up on the high ground one side of the river. A cliff rises from the lake shore and the individual houses of the hotel built at the top of the cliff look like swallows nests from the distant water.

Boat patrols went out regularly from the station to all the tribal villages and the resorts. The police boats were the fastest and most powerful on the lake. There were four or five of them, about seven metres long. Each was a sharp V-hull with inboard engines and outdrives. They all had twin motors, either two Mercruisers of 180hp each or two OMC of 240hp each; straight-six engines. Special large fuel tanks were built into the hull along each side, carrying over a thousand litres. At full tilt the motors drank 100 litres of fuel an hour. There was a recording instrument that monitored engine and boat speed and any high speed cruising had to be explained to the member i/c. The motors were opened up fully only to put the hull on the plane and then cut back to about quarter power, which was enough to keep the boat on top of the water. On long holiday weekends, top speed was sometimes called for. On those weekends there was heavy boat traffic, full of holidaymakers, and the police checked boats on the water for safety equipment. Sometimes a boat owner, thinking his massive outboards would outrun the police boats, ignored the signal to pull over and gunned his boat away. The shock on the face of such owners when run down with ease was very worthwhile.

The boat patrols that went out to visit the shore people lasted seven to ten days. The boats had two steel stools behind the high windscreen and forward of that were small day cabins. The engine covers took up most of the back with cushioned benches left and right along the rear hull. A patrol officer and constable normally did the patrol and used the high stools. There was no canopy and no cover from the sun. The lake has sea size waves and small boats rocked heavily all the time they are on the water, a tiring motion when out all day from sun up to dusk. The romance of being out on the water in a powerful boat was soon lost in the daily grind.

One evening after and long hot day I was conning the boat back towards the government harbour at Bumi Hills. The engines had been cut to an idle as it was not yet time to knock off for the day and cutting through the water at just above drifting speed used up time. The constable was sitting asleep on the stool next to the wheel and at intervals nearly falling off, but checking with a jerk. The heat and the low growl of the motors caused my eyelids to droop also. The state of near unconsciousness, almost comatose, was interrupted by a screaming, blasting, explosive devilish howl and a terrible blast of hot wind.

'The boat has exploded,' screamed the constable, and threw himself overboard.

Totally stunned, my reaction was to follow him. Luckily the wheel was jerked over to full lock on one side. The water awakened the senses fully. The shore was a couple of kilometres away. Swimming with heavy boots on is not easy. Then the roar diminished and faded and it became recognisable as the scream of a jet engine and on looking at the sky we saw a Canberra bomber of the air force at the top of a vertical climb. The pilot had seen the police boat from up high and had noted the dozing men in it. The bomber could be almost silent in a dive with engines cut right back and he had come up behind the boat in a whisper. At low altitude, and timed so the jet blast would hit the boat, the bomber engines were opened fully as it went into a steep climb. The jet blast and explosion of noise rippled the water each side of the boat. It must have been very funny for the pilot to see the reaction of the two men in the boat. It was not a joke for us in the water. Luckily the boat was going dead slow and turning in small circles. We caught on and climbed in with the aid of the swimming ladder at the back. A few days later I went to the officer's mess on the heights to look for the pilot, but he had gone back to the base in Salisbury. That was just as well, as anger was still welling white-hot.

So it went on. Each day more and more terrorist incidents were reported on the radio network, most of it on the north-west border: attacks on farms increasing; more government workers in rural areas being murdered; people being abducted for forced induction in camps in Zambia. The armed forces were forbidden by politics from crossing the borders to attack the terrorist training camps. And all the while the talks with Britain dragged on. Only black rule would suit the British. PATU patrolling also went on and for weeks at a time we chased shadows, always being deployed by office-bound senior man who knew nothing of what happened on the ground.

One hot Kariba morning, a demonstration was staged for a collection of high-ranking officers. Tracker dogs had been used with varied success in following insurgents. The dogs did not do well in the heat of the low areas in summer as they were mostly Alsatians with thick coats suited to European winters, but Alsatians were still the best dog for the job. There was a problem in that the handlers could not keep up with the dogs if they were let loose to chase down the prey. A light radio transceiver system was fitted to the dog and the handler was to fly overhead in a helicopter and relay orders to the running dog below. An old shirt had to be dragged on a rope behind me to lay a trail for the tracker dog. There was a range of hills along the north side of the road before Kariba and near the airfield. Below the range was a large rocky, wooded outcrop. The trail was to be laid from the tar road, up the hills one side of the outcrop, along the hills and then down the other side of the outcrop and back to the tar road. The braid caps had gathered at the road and could see me lay the trail although it was a forested area, because the trail went up and along and then down high ground above them and the road.

When the trail had been laid, the helicopter landed and the handler put the dog on the scent of the shirt. The helicopter climbed and the order to track was given to the dog via the radio on its back. The dog put its head down and trotted off down the scent trail. It went a hundred metres and then the midmorning sun stopped the dog in the shade of a tree. The handler ordered it on and it reluctantly walked down the trail again. A little further it stopped and sniffed the wind. A breeze was stirring and it blew the scent from the trail laid down the other side of the outcrop to the sensitive nose of the trained dog. Being intelligent and not wanting to work too much in the heat, the dog merely crossed below the outcrop from the trail going up over to the trail going down. It saw no reason to climb the hill.

Another day, while on vehicle patrol to the fishing camps along the south shore of the Eastern Basin, the constable and I stopped at the DC's rest camp near the Agricultural Research Station. Two huts with thatched roofs and half walls of poles made up the camp and a cluster of giant baobabs shaded the huts. As the sun went down and a fire was lit, a troop of baboons took to the nearby baobabs. As soon as it was dark, a hunting leopard appeared from close by and the alarm barks of the baboons rose to a deafening degree. A torch showed a big male leopard sitting on its haunches just outside the range of the firelight. All night the baboons barked and the leopard padded about.

In the rising sun the troop leader and his gang of big males began to bark in a threatening manner. The daylight cost the cat its advantage. The dozen big dog baboons now were the alpha animals and they formed a semi-circle and advanced on the cat with much showing of fangs and loud threats. The leopard snarled and feinted but gave way and slunk off. Later that morning, it raided a duck pen at the research station, breaking out thick fence poles. The duck owner, the caretaker at the research station, wanted me to hunt the cat down. That was the game rangers work, not mine.

Then there were endless parties at the Jam Jar and the cycle of sex went on. The hotels along the shoreline had a party and holiday atmosphere. There were streams of tourists, some on guided tours that took in the lake. In the evening big ferries went out on sunset cruises which were also known as 'booze cruises'. The magic of a tropical sunset, the silver water and alcohol was seductive. The liaisons were brief, as are all holiday romances. There were few single women in the village; most were in long-term relationships.

There were several people living in homemade huts in the bush, along the shore and near one or other hotel. Three men lived in a shack near the bay where the Caribbea Bay casino stands today. For some time they ran a Land Rover to the market in Salisbury to fetch vegetables for the village housewives. It was a full day's drive but they towed a trailer to be able to carry a larger load and as there was no other source of fresh vegetables in the area they made a profit. But they were party animals and all the profit was spent in wild living. Then the truck needed new tyres and brake pads and the venture crashed. They bought the remains of an iron boat and intended to rebuild that into a luxury cruiser, but one night a thunder storm and wild wind blew the iron hull far out into the lake and the lake captain blew it up as a shipping hazard.

In a grass hut near the Cutty Sark lived a dropped-out schoolteacher. He was one of those extroverts who kept a crowd entertained with wise cracks and jokes for hours on end. He played the piano and accordion well. Most afternoons and nights he was in the bar lounge of the Cutty Sark doing his one-man unofficial show. Charmed guests kept him well supplied with drink. He had an arrangement with the barman who served cold tea instead of the whisky paid for and that money later bought a meal. Many days a group of us went out on a large motorised raft, a fishing float with a 2hp Seagull and tables and chairs with umbrellas over the tables on deck. A small piano went on board with the many cases of beer. Soon music and beer were flowing and the float went slowly out to the wide water and wandered aimlessly till sundown while the crowd danced and jived. The piano man lived there in the bush for a long time and lived the life most only dream of.

Then the transfer order came to move downstream to Chirundu, next door station to Kariba. At Chirundu was the bridge over the Zambezi into Zambia; the Great North Road in Rhode's imperial dream. On the Rhodesian side there was a police station and Customs and Immigration offices on the riverbank next to the bridge. That bridge was a single span suspension bridge anchored each side in solid rock. A small way upstream from the bridge there was a lone hill about one kilometre long that fronted on the river. From one bank to the other across the Zambezi there was about a hundred metres and deep, black water full of hippo and crocodiles. There was a tarred road that branched off the road north and ran winding up the hill. At the top of the hill were a handful of government houses. The police single quarters had a swimming pool next to it; across the way was the sergeants' mess that was right on the edge of the cliff overlooking the river and on the lawn was an ornate fountain.

Scattered round the rest of the hill were the houses for the government staff, including a post office technician. At the base of the hill at the road junction there was a small post office and poorly stocked general dealer's store. A little further back south there was a petrol station and small motel with residential thatch-roofed huts hidden in the mopani and baobab forest.

Chirundu was about animals, heat, tsetse fly, heat and mosquitoes. There was no normal crime. There was, like Kariba, patrol work on foot and along the river by boat. There was boredom and heat. There were wild parties where whole sheep were roasted on spits next to the pool and drinking went on till daybreak. There were animals everywhere. Elephant and buffalo roamed across the access road at night. Rhino frequented the forest below the hill. Chirundu was a weekly film projected on a white sheet set on poles outside the police pub, where a cloud of insects attracted to the white light made the film spotty with dancing shadows. There was constant war with a baboon troop that raided the houses, immune from shooting on game rangers' orders.

Chirundu was also many weekend romances. The one S/O had a fiancée who lived in a women's hostel in Salisbury. There were many of those in the capitol where working girls preferred to board. The fiancée drove the half-day to Chirundu each weekend and brought a car load of girlfriends with her to share costs. For the city girls it was a wild and romantic place with eager and sun-bronzed men in exotic occupations; game rangers, hunters and district policemen. At night it was steamy and muggy and a midnight post-coital swim in the pool to the music of hyena and lions calling from nearby was the order of the day. In the evening and at dawn the silver river below was covered in water birds flying to and from roosts and feeding grounds and the bellowing of hippo echoed.

To work off the frequent excess, I followed my usual routine of going for a daily run. There was a track down the cliff and down and along the riverbank called the 'Ho-Chi-minh trail'. It was a steep scramble down to the riverbank and then a level run upstream along a path through the riverine forest. When the hill ended, the path bent inland along the base of the hill through the forest and then reached the tar road and the hard part of the run on up, back to the houses at the top. Late one afternoon, nearing the climb up the hill on the road and sweating copiously in the steamy heat a long, hard sprint was called for as a rhino charged from behind. It had been resting up in a thicket and was insulted by my running by so close.

# 8
# The final rounds

There are no other outstanding memories of Chirundu from that short posting. It was too short, and soon ended in another, to Makuti. Back almost to the start; back to where we had camped during Support Unit days. Then the war had once focussed on the northern border with Zambia and Makuti tent camp had been built into a large police station. There were two five-bedroom single quarters houses, a large brick charge office and office block, and a line of small houses for the married and single black officers. When the war moved east to the long, long Mozambique border, Makuti went back to sleep. By this time, I was a section officer and posted as the member in charge and the only white officer there, along with two sergeants and nine constables whose duty it was to man the charge office day and night. One patrol officer was sent down from Chirundu to man the road black for six weeks at a time.

For more than a decade the roadblock had been in place on the road north, sited in the escarpment hills near Makuti. In the early days, it had been manned day and night by four P/Os, supported by a platoon of Support Unit hidden in ambush near the roadblock. Now it had been reduced to one P/O and one constable, and they manned it only at night. Gas floodlights were set up to illuminate the area and the odd truck and car travelling at night was stopped and searched. In all the many years the roadblock was in place not one terrorist was found in any of the vehicles stopped. Then again, it was possible that it being there had discouraged the use of that road for infiltration.

For nearly a year the isolated station of Makuti was my home, and the one other man in the single quarters was seen only in the evening when he got up to do his night shift or when he came back in the morning to sleep. During my tour of duty there were only three reports made to the police. One was of a theft of a purse at the motel. On investigation it turned out that a woman guest had reported to Bob, the manager, her purse had been stolen from her room. As nothing like it had ever happened before he was rightly suspicious. When I called at the room she took me into the bathroom and indicated an open wall cabinet where the purse had supposedly been taken from. It was obvious at once it was a fake report, but I went through the motions After making some notes, I returned to the other room to find her lying on the bed on her back with her skirt pulled up to her waist. No thank you. Bob, when I got back to the motel bar to inform him, sent one of the randy young game rangers to 'investigate further'. No entry was made in the crime register either.

On the hill next to the police station hill stood a collection of tin huts, the usual government constructions of iron panels lined inside with ceiling board. The tsetse control people lived and worked at that camp. There were two white married men with their families; they were leader hunters. Another man did the office work, a retired crocodile hunter who had lost all his money running a racing horse stable. The tsetse control hunters worked in a fenced corridor, shooting all game inside it to control the spread of disease borne by the fly; infection of humans resulted in sleeping sickness. The white hunters worked with about thirty black ones, who were from the local tribal lands. The whites were tasked with shooting buffalo and elephant as the tribesmen were armed with .303 rifles, too small for those dangerous animals. They all went into the corridor to camps in the bush for three weeks of the month and then came back out and the black hunters returned to their tribal homes for a week. With all the game shot and cut into strips and dried for later eating, the titanic lust for meat of the locals was sated. The black hunters were known as 'magochas' in Shona, 'the roasters'. On the week off they made up for abstinence from alcohol in a week-long home brewed beer binge. When it was time to go back to work, a seven-ton truck was sent to round them all up. They were rested and sobered up at the camp at Makuti for a day before going out again to hunt in the control corridor.

A usual day of work at the Makuti police station meant taking the morning broadcast at 8am and then at 10am going across to the motel swimming pool and tanning the rest of the day. If the unlikely happened and a report came in, the charge office staff knew where to find me and it was only five minutes away. At sundown, the male population of Makuti gathered in the motel bar, the females in the lounge bar. The guns were put in the rack provided. There was a collection of hundreds of different calibre bullets on a rack behind the bar counter, a collection added to when hunters from all over the world stopped for a drink on the way to the valley to the government hunting concessions. A dart game would take up where it left off the previous night. There were dominoes and poker dice for those waiting a turn at the darts board. Drinks flowed. Midnight or later it was back to the empty single quarters.

The second report of the duty tour came on such a night and the charge office had to let the mess phone ring for some time before it penetrated my befuddled senses. There had been a fatal accident on the main road. At the charge office they explained to me that one of the magochas had fallen out of the truck and under a back wheel. It was a misty night and the men in the back of the hunter's truck had pulled a tarpaulin over them to keep the wet out. Like me, they were full of beer, and one magocha decided that he needed to empty his bladder and stood up in the back of the moving truck to do so. The truck lurched on a bump and the peeing man grabbed the tarpaulin for support. A random blast of wind flapped the tarpaulin sheet and flicked the man off and he fell under the double back wheels of the heavily loaded truck.

At the scene, the minced remains where gathered by torchlight and put in the body-box. The torch beams also picked out the eyes of many hyenas and jackals gathered and waiting in the verges. The steel body-box was put on the roof of the station wagon. By the time Makuti showed in the headlights, it was dawn and the sun was reddening the sky. Bleary eyed and worn out as I was, it made sense to continue on to Kariba and the hospital there, where the female government surgeon did the required post-mortem autopsy. The scant remains were placed on the slab in the mortuary and a long wait for the doctor to come on duty took place. She came in eventually dressed in plastic protection suit and rubber gloves.

A precursory glance at the remains and she asked, 'How do you expect me to examine an incomplete body? Where is the rest of it?'

'Must I fetch it? Multiple injuries will do. He fell off a truck, under the back wheels. Thirty witnesses.' It was a desperate plea.

'Certainly not. Call me again when it is all there. The one leg and the head is missing.'

It was a long, hot dry drive back to the accident scene. There was some old blood on the tar of the road and a few small bone splinters. Nothing else could be found, even after a diligent and weary search. The hyenas had moved in as soon as the Land Rover and tsetse truck had left. It was an even longer, hotter, drier drive back to the Kariba Hospital at midday.

'Well, Section Officer, where is the rest of it?' she asked, but there was pity in her eyes. I must have looked as bad as I felt.

'I really am sorry, Doc. It was raining last night and we only had torches. I am sorry – the hyena ate the rest.'

'My God! Well, I suppose there is nothing that can be done now. Give me the form, it will have to be multiple injuries, but I will not form an opinion on how they were sustained.' Which was just fine, as that was covered by many witness statements in the inquest docket.

The final case reported to Makuti that year was from a bore-hole drilling team. A new section of the game corridor fence was being put up, running to the shores of Lake Kariba. A vehicle track would follow the fence for maintenance crews and they would need water. A team was sent in to drill a bore-hole with a jumper rig. Two men were the drill crew. They had built small pole and grass huts near the drill gantry and one man's wife and child were there with him. The hole had been drilled deep enough for water to rise in it. They still had a few more metres to drill down and so the water was bailed. A long steel cylinder, sealed at the bottom, was lowered into the bore-hole, drawn up again with the gantry and the water tipped out. This was repeated until the water level in the hole had dropped and the drilling rig could be put back. It was good water and the wife came over while the draining was going on with buckets to collect the water. Her two-year old son toddled along with her. While she and the men were distracted with collecting the water, the child slipped at the bore mouth and fell. The hole was wider than the small body at the top, but narrowed further down, where it stuck fast.

The father drove the tractor, normally used to pull the drill rig, to Kariba and reported to the police. The inspector there, who outranked me, shifted the tragedy on to Makuti. A sergeant and I took the track to the bore site and the father drove back with the tractor from Kariba, getting there an hour before we arrived. It was an utterly hopeless, tragic situation. The parents held on to a forlorn hope that a policeman might work magic. The sergeant was grim-faced. It had been hours since the child had gone down. Reflecting the sun down the hole with a mirror, standard issue on drill rigs, showed only shimmering water and that water had been covering the child for some hours by then. The only thing to do was to fill in the borehole and make it a grave. They could drill elsewhere for water.

The parents refused. The body had to be recovered. I did not have the strength to deny them that. The rig had a forgery and blacksmith tools. The father took up my suggestion and at the forge built a harpoon, sharpening a steel rod and putting reversed barbs on it. The father was the only one who could operate the rig and he did so with a pained face. The small body was speared and winched up. The mother was wailing all through the procedure and rushed to remove it from the harpoon, wrapping it in a blanket. Standard police procedure and the law allowed a policeman to permit the burial of a body without autopsy if the cause of death was clear and no foul play was possible. In that case, that leeway was exercised. The long drive back to Makuti was in painful silence. Police duty can be hard sometimes.

Then there were women at Makuti. Sandy was a friend of Bob and Ingrid who ran the motel. She worked for a car hire firm in Salisbury and was given brand new cars to run in at weekends. She did the half-day journey to Makuti often. She enjoyed the attention she got from the bush men. She enjoyed my attention. It was the start of a fairly long affair. The sex was good, but the arguments were often and bitter. It was on and off for years, when I visited her in Salisbury.

New Year's Eve at the motel, the men dressed in formal suits. There was an outside polished concrete dance floor, with a big tree in the middle and kiosks each side of the floor in which Chinese lanterns hung. Every lonely man from hundreds of square kilometres of the district came to the party. Sandy was living with me in the mess that holiday. The favourite music that night was Liszt waltzes, especially the Blue Danube. Sandy was looking prettier by the hour and was almost the only single woman at the party. Every time we got up and danced some randy bugger would cut in. She loved the attention, ignoring and not caring how it made me feel. At midnight, we were dancing to the countdown when a game ranger tried to cut in again. This time I refused. After singing in the New Year, back in the kiosk the argument began again. It ended with her pouring a beer over my head and my only formal suit and moving in with Ingrid at the hotel for the rest of the holiday.

Something that gave testimony to race relations in the country where whites were often portrayed as racists by outsiders is the fact that at that time it was still safe for women to hitchhike on the country's roads. The insurgency had been on the go for years and yet young white women from all over the world still hitchhiked to all the tourist destinations. If the blacks hated the whites as the black rule advocates claimed, then it was never evident. At the later stages of the war, some eighty per cent of the Rhodesian government forces were black, need more be said?

Tourist women would hitchhike to Kariba a lot, but they would take the road from Salisbury late in the morning. Locals going to Kariba left very early. The hitchhikers would get a lift with people going to Zambia and further north. Those travellers usually stopped at the Makuti Motel for one last night before going on, and also on the way back stopped the first night at the motel. The hitchhikers would sit at the turn-off to Kariba for the rest of the day, after being dropped off by those travellers. At sunset, the gallant policeman would arrive, just as the night song of the lions and hyena began, to offer free accommodation in an empty house with all the amenities. Some of them stayed on for many days. Bush living sometimes had its perks.

There were also other activities that were invented to fill the time. Having no police work ensured the officers became creative. There was a radio mast in front of the charge office, steel latticework and three-legged. A long-standing record had been established climbing it and many tried to better the record. The station was on a hill and the wind blew gently a lot of the time, so kites were made in all sorts of shapes and sizes and long hours spent flying them. A vegetable garden was attempted across from the one house of the single quarters, but all I learnt from that was that a wide variety of animals eat vegetables and fruit. The ever-present jackal and hyena ate the carrots very young. An assortment of buck rivalled the elephant at night; when watermelons grew, the night shift constables in the charge office just over the road were given the added duty of guarding the fruit. During the day that duty went to the camp labourer.

One night returning from the pub, my batman and the labourer were lit up by the light coming out the mess window and they were throwing rocks and shouting at something in the vegetables, or what was left of them. On getting out of the car to investigate, they told me there was an elephant. Suddenly, two large white tusks loomed out of the gloom and we all retreated into the mess. In a rage I took up the FN rifle and several loaded magazines and a running battle ensued till the tusker beat a noisy and reluctant retreat back down into the nearby valley. That particular elephant had been chased off many times before. It had a habit of digging up the camp water pipes and breaking them open to drink.

Another morning I looked out the window idly to see a large baboon, from the resident troop which often laid siege to the mess, sauntering along the tar road outside the charge office with one of the last watermelons under an arm. That left only the granadilla plant growing up a tree and its fruit. The baboon was shot through the window, and later a lie was made up for the game rangers who heard about it and objected. The jackals and hyena were also off limits, even though some nights they came barrelling out the screen door of the mess as I arrived home. Other times in the night lions roared from the police camp grounds. There were many such distractions that the tourist women found deliciously alarming.

The insurgency war had moved further east, towards the Mozambique border. The farming and tribal areas on that north-east border now bore the brunt of the terrorist actions. More and more farm homesteads were being attacked at night with rocket grenades and machinegun fire. Hundreds of remote tribesmen were being murdered as the terrorist movement forced compliance from a reluctant population. Dirt roads were mined indiscriminately, with the mines often exploding under long-distance buses which serviced the tribal areas. The government forces had long used home-grown mine-protected vehicles. There was even a mobile mine detector vehicle based on a VW beach buggy with extra-large and soft tyres and a sonar scanner that led convoys over suspect roads. Many of the ordinary Land Rovers had steel deflector plates fitted to the undersides. So it was the civilians who suffered most from mines.

That end of Rhodesia was a big chunk of land and not heavily settled. The gangs had hundreds of thousands of hectares of heavily forested land to hide in. They also hid among the sparse local tribesmen. They entered the country dressed in ordinary civilian clothes for the most part and for outsiders it was impossible to tell by merely looking who lived in the area and who was an insurgent. The locals were so intimidated by the killings and torture, they seldom gave information anymore to the government forces. Unlike the terrorists, the government forces were forbidden from using force to obtain intelligence. Often on PATU patrols, it was obvious from the reaction of the locals that insurgents were in the area, and my own inclination was to beat information out of someone; that was not done, but should have been. Terror can be fought with terror, but was not done.

It was that north-eastern end of the country to which my next posting was made. It was 1975 and in the ten years I had been in service of the police I had been posted to various jobs and stations a dozen times. There always seemed to be some station needing staff and married officers were not as easy to shunt around as single ones. By this time, the rule that junior officers could not marry had been lifted. But as married men required furniture moved and schooling for the children, the remoter areas still were the beat of single men. As usual, the posting came without warning or explanation. The district commanding officer called me on the phone and curtly ordered the transfer.

Karoi was the next port of call, a small farming community. It was still in the Lomangundi Police District and had a fairly large police camp; the single quarters had seven bedrooms. There was a district prison on the edge of a golf course and the chief warden bred exotic tropical freshwater fish in the stream that ran down the middle of the course and that was dammed several times to supply water to the greens. The prison also had a vegetable garden and gangs of bandits worked there, as well as on the warden's fish. There was an old tin-roofed hotel and a few shops including a farmer's co-op. The school hall showed films once a week. The reels came by railway bus and were passed on up the road to Kariba and Chirundu. During the swapping of the reels on the projector, the audience mingled round the tea and biscuits table; there were available young women, mainly teachers. There was little social life except the sports club, the police bar and the hotel bar. The village straddled the road north.

The job of prosecutor was again mine. Other and new work was 'ground coverage'. That entailed travelling the vast area that the station encompassed, interviewing tribesmen and others in an attempt to gather intelligence on possible terrorist activity. Karoi was an extremely large police area and the first trip took over a week, driving in the Land Rover over poorly-maintained dirt roads. The sergeant and I slept over in DC rest camps at night. There was an idol called Chingombe in the Urungwe tribal lands, a rusty bit of steel that resembled parts of an old sword, and which spoke through the means of a medium. After the correct gifts were given, the medium, in a trance, said there would be hard times ahead, but refused to clarify that prophecy. We gained no important information.

At the north-eastern side of the area, close to the Zambezi, there was a mission station with an airstrip and the missionaries were from America. There was one Henry 'Chopper' Long, a man who possibly held the Rhodesia record for convictions, mainly offences involving indecent exposure. Long had secured work on a road maintenance gang and was in the vicinity of the mission at the time. Twice in the night he knocked on the door of the house where the nuns were living and when the door opened, flashed his rampant tackle and ran giggling into the night. He made the mistake of returning a third time. He knocked; the door was opened by the head nun, Polaroid camera at the ready. He flashed and the camera flashed. The sister handed the evidence over the next morning when the patrol called. Mr 'Chopper' Long did another stretch and probably still holds that record for incarceration in Rhodesian prisons.

Karoi is a corruption of the Shona word 'va-royi', meaning 'black magic witch'. The entire area was thick with the practice of witchcraft and there were dozens of spirit mediums. Near the American mission was a Zionist church built out of mud. It had high walls and watchtowers and ramparts like a medieval fort. The practitioners built it each year and each year the rain washed it all away. They all wore a belt on which there was an empty knife sheath to indicate they were none violent. A lot of time on those patrols was spent fishing for information from various black magic workers and religious fanatics, but nothing much was learnt.

And at regular intervals, the PATU patrols interrupted all other work and for two weeks the shadowy terrorist gangs were hunted in the heat of the valley or in the rough hills of the escarpment. Every day, the police radio broadcast reported mines blowing up cars and buses on dirt roads, stores being burnt down, farms attacked and people being murdered. On every patrol, the composition of the unit changed; never the same men. Sometimes the gangs were minutes ahead, sometimes days. But never was contact made. Once or twice, while in hot pursuit on tracks, other forces were put in ambush ahead and then the firefight that took out the gang was the distant mutter of gunfire. An extremely frustrating outcome when the chase had been days long and hard, sweaty, dangerous and tiring work.

In the early years of my service, and in the years previous to that, no-one was in a hurry for promotion. A patrol officer rank was one gold bar on the shoulders. After three years, promotion to senior patrol officer was automatic, unless there had been a serious disciplinary problem, and then there were two gold bars. After serving two further years, the P/O was entitled to sit the examination to section officer and three gold bars. At least five years' service was required to sit the examinations. Many did not bother for a year or two after qualifying to sit to S/O. Promotion to section officer did not change a man's life much and many did not aspire to the slightly higher rank. The duties and pay were little changed.

While in Kariba the Law and Police Duties exam was taken and passed and then it was a two week stay back in Depot in Salisbury, where foot and arms drill was brushed up. Life Saving and First Aid passes were required. Then a lecture had to be given and a final parade where uniform had to be spick and span and shining. Shortly after completing the required course, promotion came and made no difference to my duties and very little to the salary. But it did mean more postings, this time to Sinoia, another small town astride the north road but a little closer to Salisbury. Sinoia was the District Headquarter of Lomangundi and was short of an S/O to be the prosecutor. The stay there was very short as a new married section officer was brought in and I, a single member, had to be sent to fill the urgent vacancy at a more remote post.

In the morning, the iron trunk and rifle were packed and it was half a day's drive to Sipolilo, Lomangundi District, and to a posting as second-in-command to an inspector. That small government enclave was a patch of ground in Tribal Trust Land on the edge of a commercial farming area. There were a dozen houses for police and home affairs staff, a post office and a small, seldom used dirt airstrip in the bush nearby. There were two general dealers' shops in the tribal land nearby. One had a liquor section and butchery. Cattle were slaughtered in the backyard of the butchery and the carcass hung whole in a room. All the meat was one price, twenty cents a kilogram. The rump and other steak went on a first come first served basis. The liquor section had, for some unknown reason as natives did not drink it, a wide selection of good South African wine.

The nearest town, a very small farming town, was Umvukwes which was two hours north of Salisbury. The road from Sipolilo to Umvukwes was a narrow dirt strip, very corrugated, through tribal land and it was about a hundred kilometres. There was a strong soap-stone carving community in the tribal lands and excellent works of art sold along the road for very little. There were two sports clubs in the nearby farming area, and another built by the DC in the village, which boasted a swimming pool and bar. The three clubs were the centre of most of the social life. The DC's place did not compete in the sporting field, only in the bar side of things. Tennis and cricket were the main sports played, but there was also a polo field, a clay pigeon shooting range and squash court. Dances were held in a large hall.

The Sipolilo police station was just short of the hills of the Zambezi Escarpment, and a dirt road wound and twisted through the hills to a sub-post of the station at a place called Mashumbi Pools. That post was a tin, prefabricated house, with the normal radio mast outside, on the banks of the Hunyani River, just above the junction of that river and the Angwa. It was manned by a P/O detached from Sipolilo and a couple of constables, on six-week tours. It was typical Zambezi Valley there, elephant and buffalo in numbers, good fishing in the rivers. It was hot and humid almost all year round. In winter, the sky was clear of clouds and no wind blew, and by 9am, the dawn cool had turned to heat and the bush shimmered with heat mirages. In winter it did not rain and was dry and dusty.

The week of arrival saw orders issued for another PATU patrol. Sipolilo was 'hot' and there was terrorist activity all over the area. Again, the patrol was made up of five strangers from different stations, although the constable had worked with me sometime previously. He was a good bushman and tracker. Two of the P/Os were almost raw recruits and had done almost no bush patrol work, except for some compass marching practice. The stick was to go to a point in the tribal lands where a path led down through the mountains to the Zambezi Valley in the vicinity where the Hunyani River came out through a steep gorge, and was to follow the path all the way down to where the river exited the mountains. The reason given was that maybe terrorist gangs were using the path to enter the populated tribal lands above the escarpment. The patrol would be dropped off by vehicle where the path began to descend the mountains.

The area was as yet unknown to me. There were maps covering it all, in the right side pocket of my trousers. The vehicle driver had been stationed at Sipolilo for some years and knew the area. At midday, he stopped near a kraal of huts and scattered maize lands with hills looming behind. The driver said the path started just behind the furthest ploughed land. After the vehicle left, the backpacks were hefted; there was also a single side band radio set to carry, which weighed about twenty kilograms. A quick assessment of the physical qualities of the stick showed only the tracker and I were able to carry the set in addition to the normal load, so we took it in turns. It was a typical hot summer day, the sun silver in a pale blue sky and not a breath of wind. The tracker called to a tribesman at one of the huts and asked where the path down to the valley began.

'Sir, he says two hour's walk, to that hill there.' He pointed to a peak still blue in the distance.

'Are you sure? Is there not maybe two paths?'

He shouted again and listened to the answer. 'No, sir. There is only one. The driver dropped us at the wrong kraal.'

So it was back to the map reading and after a while bent over the map on the ground, it was found the patrol was a good ten kilometres from the intended start point. By the time the cultivated lands were left and the start of the path found, it was mid-afternoon. The path down the mountains was just on fifteen kilometres. The two novices were already looking tired. The only thing to do was go on down and if the walk was too far the patrol would spend the night in the mountains. It is easy to overlook the obvious; there was no water on the mountain. The patrol went on down at my command. The path turned out to be very steep and not all downhill, as at intervals it climbed before it dipped again. An hour before sunset was the time to stop and it was only then a check on water revealed the only water left was in the tracker and my bottles. One of the novices complained of a hurting back, a cut or something. A check revealed his pack was rubbing the skin off his back, leaving it red and raw. The patrol had to go on. Spending the night on the track would bring more problems than going on. Another check of the map also showed the river gorge extended out in a ridge a kilometre long from the base of the mountains before reaching level land out in the valley.

In Africa and many other countries, steep paths have cairns of stones next to them. Travellers put a stone on the cairn to mark passage. In Asia a prayer is offered, in Africa it is thought the stone lessens the burden of the climb. With the loud panting of the men in my ears I placed stones on each pile on the way down and did some praying as well. The novice's back was bleeding and he was in pain, the rest were worn out. There was still at least an hour's hard walk to go. It was dark and only the stars' light illuminated the hard-packed path. The men were all panting open-mouthed and reeling. Walking on a slope uses four times the energy walking on the flat takes. All the water was now gone and lips were cracking. Suddenly the ground was flat, but the neck of mountain loomed on the right, black against the navy night sky. Concern for the other men in the stick had faded as the urgent need for water rose. They were scattered far behind in the dark, just the distant clump of boots marking where they were.

Suddenly, the black high ground on the right gave way to trees silhouetted against the starlit sky and veering towards them there was at last river sand underfoot. Water glittered silver in the dim light and without shrugging off the pack I fell face down and sucked water. The tracker was a few seconds behind me and as we lay regaining breath and swallowing sweet water the laboured passage of the other three could be heard coming closer and they joined us on the sand bank face down. Once the thirst was no longer urgent, it filtered through that the Hunyani here left the hills in a wide deep flow and held many crocodiles. It would be prudent to move back and make a fire. There were also hyena, leopard and lions. By the light of a bonfire, lit with the brush wood found along the bank, a few tins were opened and then sleeping bags rolled out. The men quickly slept, totally exhausted. Any terrorist gang or predator nearby would have had easy pickings that night. And on another day another line was drawn on a map in an office and another coloured pin pushed in to mark an area patrolled and cleared.

In the cool of dawn the fire was stoked and water heated for coffee and tea. The man whose back had been rubbed raw was in a bad way, his entire back raw flesh, and there was only a small tube of iodine ointment to treat it with. While he was walking, the extent of the damage had not been so apparent. The option was to call for a helicopter to evacuate him or carry his equipment. With two weeks of rations, water, ammunition, heavy radio pack and spare batteries no-one would be able to carry the injured man's load for long. The bank of the river was shaded by evergreen trees and was soft, clean deep sand. The sand was convoluted into dunes which were a good place to conceal a base. The river was good for fishing and I always carried a hand line and hooks when on patrol to vary the diet of tinned food and boiled rice. For three days, the patrol lazed next to the river in a dip in the sand with a sentry posted as a look-out. The men stripped to underpants and tanned while one fished for the next meal. On the fourth day, the novice's back had recovered enough and we went on to the sub-station at Mashumbi Pools, sharing the injured man's load. A vehicle was called for from Sipolilo to take the man to a doctor at the clinic. As the patrol was now reduced to four, new orders were issued to patrol extensively in the area of the Mashumbi base camp, along the Angwa and Hunyani Rivers.

Mashumbi sub-station was an oval tin building lined inside with ceiling board. There were several rooms and the hut served as living quarters and office. There was a thatched roof, open sided home-made bar outside, with a fridge and a dart board and a record player on the rough counter, run off a vehicle battery. The bar had many times been shot up in drunken binges and was pocked with bullet holes. Across the other side of the narrow dirt road which ran along the north bank of the Hunyani was another oval hut of poles and thatch. Every three months, nurses from the national eye clinic used the hut for a week while doing their work among the tribesmen who sometimes walked hours to reach their help.

A P/O by the name of Geyser had made Mashumbi his home. Geyser had arrived many years before on a posting to Sipolilo and had been sent to Mashumbi on the usual six-week stint. He had volunteered to do longer stints and, as not many other P/Os wanted to do the isolated duty, he was allowed to remain there for long periods. At first he was rotated after several months, then he refused to leave. When he was called on the radio with information of a duty change, he would vanish. The constable and P/O stationed there patrolled on bicycles along the footpaths to the scattered kraals. When the relief P/O arrived he would find Geyser had ridden off and refused to answer on the mobile set he carried. His hair was as long as a girl's by then. He trained a pride of semi-wild cats to parachute from the thirty-metre high radio mast. Each cat had a name and a hand-made parachute and the cats enjoyed the experience, demanding to be taken up and dropped again. When he put a small crocodile in the plunge pool to scare off the visiting inspector things came to a head and he resigned rather than agreeing to a transfer.

Geyser rejoined the force a short while later and after a shortened Depot stay, requested and got transferred back to Sipolilo. By then the officers who had been there previously had all been transferred. An easy going Welshman, Taffy, was the station inspector and Geyser was allowed, on his request, to return to his Eden at Mashumbi. Occasionally, he consented to return to Sipolilo for the weekend when he bought a crate of vodka and another of orange squash and lay on his bed in the single quarters, coming out only once a day to eat. Taff sent me down to capture him during my tour at Sipolilo; to force Geyser to take a break in Salisbury and civilization. We had learnt that the way to capture him was to sneak up on the base, not call to warn him, but to leave the Land Rover out of earshot and walk through the bush to the base.

The sergeant and I managed to grab him by the belt as tried to walk away and bundled him into the station Land Rover and drove him to Sipolilo. Geyser had been booked into the Windsor Hotel in Salisbury for three days. The costs had been contributed to by the DC's staff and the police. A police vehicle drove him to the hotel and saw him booked in. Then the escort did some shopping and returned to Sipolilo. Geyser beat them back, hitchhiking. Taffy was easy going but had his limits and after a few more skirmishes with Geyser, laid down the law; no more Mashumbi, only a future of police work. Geyser resigned again and at his farewell party got so drunk he wrote off the car he had borrowed for the night by hitting a culvert near the country club. The car was going backwards when it collided with the concrete stanchion.

Sipolilo was tennis, cricket in perfect winter weather, and clay pigeon shooting at the country club. It was also endless party nights. Jerry, son of the legendry Colonel Hickman, was the second S/O at Sipolilo and had been there for some time. There was a lot of terrorist activity and many rural stores had been burnt down and looted. Jerry had collected debris from those incidents and built a bar hut in the grounds of the police camp under a big, wide-spreading marula tree. Strictly against the law as an unlicensed liquor outlet, but the most popular gathering place in the area. It was a mud and pole thatched room of about ten metres by ten metres, and one end of the room was a stone fireplace with a chimney reaching up high above the thatch. A darts board hung over the fireplace inside the room, and there was a long bar counter with freezers behind it for beer and cool drinks. A carved soap stone sign hung outside the door on the marula tree; it said 'Jerry's Erection'. Many nights the entire white population of the village gathered there.

When the South African Police were still assisting the BSA Police they were in Jerry's Erection every night. Four SAP Special Branch senior officers were stationed at Sipolilo, and they were enchanted with the wild nights in that bar, eagerly looking forward to them. When the singing started, they chipped in with a number of new songs that then became a part of the bar repertoire. Raymond, one of the SB men, became a friend during that time. The love of vodka rather than beer was the common link, and many nights a bottle was shared. He had been in South West Africa for years and then in Rhodesia for more years. His home station was Johannesburg, but he had not been home for a long time and had been living on field allowance, so his normal pay had been banked for many years untouched. Some years later I visited him in his hometown, and he had bought a number of Johannesburg apartments which he rented out and a new Mercedes; a wealthy policeman is a very rare thing.

The four SAP men came in one night very subdued. Orders had come that the SAP were to withdraw from Rhodesia. It was 1975 and the politicians had decided that if South Africa abandoned Rhodesia the world would stop badgering them about South West Africa and their racial policies. The Special Branch men and all the BSA Police officers knew that was a completely false presumption. The support of that well equipped, armed and financed force would have made all the difference to the outcome in Rhodesia. Farewells were bittersweet. The SAP officers had been living in one of the DC's houses and had reared a pig for slaughter. The pig had grown enormous and fat as the SAP did not have the heart to eat it. This happened often on temporary camps. They handed the pig to the BSA Police mess and it was in the fridge and freezer within days. The crippling sense of doom that gripped me at times when alone in the dark was particularly strong that sad night.

The DC, Jim, was an intelligent and very sociable man, a raconteur of note, and had a hobby of assembling radiograms in old wooden ammunition boxes. He and the station inspector, Taff, sang in close harmony and had a vast range of songs. As the beer flowed and the stars wheeled in the sky, the songs became more and more profane. The few wives in the pub joined in lustily, enjoying the robustness of it all. When it happened, Taff was on leave at the time and as my promotion had been a few months before Jerry, the station command was mine. It was a Friday night and the pub was packed with the police and internal affairs staff, as well as a number of farmers and their wives. The monthly meeting with the district commanding officer at Sinoia, three hour's drive over bad dirt roads away, took place at 9am on Saturday. Because of that, as well as the unnerving attention of one of the wives, I left the party early. At 5am, I was on the way to Sinoia, before the rest of the mess had turned out for stable parade.

The CO was a fair, decent man. Seeing me in the corridor of the office block, he beckoned me to his office.

'Ah, S/O Smith, how are things going at Sipolilo?' He said from behind his desk, watching me carefully.

'Fine, sir. Everything is fine, no problems.'

'Are you absolutely sure you can take care of things, Smithy?' Again, close scrutiny.

'There are no problems, sir. None that cannot be taken care of.' A feeling of missing something was strong.

It was only late that afternoon on return to the mess that a P/O gave up the story. The previous night, late, Jerry had wanted to close up and go home to his married quarters. Jim had objected, and a drunken melee took place, with people on both sides of the argument. Jerry padlocked the beer coolers. Then he wanted to switch off the lights. There was a gun rack in all police pubs at the time and Jim's Uzi sub-machine gun was in it and he took it up and shot the padlocks off the coolers. Then he grabbed a shotgun and scored a bull first shot on the dartboard. Jerry protested loudly, still trying to switch off the lights. Jim carefully shot out each of the five globes, drained the last of his beer and walked off home, singing bawdily.

Jerry was still in a rage in the morning. In anger he did the unthinkable, he opened criminal dockets to charge the DC. On a district station the DC was one step above God; he was The Law and not answerable to any other law. A feud between the police and the DC was the worst possible scenario. It was not the first or last time that sort of thing happened in the local bars. All the men were wound tight by the constant threat of terrorist attacks all around the area. To compound matters, Jerry had made several entries in the crime register. Malicious damage to property, drunk and disorderly and discharging a firearm dangerously were some of the charges. The crime register was the holy of holies, tampering with entries in it was a capital offence in police circles. The crime register was removed to my office and the door locked and curtains drawn. The crank was worked to open the binding and the offending page removed and replaced with a clean sheet, the register numbering fixed. Then the evidence was burnt in the waste basket.

Jerry was in an unforgiving mood. It took some time to swing him over, but we eventually destroyed the dockets together. Then there was a visit to the DC in his office to explain what had taken place and when he heard about Jerry's anger he at once called him on the phone and offered a sincere apology and payment for any and all damage. There was a surprise call from the OC district later in the evening.

'Ah, Smith, my good man. Just calling to confirm everything is alright there; as we discussed this morning.'

'There was a bit of a problem. It arose last night and I did not know about it till I got back here. But don't worry, sir, it has all been smoothed out and no more of a problem.'

'Are you sure?' Bringing charges against a DC was a catastrophe of note.

'If there is reason to call you I will do so at once, sir.'

'You have handled it very well, Smith. Good man.'

That was not the end of the matter. Understandably Jerry's feelings were hurt, and relations between him and Jim were still strained. The mood in the pub was not yet good. Then one night after a few beers the DC asked Jerry what he could do to make things right. Jerry, taking a chance, at once asked for a licence to hunt a bull elephant. The DC had authority to allow some bulls to be hunted in the Angwa Tribal Trust Lands. Jim took out a pencil and wrote a note to the postmaster, who issued game licences, on the back of a bit of cardboard torn from an empty cigarette package. I stuck my hand up also on impulse and he altered his permit to two elephant.

September 1976 was the date I hunted an elephant for the last time in my life. It was also the last time I shot anything for trophy purposes. It was a short hunt for me, guided through the thick riverine forest of the Angwa River by a local tribesman with Jerry as back-up gun. Using a borrowed Holland and Holland take-down rifle in the powerful Holland and Holland .375 magnum calibre, it was also a one shot kill. Within hours, a swarm of tribesmen had reduced the bull to skin and bones, and the tusks were on the back of the truck. Then it was time for Jerry to take his bull. That was when he confessed that he had never hunted anything, certainly not an elephant. His bull was shot later on open ground in the area just south of the Zambezi. The licence cost just one hundred dollars and there was a good profit from the ivory. That day, an immense sadness gripped me as the elephant died, and it still grips me today when I recall that senseless hunt. Times had changed, ethics had changed, I had changed.

In the Angwa tribal lands 'keeps' had been built to protect the population from terror attacks. The keep was made of a vast, thick circular wall about three metres high, put up by bulldozer. The locals were free to build a hut inside or not as they desired. The place was under protection of Guard Force, a sort of reserve force run by internal affairs. There were muzzle-loading cannon on the ramparts, guns made in internal affairs workshops. The pieces were called 'garden-boys' as they were charged with a bag of scrap iron, nuts and bolts and nails. When touched off, the vegetation in front of the weapon was mowed down for a long distance; trees stripped bare of leaves. The keeps were seldom attacked. On the elephant hunt we slept the night in a tin hut in the one keep near the Angwa River. It was virtually unknown for the terror gangs to attack armed government forces. They preferred to murder unarmed civilians.

Rex Nongo was the name of a successful terrorist gang leader who rampaged out of Mozambique on many bloody-handed raids into the north-east of Rhodesia. While on PATU duties, my stick had often been close to him while tracking down his gang, but he lived a charmed life. He specialized in mutilating tribesmen suspected of assisting or cooperating with government forces. He chopped both legs off at the knee on one man with a wood axe. Considerable resources were concentrated on his elimination. Special Branch gleaned information that he was on his way back to the camp in Mozambique. It was known that his gang regularly used the same pass through a mountain range near Sipolilo. Six sticks of PATU were deployed to flood the area of the pass specifically to do away with Nongo. My stick was part of the operation. The deployment was at night and by a long march because the terrorists seldom moved at night, as night warfare requires extensive and specialized training.

By sun-up the sticks were in place. The shadowy side of the slopes gave more cover, and the six sticks of men saturated the pass which was less than a hundred metres wide. Then the long, long wait. The men had to stay absolutely still and silent, an easy thing to do for a short time, but hard to maintain for hours, especially if the intended prey was in doubt. There was no certainty that Rex Nongo and gang would do the expected. The same old problem confronted the patrols all the time. The bush was wide, thick and almost endless, even on farms the forests were larger than the cultivated land. For the most part, the land chosen by this gang to enter and leave the country was empty of people so informers could not be used against them. The insurgents were always in deadly fear for their lives but Nongo was ultra-cautious; he knew from bitter experience that contact with the government forces meant certain death or capture. Lady luck, the roll of the dice, how the cards are dealt always plays a part in war. This particular day the fates chose to favour Nongo and company.

The last PATU stick at the end of the pass began to fire and there was brief return fire, the stutter of AK rifles. In seconds it was over. The radio gave the information that the gang had been seen when they were already some distance past the ambush site. The other five sticks had been, somehow or other, avoided by the gang. The fleeing gang was chased hard and fast till sundown. There was no blood spoor and they had thrown off packs and other stuff that weighed them down. They ran at pace and the followers could not do the same carrying weapons and packs. The next day, a post-mortem of the incident was held by going back to the pass and examining the gang's trail. They had gone by each part of the ambush within easy sighting range and yet no-one had seen them. It was hard to explain. These near misses by the government forces enhanced Rex Nongo's reputation.

In later years, taking on the name of Majuro, he became the commanding general of Mugabe's army. There he continued his career in brutalizing the people of the country. He helped himself to a dozen white-owned farms, long before it became the fashion. During the recent meltdown caused by the destruction of the white farms, his troops committed many atrocities to intimidate the locals into voting Mugabe in for another term. His armed soldiers made a habit of stopping buses from rural areas on the outskirts of Harare and forcing the passengers to lie on the ground. Then the passengers were stamped on heavily, some having heads fractured and dying. Another night, Majuro's troops entered a nightclub in an area of a native township south of the town centre and ordered all the patrons to strip naked. The order was then given for patrons to have sexual intercourse with the person next to them regardless of gender.

In the Mugabe era, Majuro lived like a feudal king in a large mansion in a security complex in a wealthy suburb of Harare. All the benefits of supporting Mugabe were his. His wife is the Vice President. A large slice of the proceeds of the biggest diamond mine in history recently discovered in Zimbabwe went into his pocket. In the middle of 2012, there was a mysterious fire at his palace. There were a dozen armed bodyguards on duty. The press reported he had burnt to death in his bed. The matter has been hushed up by the Mugabe government. Justice has finally arrived for all those he killed and tortured. It is an enduring regret that the man was never in my rifle sights.

With the never-ending drinking and partying and socials at the sports club it was inevitable that women came into the equation. The strange thing was that, unlike previously in my life, those women at Sipolilo were all married. The troubles meant that men all over the country were regularly called up to reserve and territorial units. Like wartime everywhere, normal morals and ethics were abandoned. There were normally only single women in my life, but it was hard to resist blatant offers. There were penalties to pay; subterfuge and evasion which left a bad taste in my mouth, but most of all there was a pall of guilt. My will was not strong, but luckily a farmer's daughter, half my age, came to the rescue and made sneaking around a thing of the past.

At one of the parties at a farm, a white Alsatian puppy was given to me. It came from highly pedigree parents, but as a colour throwback would have been put down by the breeders if I had not taken him. Spook, as he was named, turned out to be a magnificent animal. Once grown, he was a massive and strong dog, and had intelligence that was uncanny at times. Without any formal dog training he did things that only dogs with intense schooling normally did. Most uncanny of all, he understood hand signals. The white dog gave me a great deal of pleasure for the time he was with me. A favourite sport of his was to range ahead on the road during my afternoon run and chase up game birds.

Circuit court was held in a dedicated courtroom at the Sipolilo district commissioner's office complex. The magistrate's courts were all the same pattern. A high, solid and imposing bench; heavy wooden docks for accused and witness; solid tables and chairs facing the bench for defence and prosecutor and behind those, rows of hard wooden pews for the public. The rooms all had the same smell: wood and floor polish and the mouldy smell of very old books. The Sipolilo circuit magistrate was young and a squash fanatic and the court role had to make provision for a two-hour lunch break for a game at the sports club and a shower afterwards. There were still odd occasions when I was the investigating officer in a case and had to give evidence as a witness and also prosecute. It was always a strange feeling to call the next witness and then hurry to the witness stand. The evidence was given in the correct order, pausing for the magistrate to record it all by hand, and then a hasty crossing of the room back to the prosecutor's table. By now it had become a practised routine, but not one easy to get used to.

There were good days and bad days while doing routine work, but it was sometimes hard to go on as normal when all around the area a terrorist war was raging and people were being murdered. Axel Van Heerdin was, in fact, Alex MacPherson. We had been stationed together at Kariba. Axel preferred lager over his national drink, but his brogue was as thick as any Highlander. When the heat of Kariba had been quenched by plenty of cold lagers, the slur and the burr combined to muddle his speech almost totally. He had introduced himself to a group and they thought he had said Axel Van Heerdin, not Alex Macpherson. Axel was his moniker thereafter.

Axel was duty dog the morning a report came in of four tribesmen shot to death after being accused of being informers. The terror gang had ordered them buried in the sand of the dry river where the murder had happened. It was at the time that the station inspector was on leave and I was acting member i/c. Alex was sent out with five armed constables and a sergeant in two Land Rovers carrying four body-boxes. All murders required post-mortem examinations done in case they ever got to court. The nearest district surgeon was at Umvukwes at the small clinic there. The doctor was an Italian. He was on leave for two weeks, but Alex did not know that and none of the clinic staff told him either. The mortuary was a small box of concrete without a cold room or windows and Alex tied labels to the deceased's toes and left them and the paperwork for the doctor to attend to.

Two weeks later the phone rang and it took a while to decipher what the excited Italian was saying. The phone had to be held at arm's length to dampen the volume. How did the member in charge of police expect a doctor to work under such conditions? Did that chief of police not know the doctor was an educated man and not a butcher? It was impossible; all that was left to do was at once remove the cadavers from his mortuary. It was impossible to do anything with the remains, now almost just bones anyway. How could the chief allow this? After ten minutes of profuse apologies, the phone the other end was slammed down. Alex was crestfallen and it really was not his fault. No-one had said the doctor was on leave when he left the already ripe bodies in the room. The armed convoy collected the remains and took them to the tribal area where they were handed over for final burial without post-mortem examination. Sometimes it is prudent to make exceptions.

'Tell you what; I could do with a drink.' Alex's face was screwed in anguish. His uniform smelt of decaying flesh. 'Should have listened to my mother and never come out to this heathen country.'

'What time is it? Half past three. Pub closed till four.'

'Bejesus, boss. I need a drink bad.'

'OK. Let's go. Half an hour won't kill anybody. Was it bad then?' I tried to keep a straight face. The cloying smell of decaying flesh called in flies that buzzed round him. He had earned a drink.

Then, a good day. A notorious thief had been rampaging through several police districts. He mainly attacked farm stores in the night, forcing the storekeepers to unlock the safe and making a habit of raping a woman at the same time. The man had been arrested twice before but had managed to escape. For months a dedicated CID task force had been on his trail, but virtually every night he struck again in a different area. At the Saturday morning district commander's meeting in Sinoia, photographs of the man were circulated and a lot of time spent on explaining that the man was dangerous and his arrest was urgently required and all officers were to be made aware the case. The previous night he had raided the farm of Graham, the Minister of Agriculture, whose farm was on the side of the main Salisbury to Sinoia road. Graham ran a Brahman stud, and the farm store had been robbed and a woman raped and also Graham's car had been stolen.

The road back to Sipolilo from Sinoia went through tribal lands. Near a collection of huts at a crossroads a shiny black Ford Galaxy was parked under a tree. It was a startling sight in an area of no motorcars, and it was the car stolen from Graham, Duke of Montrose. The hut owners told me that a stranger had arrived two days previously in another car, but during the night had come back with another man and they had left the car there. The two had driven off up the other track and had said they would return shortly. Taking my FN rifle from the truck, I hid the truck behind huts and set an ambush. Within about ten minutes a distinctive red Mercedes, also recently stolen from another farm, drove back down the track to the parked Ford. Before the two men in the Mercedes could do anything the barrel of my rifle was tapping on the window of the driver's side. The desperado's eyes popped and his hand crept along the seat towards a revolver. Then he thought better of it just as my trigger finger was tightening. His life was not worth much just then and he possibly realised that.

With the help of the local tribesmen, the two were bound hand and foot with rope and made to lie flat in the back of the Land Rover station wagon. Back at the station, there was an instant hubbub when it was realized who the prisoner was. The airwaves were full of disbelieving voices. Eventually the CID inspector in charge of the task team demanded to speak to the member in charge.

'You want to speak to me? Over.'

'Confirm you are member i/c.'

'Affirmative. Go ahead.'

'Please make sure that the accused is held in a secure place. I will personally collect. Confirm also you are sure he is the right man.'

'All confirmed. Two cars recovered but still at the scene. On your way here please bring them in. One is Graham's.'

'Will arrive there in three hours, say again, three hours. Confirm that is in order.'

'Roger, wilco, out.' Really the fuss was over the top. It had been pure luck, the sort that is often needed in police work. It did put my stock up with the commanding officer though.

The 7th Duke of Montrose, James Graham, signatory to the Rhodesian Unilateral Declaration of Independence, Minister of Agriculture in the Ian Smith government arrived to collect his Ford the next day. There was no ceremony as he was just another down-to-earth Rhodesian farmer. But he was very pleased when Alex talked to him in his native Gaelic. Then it was on to Jerry's Erection for cold beer and amiable talk, and he was intrigued to find out that the Jerry in question was Colonel Hickman's son and brother to the army general. That few days gave me back the feeling it was worth being a policeman sometimes.

Then there were bad days, and some of them were very bad on my watch, while Taff was still on leave. The start of all public holidays is busy time for policemen. There is a rush to leave and the roads are crowded. There is carnage to clear and long nights of no sleep. Sipolilo had little in the way of traffic rushes, but a small increase of rural bus traffic did take place that Thursday before Easter. A P/O, newly out of Depot, caught the standby duties for the Easter weekend. Friday morning, the members of the single quarters went off to the country club leaving him to deal with any calls. On return in the late afternoon I asked the duty man how the day had been.

'No, well, just fine. You all said it would be busy, but there have been no reports.'

'That's how it goes sometimes, but don't tempt fates by saying nothing will happen.'

'Well, all I know is that there has been sweet stuff-all doing today.'

The phone rang and he picked it up and as he listened his eye grew wide and he handed the phone to me.

'Hello, what are you reporting?'

'They are all dead, everyone is dead,' said a voice recognised as one of the station's constables, 'the sergeant and everyone.' The voice was hysterical.

'What happened? Where are you? Slow down and think.'

'We are on the road to the store. All dead. The truck had an accident, everyone dead.'

It took some time to drag information out of the obviously shocked officer. It was a cold wave of icy water as it sank in. There had been a major accident involving the station seven-ton truck carrying the majority of the black police from the station and also most of the staff from the district commissioner. It was difficult not to get very angry as the details came out. The inspector, Taff, was still on holiday and I was next down the line but had been bypassed and Jerry had been approached. Always ready to please he had allowed the truck to be used to carry all the off-duty staff to a football match at a small commercial centre in the nearby tribal lands. They knew my permission would have been refused. There was too great a risk of landmines or ambush by a terrorist gang. It was now too late to do anything about that, permission had being granted.

Two senior sergeants had been in the cab, the one driving a good reliable man. The truck had been mine-proofed by lining the back floor with sandbags. Two wooden benches, long and low ones, had been placed down the middle and men had sat, squashed together on the benches with their backs to steel body sides. The football games had lasted all day and it was a cheerful bunch who had taken the road back to the police camp. Crowded on the returning truck was the entire compliment of black officers not on duty and also the entire staff from the other government departments. The back of the truck was closely packed with men, grossly overloaded. The road was a twin track of hard earth through grass and bushes little used by vehicles. The speed of the truck was less than 20kph. A deep patch of loose sand had veered the truck slightly off the track. The front and rear wheels on the one side had bumped over a small but hard anthill. The anthill was about the size of a medium tortoise and the bump was not so bad as to cause alarm in the driver's cab. The two sergeants in the cab in fact laughed at the mishap. Then the screaming came.

The closely packed standing men had all lost balance and had been thrown to one side and those on the benches also fell over en mass. The falling mass of men crunched into those with backs against the hard steel of the sides. The side panels came up to the mid-torso level and a lot of the mayhem that ensured was from that. The mine-proofing sandbags were given enough momentum by the speed of the truck and the bump to become airborne cudgels of great weight. The one dead, a popular sergeant, was on the steel floor of the truck with his skull smashed by a sandbag. The carnage seemed to be far out of proportion to the minor mishap, but major carnage it was. Four policemen dead. The sergeant, one married constable with a fractured neck, two single constables with spine and many other bones broken. There were also eighteen others with serious internal injuries and bone fractures. None of the men in the packed back escaped without injuries. Human bodies are frail.

A major medical evacuation had to be put in place. The three station Land Rovers were at once used to take the most urgent to the Umvukwes Clinic. The police at that station were called by radio to dispatch all their transport. Government ambulances from Salisbury were called for and at once dispatched. The P/O on duty and I first arrived at the scene at about 5.30pm, and I drove the last truck back to the station at 8am the next morning. The accident photographs and sketch had been done, and done thoroughly and carefully as there was inevitably going to be many questions to answer. Relations with Jerry were frosty.

My stock of kudos with the OC district had all been used up before the dust storm raised by the accident had settled. Station transport was not permitted to be used for private purposes. By calling the football match 'official recreation' that rule was skirted, if only narrowly. The next problem was that only the member i/c could permit the use of station transport for recreation. Had I, the superintendent, he wanted to know, given that permission? There are times when it is prudent to lie. If the trip had turned out to be not officially sanctioned the repercussions would have been unbearable, with criminal charges filed against all involved. Jerry watched me with great anxiety for some days, and I left him stew before admitting to lying to protect him.

For some months, the majority of black government staff at Sipolilo limped or walked with crutches or with plaster casts and white bandages on one or more limb. All through the war, accidents claimed Rhodesian armed forces lives. Certainly many more men were killed by accidents than by the enemy. Vehicle accidents were a major cause of loss. There were flying accidents, crash landings, helicopters hitting power lines or each other and so on. Then there were rifles accidentally being fired and, at times, men killed in mistaken identity incidents. The reports when read had always caused a feeling of disbelief. How did they happen? Now it had come home to me; it was not something that could have easily have been prevented. When a bad day comes, it is always a surprise.

Another bad day came and, fortunately for me, when Taff was there. A Catholic bishop from Salisbury was firmly on the side of the oppressed. That covered all blacks as he saw it. Jim, the DC, had for some time applied his own laws in his own district. Any chief or headman who gave any indication of siding with the terrorist was removed from his kraal and installed in housing in the DC's compound. There they remained under house arrest and worked at gardening and keeping the area clean. The bishop had become aware of the labour gang and had begun to harass Jim. That had no effect, but the bishop did return again and again to Sipolilo on his mission. One day, Jim saw his car arrive and jumped out the window of his office and rode his Vesper scooter down the road to the police station. On passing my office on the way to hide in Taff's, he told me to tell the bishop to do things Catholic priests take oaths not to do. The bishop arrived red-faced and demanded to see the DC. I tried to stop him, but he ended up pounding on the member i/c's door. Jim stormed out and used language a sailor might understand, but not a Bishop; the cleric left defeated.

Shortly afterwards, the Sipolilo police arrested a Catholic priest at one of the missions near the station. He had embezzled large sums of money and his fellow priests had called the police. There was overwhelming evidence and the priest, a black man, had been put in a holding cell. The case would be heard in front of the circuit magistrate in a day's time and I, as prosecutor, made sure all the witnesses were subpoenaed. Next morning, the Bishop arrived and came in irate and prickly, accusing police of being Gestapo and demanding immediate access to his maltreated brother. There was no reason not to take him to the man in the holding cell. On opening the door it took a long minute to take it all in. The priest's shoes, socks and belt had been removed before he was placed in the cell; standard prison procedure. There was a ring bolt in the floor in the middle of the cell, usually used to chain violent prisoners with leg-irons as a restraint. The priest had twisted his shirt into a rope and tied a slipknot round his neck with it. He had tied the other end to the leg iron and had hanged himself from the floor. It required a hard pull on the home-made rope to tighten the slip knot. That cut the blood supply to the head and restricted breathing resulting in unconsciousness and eventual death from asphyxiation.

It seemed impossible, but the disgraced man had been determined and had managed to commit suicide. Naturally we, the police, had confirmed all the suspicions the bishop had and he was not shy in saying so. The hullabaloo became too much for me and I had to walk away, leaving Taff and Jerry doing their best to smooth things over. A post-mortem report vindicated the police. That suicide ranked up there with the man I told to go elsewhere and hang himself while still a shiny new recruit. Two other weird suicides that happened during my service come to mind. One was a man wronged by his wife, who brained himself by running head first at full gallop into a tree. The other was a man who killed himself with an electric drill, putting several holes in his own skull before it worked.

Zambezi River from the south bank. (© Ted Ayers-Hunt)

Zambezi river patrol. (© Ted Ayers-Hunt)

Police launch – Lake Kariba. (© Ted Ayers-Hunt)

Bridge across the Zambezi looking towards Zambia – taken from Chirundu. (© Ted Ayers-Hunt)

View looking north from police mess building – Mozambique border. (© Ted Ayers-Hunt)

The police pub at the single quarters at Chirundu. (© Bob Belder)

Mopani scrub – Zambezi Valley floor near Chirundu. (© Ted Ayers-Hunt)

Tsetse fly ranger's camp – Mozambique border. (© Ted Ayers-Hunt)

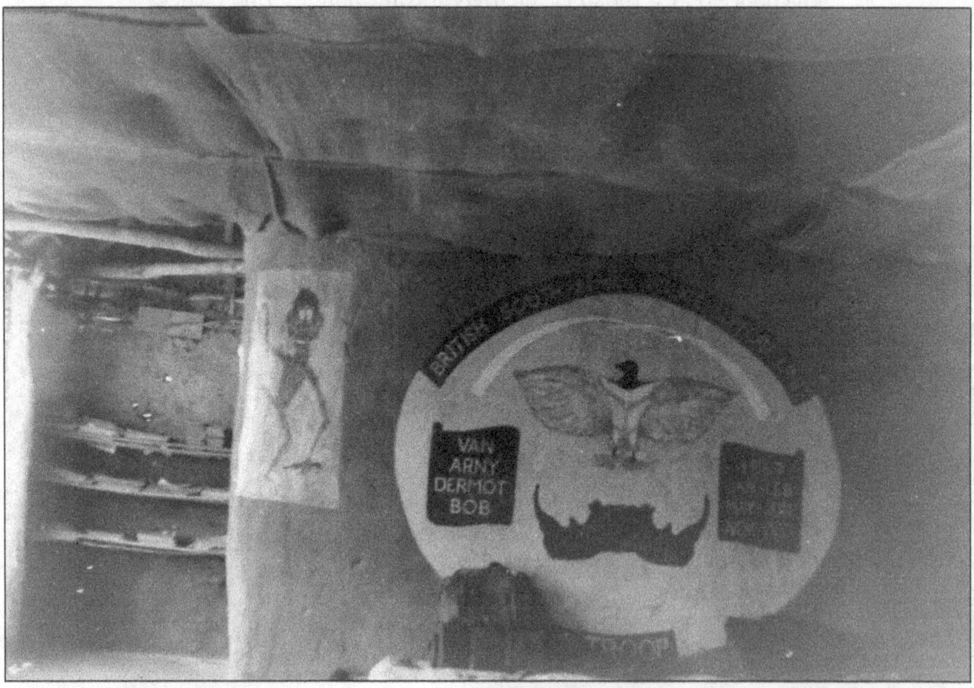


Insignia in thatched living quarters – Villa Salazar 1968–70. (© Ted Ayers-Hunt)

The Mashumbi Pools police post, in the Zambezi Valley below Sipolilo on the banks of the Hunyani. (© Bob Belder)

Fishing lodge on Lake Kariba. Visited by lake boat patrols. (© Bob Belder)

Villa Salazar Support Unit camp viewed from the top of the water tower – 1968–70. (© Ted Ayers-Hunt)

Karoi Motel in the 1960s. A police watering hole. (© Bob Belder)

Entrance to Support Unit camp at Villa Salazar –1968–70. (© Ted Ayers-Hunt)

'D' camp, Zambezi River, 1968/9. (Left) Louis Fourie, (middle) Ted Ayers-Hunt, (right) Dick Cotton. (© Ted Ayers-Hunt)

(Left) Louis Fourie, (middle) Chris Phillips, (right) Dick Cotton. (© Ted Ayers-Hunt)

Clowning around outside Villa Salazar living quarters. (© Ted Ayers-Hunt)

Unknown 'A' Troop member admiring mango trees – Villa Salazar. (© Ted Ayers-Hunt)

# 9
# The knockdown looms

My Alsatian was full grown, but still a puppy, when the next transfer came through. It had been nearly ten years in the wilderness by then. Small communities are friendly, but the chance for new personal friendship very limited. There was tea and lunch at the sports club, but there was no nightclub. There was hunting and there was fishing, but there was no crowded shopping centre with a Chinese restaurant. The choice of females available was limited or dangerously married. For some time at station inspections and other times when with senior offices, I had agitated to be posted to 'town'. That feeling of missing out on something has always been part of my life. When in the remote bush, the cities call. When sitting in a nightclub watching strippers at midnight, then the forest and the elephant call. During my lifetime, over fifty places have been called home and none of them has felt permanent. The requested posting came unexpectedly, but it was not to a big town but to Marandellas, a small village about forty kilometres out of Salisbury on the Umtali road. My batman packed the iron trunks and we took the road again, only this time Spook sat on the back seat, head out the window and tongue trailing in the road wind.

Marandellas was a relatively big police big station, with a chief inspector, inspector, two section officers and half a dozen patrol officers. The African compliment was also large. As usual, the police social life focussed on the bar in the police camp grounds. Although the regular PATU patrols remained part of it all, most of the work was normal police work. The prosecutor's post was again mine and the court was a proper one, not a makeshift one put up in the tea room or an empty office. The court sat three times a week. There was a complete volume of statute law on each station, hundreds of Parliamentary Acts, that ran to a score of thick tomes. All additions, amendments and gazetted proclamations had to be annotated in those books. At Marandellas a long backlog had been allowed to develop and that backlog was handed to me with the prosecutor's job. It took weeks of slogging away to catch up.

The Marandellas Police District included many commercial farms and several Tribal Trust Lands and it was near enough to Salisbury to be an attraction for the city's criminals. Many of the housebreakings and stock theft cases were by criminals who came out from the capital at night. For a while the PATU call-ups were put on hold as prosecuting required someone who was available every week. The insurgency was heating up, and many of the country's white male population were being called up to reserve forces several times a year. It was also a time when the Rhodesian government was trying hard to find a political solution.

Talks with Britain had never stopped, and a solution had been sought by talking to the black population. In the early 1960s, the government of the country had agreed to far-ranging concessions to allow the black population partial representation in Parliament. A referendum was held for white voters and the agreement was passed by a small majority. But the British sent a commission to see if the blacks in fact wanted the agreement and Bishop Muzorewa formed a new opposition movement and convinced the British government to veto the proposals. Now in 1976, the Rhodesian government had put another dispensation in place that gave blacks voting rights and equal seats in Parliament, and Bishop Muzorewa was made head of the government after a general election. The two nationalist parties involved in the terror war refused to recognise the Muzorewa government and the war went on. With a black government in place, the politics became murky. As blacks were now considered to be in power it was decided that black youth inside the country should be called up to do national service like the whites were required to do, and laws to that effect were passed. The daily reports from operational centres showed a big increase in the number of people in rural areas being murdered. A lot more men were needed for government forces.

There were protest marches by black youth in urban areas and, under the security legislation long in place, all such marches were banned. There were several senior schools near Marandellas and one morning about fifty black pupils gathered at the square in the centre of the village with placards and milled about chanting. They were protesting possible call up. It was my week on standby and the charge office called me in the S/O's mess. It was 7am and a sunny day. Spook, the Alsatian, had filled out and was a solid, big dog of about 100 kilograms and worked with me, obeying hand signals and minimal spoken orders. At the charge office I collected an automatic shotgun and a belt of cartridges, a constable similarly armed and I had Spook walk at heel. My own anger at all the wrongs the Rhodesian whites were subjected to had boiled up and my blood was hot.

The three of us arrived on foot where the demonstrators were milling about, some blocking a road. The crowd fell silent, some looking bashful. It was plain to see the mob did not really have any heat and hearts were not in the demonstration. They were all ordered to form a crocodile, two abreast on the road. One boy shouted something in defiance and I pointed to him and told Spook to demonstrate. The white dog loped to the indicated young man and crouched in biting distance and snarled deeply showing his knife blade teeth. The now silent crowd at once formed into a long line, two abreast. We marched them to the nearby police station grounds. There they were ordered to sit and remain in formation. The constable walked down the line taking each person's name.

More staff were sent for and everyone in the line was fingerprinted. While they sat outside under guard by Spook and a constable, I went inside and typed an indictment and attached a typed list of the names. At 9am, the line of demonstrators was standing obediently in front of the Marandellas Magistrates Court bench and I read the indictment to the presiding officer as the first item on the roll. They all pleaded guilty, most of them totally stunned at the turn of events. By 9.30am they had all been fined twenty dollars or two days gaol time and allowed time to pay. By 10am the docket had been closed, complete, and the fingerprints and record of the conviction sent off. Some sort of record must have been set that morning. When we played squash at lunchtime the magistrate could hardly stop laughing as he recalled the faces of some of the stunned scholars.

The main single quarters at Marandellas were full, and the single S/Os had a house at the side of the police camp allocated as living quarters. It was an old residential house that had been incorporated into the police camp and each side of it were normal suburban homes. There were several rooms, wooden floors, bathroom and kitchen, which was never used as I ate at the single quarters. It had a hedge in front along the road and a fence all round. There was room enough, but Spook was used to wide open spaces and at times fretted. At times he lay with his face on his front paws facing the front gate, his tail wagging when he heard me come up behind him, and when I did not open the gate, his ears drooped and he turned sad eyes on me.

At night, lying in the dark, my thoughts were more and more filled with doubt. There were still too many restrictions on the forces combating the terror war. There were too may senior officers who still had little idea of what went on in the field. The country and government were under attack from all sides.

The men in the field were determined and skilled. In combat they were never beaten. The enemy were in deathly fear of the government forces. But those were never fully unleashed; the field commanders were always subjected to the politics. There were also far too many of the Rhodesian police who still had a foot in each camp, who always regarded the country as a place to earn a pension and then one day to retire 'back home'. When the gloomy thoughts hit, the looming disaster seemed to be unavoidable, yet to the very end I could not accept that black rule would come and destroy it all. Rhodesia was too much a thing of beauty for it all to vanish. The agitation against white rule was almost all external. The black people who I had grown up with were against the black nationalists and could see that it was a foreign concept they were trying to force on the country. There is no justice in politics or much common sense.

The situation in the country was seldom discussed in the police bar or the Three Monkeys Inn, which was the other place the police used often. There was a saying that in Rhodesia that you did not discuss religion, politics or dogs. There was too much passion in these subjects. There was widespread terrorist activity and yet life went on as normal, almost. Those civilians who were called up, and that was nearly every white male, went off and served and came back, and in social situations the war was not discussed. It was not something that needed to be talked about. The government forces were the winning side; all that was required was for no-one to weaken or become defeatist. As long as Smith remained defiant of the British, things would not go wrong. So life went on as normal and the dockets piled up on my desk before each court date. It was a round of investigating traffic accidents, housebreakings, stock theft and murders, interspersed with representing the attorney general in the magistrate's court. There was a hiatus in the PATU work. The sticks formed locally were made up of men who worked together all the time, as planned in the original concept, and so my service was not needed. A complicated relationship with a young schoolteacher took a lot of my attention and free time.

While stressed with worry, a sad event added to my gloom. Spook had always ridden in the station transport with me on the remote bush stations and saw no reason not to continue to do so. The other officers enjoyed the big dog prowling at their side when they went to crime scenes and allowed him to ride in the transport. The member i/c, a chief inspector, thought otherwise. The long white hairs shed from the dog stuck to his uniform when he drove the trucks and he issued instructions banning the dog from police transport. But the other officers ignored it and it became a matter of conflict. There was also a constant stream of black school children walking along the pavement in front of the house the other side of the hedge. Some of the young boys thought it was amusing to throw stones at the white dog; it made him rampage along the wire, barking in anger. It was a big game until one morning Spook had enough and took a flying leap over the wire and scattered his tormentors with several being bitten. He was a bush-reared dog and the city life was not for him.

There was a farmer who used the Three Monkeys Inn. He had recently remarried and his and her children from previous marriages had all come to the farm. Spook delighted in children and loved to be ridden and to wrestle with them. The sense of loss was something physically hurting. Some weeks later I drove to the farm to make sure the dog was alright. On the way to the farmhouse the road went by a big dam. Spook and a dozen young children were playing in the mud and water and even from the distance I could see the silly grin on the dog's face. He had not noticed me and I drove away. That was the last contact with an exceptional dog.

There was more than just physical attraction between the teacher and me. It scared me and at times confused me. It was impossible to take things further and take on responsibility at a time when I felt the world was falling apart. Yet it was hard not to get emotionally involved. The affair went on; we stayed in touch for years. There was a daughter born and her mother and she are my family today, although we now live thousands of kilometres apart from each other. The relationship that started then has lasted over thirty years and more.

The BSAP members were entitled to more leave than they could possibly take. Police pay is always minimal, like that of nurses and teachers. So it was hard to go away on leave. The leave was fifty-eight days per year vacation leave and also six days occasional leave that could be taken at short notice and at any time. Those six days went up to twelve after ten years' service. Leave could be accumulated to a total of six months, again rising to nine months after ten years' service. Being stationed in places that were considered holiday destinations or tourist spots meant that taking leave would probably mean going back to the vicinity of a previous station. A lot of my service had been a holiday anyway.

The situation in the country was very bad, with terrorists flooding into the country from Mozambique camps in large numbers. The installation of a majority black government made no difference. Bishop Muzorewa was now officially in charge of the armed forces and that made life difficult for them. They had been fighting with one arm tied behind their backs and now it was worse. The terror attacks were reaching further and further from the borders;

farm homesteads attacked in the night with rocket grenades, landmines on dirt roads, more and more black civilians killed daily; torture and mutilation on a large scale. And over it all, my experience of being sent out to chase terror gangs in places where they did not exist, sent out by senior officers who had little or no idea of what happened out there in the bush, I was sent out with a stick of five men who had not trained together to fight well-armed gangs of up to forty strong.

So it was time to take leave, time to distance myself from the problem of war and the woman. It was time to go far away and look back and consider what to do. It would be easier to see things clearly from a distance. It was while sitting on the Marandellas Hotel veranda waiting for a waiter to bring beer that the idea to go on holiday hit. Then the idea swelled. It was many years since the sea had been seen. Just the thought of salt water, swimming and fishing sent a thrill through my body. There was no reason at all why a trip to Durban could not be done. Little money had been needed the last few years so there was enough to go to the coast and spend a week or two in a hotel. A coastal holiday would give perspective to my troubled life.

The Lonsdale Hotel at the end of West Street in Durban charged two hundred rand, then on a par with the Rhodesian dollar, for two weeks full board. It was paid in advance. The next morning, fishing tackle was bought and used from the pier near the hotel. There was a permanent band of fishermen who lived on the pier and who tried to make a living out of catching fish from it. The only thing I caught was a small shark and it was already entangled in a dozen hooks and yards of cut-off fishing line. There was a nightclub near the hotel where there was live music and singers. There was an eatery specializing in prawns next to the hotel and the prawns were big and succulent. But I was a stranger in a big town and did not fit or want to fit. After two days, I requested and got back my money and took the road home. The only sign of the war when crossing the border was that armed vehicles were supplied to escort cars formed into a convoy from the border to Ft Victoria.

Kyle Dam sprawls between hill and mountain ranges just outside of Ft Victoria. There are many inlets and gorges and the banks are forested and full of game. There were a dozen resorts along the shores. The chosen chalet was wooden and had a sheltered veranda from which a line could be cast to the water. A big Canadian trapper style canoe came with the chalet, and each morning while the dawn chorus of birds was crackling out, I took a packed lunch, fishing tackle and a flask of coffee and spent a long, quiet day on the water. After a contemplative ten days, the worries of the love and war still had not been resolved. Nothing had been solved by running away. Things would have to take the ordained course, they always do.

The first day back at the station from the holiday, orders were given to report to Mtoko, a small farming community in the heart of massive tribal lands on the northern border of the country. The troubled times had led to a massive increase in stock theft that was threatening to do what the long war had not done, move farmers off the land. A stock theft unit had been set up at the station to deal with it. The S/O in charge of the unit had gone on leave and had to be replaced temporarily. So the batman packed the tin trunks again and at noon we left, without hello or goodbye to the woman. A recent law had been passed making a nine-year sentence mandatory for each count of stock theft. It was hoped that it would help curb the theft of hundreds of cattle a month.

Mtoko police camp was part of an enclave of government offices surrounded by tribal land on one side and commercial farmland on the other. That part of north-east Mashonaland is remarkable for the uncountable number of kopjes, jumbles of piled up granite castles as far as the eye can see; some of the rock outcrops were solid unbroken granite massifs welling up in mountains skywards. It is prime farming country below the kopjes. The buildings at the government station were all from the turn of the century, the standard brick under tin with the wrap around gauzed-in verandas. The entire open space between buildings was covered in mango trees, and the fruit was ripe when I arrived. Each morning early before going for a run, several sweet juicy mangoes made a pre-breakfast snack. The main roads were jammed with trucks taking cargoes of mangoes to Salisbury. The only social life outside the police station, and the only pub, was at the inevitable sports club. So it was back again to the familiar remote bush station. Fortunately it was temporary as my temperament was getting very brittle. I was angry with the constant shifts to isolated small villages. This was a new thing, as previously it had been accepted as the norm.

A few days after my arrival, while sitting in the sun outside the mess after lunch, a uniformed district commissioner's messenger, a sergeant, complete with red-banded bush hat folded up one side, approached and saluted snappily. He had been told, he said, that I was now the head of the stock theft unit. When I confirmed that he went on: an informer had arrived and reported that a gang of stock thieves was busy slaughtering stolen stock in a cave nearby right at that time. Would we be interested in arresting them? He indicated the massive granite mountain looming high behind the single quarters. The posse was summoned and I collected my FN and strapped on my spare magazines quickly.

The caves were the other side of the range behind the police station. The sergeant and one constable went off around the mountain at ground level, weaving through the trees. The DC's messenger guided me up and up over the massif, a steep and hard climb and a hike of about five kilometres. As the summit was crested, a commotion of angry voices drifted up from below. Half a kilometre away, the men of the stock theft unit could be seen, and there were three men armed with axes at the ready advancing on them, intent on grievous bodily harm. A couple of warning shots across the bow at once changed the power ratio. With a few claps and kicks, handcuffs were administered. On my arrival at the scene the stock unit men were still seething at being threatened and had to be calmed. The entrance to a cathedral-like cave was next to where the melee took place. Inside the cave were the carcasses of nine cattle, some only recently axed to death and some already partly butchered. The stolen meat would later have been sold in the tribal lands, and the cave an illicit butchers shop.

Before the crestfallen thieves had time to gather courage and concoct a story they were questioned separately. The sergeant and other stock theft unit members had picked up the dropped axes and might have held them in a manner seen as threatening, but they would swear in court that it was not so. My rifle might also have been pointed. For whatever reasons, the thieves quickly agreed to come clean and confessed to many counts of stock theft over a period of many months. It was one of those lucky jackpots police work sometimes gets. For two hours they took us from crevasse to crack to cave and at each location the skins of cattle previously stolen and butchered were found stuffed into the rocky holes to conceal them. Fortunately, the local commercial famers were careful to brand stock. It was a record haul for any stock theft unit. There was, in the small area searched, evidence of at least twenty previously reported cases, covering a period of many months and scores of cattle.

The dockets for court were prepared by me over two days of very intensive typing; the farmers were glad to come in to give statements and return on court day to give evidence a few days later. It was important to try the case before the culprits had time to concoct stories. A special sitting of the circuit magistrate's court was arranged. The case dragged on for most of the day as the thieves suddenly, but belatedly, realized the trouble they were in and began to contest all the evidence. The case was watertight. They had been caught red-handed and had also indicated to the stock theft unit posse evidence linking them to numerous other cases. The small court was packed with spectators. The gang was very popular in the tribal area as suppliers of cheap and plentiful top quality beef. They had many supporters. Possibly a collection had already been made among the supporters and when the option of a fine or gaol was given, the fine would be paid by the community. The magistrate was aware of the support and in other times would have been obliged to give the option of a stiff fine to go with a short sentence. However he had a thin smile on his face as he dropped the bombshell. The new law made it mandatory for him to give a sentence of nine years without the option of a fine per count; each count to run in succession and not concurrently. The total sentence was over two hundred years. By the end of his verdict and sentencing there was total silence in court. The stock theft unit members wore smug smiles.

The word spread like a grass fire in a gale. By the next morning, stray stock was being reported from all over the tribal area. Those tribesmen holding stolen cattle in hidden kraals in the bush hurriedly shooed the cattle away. The stock theft game had become too risky. There was also the fact that the evidence in court had revealed an informer had grassed on the butcher gang and that was not lost on the locals. The identity of the informer had been kept a secret, so all tribesmen engaged in the stock theft were under equal suspicion. There was an airstrip near the government offices which was fenced. It was turned into a temporary pound. Over some days, hundreds of stolen cattle were rounded up and returned to grateful farmers. It was a magnificent triumph, made all the more sweet by the contrasting flow of bad news from the war front.

A few days later the section officer leading the stock theft unit returned from leave and after the dockets had been handed over, it was a few hours' drive back to Marandellas. A month later, the stock theft unit at Mtoko received a Commissioner's Commendation for good work. My role in the matter was too minor for the commendation to include me. That was obvious, as all the ground work had been done before my arrival, but it did leave a feeling of bitterness. And that discontent soon increased. Orders had come for a transfer to Nuanetsi again. The matter with the schoolteacher was still not resolved one way or another. The request to be transferred to town had been lost somewhere, or the short spell in Marandellas had been counted as enough town service. The trunks were again packed and put on the roof-rack. It was a sad farewell to the woman and a long day's drive south, through Ft Victoria, town of my birth and childhood memories; through the mountains on the edge of the high plateau of the country and on down to the low veldt, the heat, thick waterless mopani scrub and land of a thousand wild animals.

## 10

# Getting up and going on

Normally a visit to Nuanetsi and the prime hunting country excited me, and underlying my feeling of doom and discontent at the transfer there was still an edge of excitement. The small colonial government settlement had not changed much since school days in the 1950s or my last posting there over ten years back. The DC's office and three houses were exactly the same, as was the single quarters with the saddle racks in the bedrooms. The new charge office block stood next to the old oval thatched roof rondavel, that was still used as an office. One of the old camp storerooms had recently been converted to quarters for a section officer. It was a square room with an alcove for a toilet, bath and shower. It was furnished with a bed, table and chair. The tin roof had no ceiling or other insulation under it. It was hot as a sauna inside. There was a bougainvillea creeper next to the room with a trunk grown to the size of a man's torso; the creeper had been planted many decades ago. At the back of the mess next to the wood-fired water boilers there was another jungle avenue of the massive purple-flowered plants. There was also a hedge in front of the mess of four metre high pomegranate trees. None of that had changed, only grown bigger. Both those plant species are well adapted to heat and dryness. There were large servings of both of those, also high humidity during the wet season.

The section officer's quarters were an oven in summer, and merely very hot in winter. Electricity had recently been installed at the camp. Fans were almost impossible to find in shops as sanctions had been in place for years. It was impossible to sleep even with the doors and windows wide open. My brother was an air force pilot on Dakotas and flew round the country on various duties. As an urgent mission he scrounged an electric fan on a stand for me and flew to the local airstrip just to drop it off. The mosquito net, absolutely essential even with regular anti-malaria pills, was soaked in water. The sheets on the bed were wetted as well. The fan was put on full speed and directed at the bed. That was enough cooling to allow a bit of sleep. Later in the night when the water had evaporated, the outside air had cooled down enough for the fan to work on its own. The door had to be left wide open and often snakes came through it. In the mornings I had to be careful until all the hiding places had been checked. At that time of the year, when typing in the office, a towel had to be kept close to wipe sweat from hands and chin or the papers became soggy.

At the ancient clay tennis courts dating from the 1930s, a small wooden clubhouse of two rooms had been recently been built. At the club, a small swimming pool had also been installed with a filter plant driven by a diesel engine. There was a bar counter in the one room and a fireplace which was never used. The other room was empty. The other new thing in the police camp were two long wood and tin barrack-type buildings. They were sleeping quarters for the police reservists called up to act as guards at the scattered ranch homesteads. The called-up men were known as Bright Lights, possibly from the radio code name given to them. Most were over forty-years-old and most of them were farmers from areas where the terrorists had not yet reached. It was natural that they resented being called up to national service, being forced to leave their own farms to protect others. They were sent out for six weeks at a time, two or three worked together to bolster the defence at the isolated ranches. They rotated with other reservists from their home areas. There was hardly a white male in Rhodesia at that time who was not being called on to give national service.

Also new was an alarmed diamond mesh fence right around the entire police camp. It needed to be kept clear of vegetation, and that was a major maintenance job. The alarm was set off when a wire stretched tight through wire rings and touched the side of a ring. Creepers and grass growing against the trigger wire could set it off. A variety of snakes and small animals set it off. It was one of those ideas conceived in an office somewhere which looked good in theory but was totally useless on the ground. As the frequent alarms were always false the fence was left switched off for long periods. The truth was that few places in the country manned by armed government forces had ever been attacked. Even the three of four armed men on the remote ranches deterred the insurgents from determined attacks on the isolated homesteads.

The old thatched jail still stood and the two cells were in use by the personal batmen of the police members. The rooms were infested with bed bugs, an insect hard to get rid of as it hides in cracks and crannies during the day and comes out at night. The other batmen had not reported the problem to the men they worked for, but mine did. He was a quiet, mild young Shona and had been with me for some ten years, enjoying the constant change of scenery as an adventure. He had been with me long enough to know he could bring a problem to me. The bed bugs required repeated attacks with room foggers and tin after tin of long lasting residual insect spray. The bandits must have suffered a lot during their tenure of the jail.

There was a problem with the Bright Lights. There had been no section officer at Nuanetsi for some time and now the problems normally dealt with by that rank had built up and were inherited by me. The reservists ate at the single quarters. A spare table had been squeezed into the small dining room and all the reservists crowded in at meal times. The kitchen was a room outside the mess, linked by a covered walkway. The stove was a very old wood burner. The washing-up facilities were a concrete basin fed by cold water. The cook was a local Shangaan who was saving his wages to buy a wife, and his cooking skill consisted of being able to roast meat and mash potatoes. Normally, the single mess had four members. The patrol officers could and did at times take over cooking a meal when variety was called for. The various batmen were tasked with keeping the rooms and communal area of the mess clean. The reservists received a small field allowance and that was paid to the mess account. It barely covered one meal a day.

A delegation of Bright Lights called on me in the office one morning. The food was not up to standard. What was happening to their field allowance? Their barracks behind the mess were not being cleaned. There were not enough chairs in the living room of the mess or out on the veranda for all. It was just general discontent, but they made it my problem. It was pointed out to them that the mess was home to the four single police officers and that the reservists were uninvited guests in that home. The furniture catered for those four men. The police who lived there tried to be good hosts, but with the large numbers passing through it was difficult and unfair on them. The field allowance? The mess accounts were shown to them and it was obvious enough that the allowance did not cover food supplied; some of the cost was being carried by the mess P/Os. It was a minimal subsidy because most of the meat was hunted venison and free. If any of them wanted to cook or teach the cook new tricks they were free to do so. The cleaners in the mess were personal paid servants. The camp labourer would be ordered to sweep, clean and dust the barracks but if they wanted more service they could hire a man. It cleared the air and that evening we all drank lots of beer in the small wooden clubhouse together and told jokes till midnight.

The other small change from the early days was a shooting range of about seventy-five metres in length. A bulldozer had pushed up a five-metre-high bank as a backstop and cleared the range of scrub and trees with its blade. The range was at right angles to the river, outside the security fence that ran parallel to the river that side of the camp. The bush corridor between the camp and river was about two hundred metres. The range was at right angles also to my office window which looked out over it. When meat was short at the mess, the cook came to the office to tell me. If it was late afternoon there would be impala and warthog on the cleared shooting range. The rifle cocking and a shout alerted the other policemen in the charge office. A marksman's badge was not on my uniform each year for all my service for nothing. Normally, it was possible to shoot one animal, and before the confusion of the shot cleared, shoot a second. The cook and the camp labourer then butchered and fetched the meat on the shooting range with a wheelbarrow. The hindquarters always came to the mess; the cook had the say over the rest of the animal.

There was still hunting enough, still the thrill of walking pristine bush and shooting a buck to eat, walking through the smell, sound and sights of the bush. Nearly every Sunday it was hunting all day for me with the hornbills honking, the chattering of guinea fowl and francolin, the brown eyes and white jug ears of alert red impala. The waterholes in the sand bed of the river steaming in the dawn as majestic spiral-horned kudu drank and hawks circled overhead waiting for the droves of prey doves to come to the water. There were early memories; there my brother shot a cow kudu. There the first wildebeest dropped after three hasty shots. The man-eating crocodile had been stretched out just there next to the DC's court, stick propping the mouth open. And there the heat that crackled at midday from a slate sky with a silver sun. But now there was always the FN slung over the back and extra magazines on the belt when the hunting rifle was carried and always that edginess guarding against ambush. Armed gangs numbering thirty or forty men were flooding across the Mozambique border, crossing the Nuanetsi police area, heading north to Mashonaland and west to Matabeleland.

Twelve years after signing on, the inspectors written and physical examination was taken and passed. It was really a repeat of the examination for section officer rank. There was a list drawn up of all those who had passed the exam and as vacancies opened on stations, men were promoted by notice in the Police Gazette. There was some sort of order of merit, but the senior officers at the intended station also seemed to have a say. Six months after passing the examination, still no promotion had come. This had been expected by me. Each time I was posted a new group of officers were my companions. Then at other times the senior officer at the station was transferred and a new one arrived and that did not help them to know my work. My official record was blemish free. It did bother me, not being made up, and a close watch was kept on the official gazette when it arrived in the mail. When men junior and less experienced were promoted, it did begin to bother me a lot.

Ken was not an Englishman, but behaved like one. He was married to a South African woman and was English-speaking South African. He took over as station inspector at Nuanetsi when the incumbent inspector was transferred during my tour of duty. "Englishman" defines a certain something in attitude. Ken was a bright, friendly man but there was a slight condescension in his manner, especially, I thought to home-born Rhodesians. It was not obvious, but he could not hide it from me. He was an excellent tennis player, and when he discovered I played the game he insisted we play most afternoons. My game was of a social standard, his nearly professional. As a gentleman he tried not to crow at his superiority, but could not stop insisting we play again soon. It would have been more pleasant to play doubles, but he always singled me out on those days at social tennis. He played a role in my career in the future. After Mugabe, Ken went to Johannesburg and was murdered in his garden one afternoon by intruders. My most vivid memory of him is one of a slamming forehand directed at my feet.

On some nights during that time some ranch homesteads were attacked from the distant surrounding bushes. During the day, landmines went off under vehicles on dirt roads. In the nearby tribal lands, the terrorist harvested a quota of murders each week. These things did not curtail my hunting and often I fished in a weir just upstream from the bridge over the Nuanetsi and watched the twice-daily escorted convoy of vehicles travelling to Beit Bridge and the border, or the other way, go by on the nearby road. Some members of a South African motorcycle club on a rally were ambushed one day and one man killed on the road near the police camp. Talks between Britain and the Ian Smith and Muzorewa government rolled on and on. Waking in the grey dawn light in the fan breeze with the hum of mosquitoes loud in the hot room, depression and feelings of helplessness would grip me. Someone had to take charge and do something. There was a terrifying inertia from the most senior officers.

Still the call out for PATU duties came, now from District Headquarters in Ft Victoria. There was an area known as Buffalo Bend on the Nuanetsi River at Malapati Pan, near the Gonarezhou Game Reserve. An old time DC, Wright, had built an observation tower there from which elephants could be watched drinking in the river. It was known as Wright's Folly. He also wrote a number of books about the area, one being about those elephants, *The Grey Ghosts at Buffalo Bend*. There was also an extensive DC's camp on the riverbank. Special Branch had established themselves at the camp, which had been sandbagged in case of attack. The call-up mission given was to go there and act as guards for SB. If they needed to travel by vehicle they were to be escorted by PATU. That was totally out of order. PATU was trained to track and attack in the bush, not do sentry duty. There was a slow anger beginning to build in me that could no longer be ignored.

Since the first VAT patrol, over a decade ago, and the meeting after it with senior officers at Police Headquarters to discuss uniform and equipment, nothing had changed. PATU still had not been issued with camouflage or suitable weapons. The Support Unit had by this time been turned into an infantry brigade and they had all the equipment of the regular army. PATU still made do with what they cobbled together for themselves. My patrol uniform was a pair of dark khaki trousers bought in a shop, a camouflage jacket that was long and loose reaching down to the knees, scrounged somewhere. The calf-length leather boots were from Bata shoe store, soft and comfortable. My headgear was a bush hat, issued by the police as a stable hat. It had a high round peak and wide brims, one side of which could be clipped up and chin strap. It was old and floppy and broke the outline of my head well. Over the years it had become very floppy with age so the rims covered most of my face and head. It was made of felt and was often used to filter dirty water for drinking.

My backpack was bought from an outdoor store. It was a smallish, steel frame climber's backpack. They were made commercially for the Rhodesia forces. The main part of the pack had a flap that covered it, on long straps that allowed the pack to be over-filled. The cover flap had a pocket that fitted the small gas burner with the folding pot holder, and also a plastic lined map holder. The main pack also had several external pockets, one of which fitted the folded-up mess tins. Those were the WWII British Army issue, two square pans with folding handles, one of which fitted inside the other for storing. There was a metal rack at the bottom of the backpack on which the bedroll was strapped, usually a sleeping bag and issued poncho. The poncho was a large square waterproof cape that could be rigged as a small tent.

An army web belt had also been scrounged along with the magazine pouches that threaded on the belt. Four spares were carried on the belt, and two more in the side pockets of the backpack. The belt also carried two plastic water bottles in khaki pouches. There was a bush knife that was the only weapon besides the rifle. That had been obtained in the Support Unit days. It was an old eighteen-inch bayonet made by Wilkinson Sword, and cut down in the police armoury to twelve inches. The knife was used to open cans, chop firewood, gut animals and a thousand other tasks in the bush. The rifle was still the ancient FN issued in Depot, the one the armourers each year tried to replace, as it was fully automatic and did not have a flash hider. Each year I managed to keep it by one or other trick. A rifle is a very personal thing.

Each member of PATU had to patch together his own gear. They did so because their lives depended on it, and anyway, most savvy bushmen prefer to make do their own way. The official police issue was still 'riot kit' or dark navy blue trousers and bunny jacket over grey shirt, blue floppy hat and WWII webbing, with the web belt and straps over each shoulder, carrying ammunition pouches. The old hands in PATU accepted the way it was and did what needed to be done. Using your own equipment and finding it works well gives satisfaction. But still I often wished the stick could carry a belt-fed MAG. For that I might even have swapped my old faithful rifle.

It was with ill-grace and resentment that I went off to carry out the duties of sentry and vehicle escort on that particular patrol. The Buffalo Bend SB details inevitably had a fat pig that rooted round camp all day. It had, as usual, been bought as a piglet to fatten for the spit and had turned into a pet. The PATU stick had been allocated a tent with stretcher beds. The pig was fond of lying up in the heat of the day on the beds. It was foul smelling and left oily, filthy droppings on the floor and beds while the stick was out of the tent. One evening on returning, the animal had made itself comfortable on my bed and the tent reeked like a pig farm. Snatching a nearby broom I laid into the animal, it fell off the bed and ran squealing round the tent as I rained blows on it. The whipping went on outside with the pig trying desperately to waddle away from the blows to its backside. The bellowing, high-decibel squealing made baboons far in the bush bark in alarm. At last, the pig could run no more and my rage had been used up. For now I felt better. The fat porker gave the tent a wide berth afterwards and no-one reported me to the SPCA.

The patrol was due to finish on the morning of Christmas Eve. The JOC at Rutenga had been contacted on the radio network and a Dakota was promised to take the PATU stick back to Rutenga and Nuanetsi. Those aircraft flew several circuits every week to the remote airstrips. The Mabalahuta airstrip was some distance from the Buffalo Bend camp. The plane was due at 7am and it was raining hard then. The stick was dropped off with backpacks and tin trunks at 6.30am. The rain was cooling, not unpleasant. The plane did not come. The small mobile radio set could not reach Rutenga, but the SB base camp was raised. After a long wait, still in the hard rain, the answer came. The Dakotas were not flying, but a reserve air wing small plane doing the rounds with mail and Christmas cakes would collect the stick at about midday. After six hours the cooling rain had become cold water. A small plane landed. The pilot came over. There was a problem, carrying rifle and packs only four of the stick could fit in the plane. He laughed at my burst of bitter swearing.

'Right on. Know how you feel. But look, S/O, there is another aircraft just behind me. Hang on. I will call them.'

'Please do. You four. Get aboard. I will wait.'

'Right on. The aircraft will land in half an hour to uplift you. He is also doing the milk run.' Delivering mail and cake.

'Thanks. Beginning to rust.'

The other small plane landed. There were only two seats and a cargo bay. Finally after six hours in the rain, we took off with me in the co-pilot's seat. There was one stop to go before heading to Rutenga and that was to Tsoropadzi, the place where a decade ago, the ANC terrorist had been captured. The DC's camp was now a substantial army base and the airstrip newly built and long enough for Dakotas. While in the air, the extent of the vast mopani tree ocean down below could be seen, green and yellow from curved horizon to curved horizon. Using the aircraft radio, contact was made with Rutenga and a message conveyed to the police station at Nuanetsi. A truck should be sent up the road to the JOC at Rutenga in two hours, the estimated time of arrival. The receipt of the message was confirmed. I was almost home for Christmas.

The small plane banked to line up with the dirt strip at Tsoropadzi and below was a convoy of three mine-protected vehicles heading to the airstrip to meet the plane. Then there came the distant sound of gunfire and explosions faintly over the hum of the feathered-back engine. There was black smoke and flame from the one vehicle and scurrying men down there below. The pilot pulled out of the bank. The radio informed him the convoy had been ambushed by a handheld anti-tank rocket. Two men were hurt. One needed to be taken to hospital urgently. As we landed the wounded man was rushed to the plane, with a drip in his arm and bloody face.

'Right on. Sorry S/O Smithy. To take the stretcher that seat must come out.'

'Murphy's law. Will you return?' My face must have been mournful.

'Right on. Well look. This aircraft has no night flying instruments. But yes, OK. Will give it a go. Maybe an hour. Wait here.'

At least the rain had stopped. So there on the strip, the wait to go home continued. The ambushed troopers were all talking at once while listening to an army radio set nearby. The rocketed vehicle still gave off a pall of black smoke. In the bush not far off, a company of very angry soldiers were in hot pursuit of the ambushers. It was now after 4pm on Christmas Eve and a flight that should have taken an hour had taken all day. The light would go at about 5.30pm. By 5pm I resigned myself to spend Christmas night in the army camp. A few kilometres into the bush a firefight broke out. The radio chattered on and a cheer broke out among the listening troopers. The attackers, extremely rash so close to a major base, had all paid the price for excess boldness. The small plane glittered against the rosy sundown. It came straight in, fast.

'Right on. Hop aboard, S/O Smithy. Don't guarantee it. But we should make it OK. There are runway lights at Rutenga, so have no fear.'

'Where do you keep the parachute? How's the troopie? Glad to hear that.'

The runway markers were on and the plane landed. It taxied to the end of the runway where the buildings stood. The pilot was at his temporary call-up home. Mine was still twenty kilometres down the road. Transport was supposed to be waiting at the guardroom. There was no sign of it. They had a police radio in the control room. Nuanetsi answered and music and drunken shouting could be heard in the background: a Christmas party in full swing. A slightly drunk sergeant jovially collected me half an hour later. He could not say why transport had not been sent earlier. No one had told him. Big party at the mess and African lines! Plenty beer. Angry, tired and hungry, the drunken shouting at the mess seemed out of place. What right did they have to be so happy, did they not know what I had been through that day?

The use of alcohol fuelled all social occasions in police circles. Many of the owners of the big ranches were of Afrikaans stock where drinking was not socially acceptable. When the Nuanetsi ranchers gathered for a party many of them carried hip flasks and hidden bottles, and had to go and hide from their wives before taking a nip. Two officers who were at Nuanetsi with me at different times were killed by excess use of alcohol. Another who had problems with demon drink was Uncle Reg of Support Unit days, who was eventually invalided out of the police as an alcoholic. But two officers who crossed my path actually died from over indulgence in drink.

There was a very eccentric officer, 'Pom-pom' Castell. He arrived at Nuanetsi one afternoon late in a vintage Armstrong Siddeley, with a vast collection of hunting rifles. He was a collector of weapons and an expert of sorts. At that time, the hunting magazines carried adverts by the American Winchester Company. There was a photograph of Pom-pom, with rifle resting on a dead buffalo, showing also a box of bullets and a caption, 'Our man in Africa uses Silver Tips'. Experimenting one day with an old muzzle-loader, he managed to blow his trigger finger off. We were also briefly stationed together in Karoi, where there was an illicit copper pot still in his room. One night on the way home from the bar he came across a puff adder in the road. Being full of his own home-made seventy per cent proof alcohol, he decided to remove it to the grass verge. It bit him on the thumb. He was a snake expert and dosed the bite with raw liquor and went to bed. Gangrene cost him the thumb.

As he walked into the mess at Nuanetsi that night, he asked if the local store sold brandy and if they allowed sales on account. Then he sent a batman to buy six bottles of brandy and mixers on tick, and insisted after dinner that night all the mess members sit and drink with him, a full bottle to a man. It was said that he was the only man ever to leave the BSA Police on the same rank as he joined. He had signed on in the days when pension was paid after twenty years, not twenty-five as in my case. On many occasions he was promoted only to be demoted again. Once he lost his rank by insisting on rooting up a vegetable garden he had grown at the single quarters on being transferred. His last days were poverty stricken, living in the back of a battered car, held together by duct tape and wire. At night he roamed the bars of Salisbury in torn and tatty clothes, bumming drinks and food from his old comrades. It was after I had left the police and was living in Salisbury. He died in the night after yet one more binge.

During that brandy-fuelled night at Nuanetsi one of the younger officers was Doug, a cadet. Cadets were signed on at sixteen and served to eighteen when they were enrolled as patrol officers. Till that night, Doug drank cream soda at the Lion and Elephant, and preferred coffee in the mess. I remember him from the incident with the corpse. One day, a corpse was taken from a dam. The decomposed body was left in the body-box on the Land Rover roof, pending transfer to the mortuary at the hospital the next day. Bodies fished from water give off several different gasses, all unpleasant. The eager cadet said he had never seen a corpse and asked if he could look in the box. Ten minutes after he went outside there came the sound of someone loudly barking at the ants. Pom-pom gave him his first drink that night and it killed him.

He became addicted very quickly. Some people react in that way to liquor. In very few years he was discharged for continual offences under the Police Act and Standing Orders. At times I saw him at various bars in Salisbury. A year or two after that, I was living at Kariba and Doug appeared there, on honeymoon. When going off in the morning fishing I would see him drinking, and on returning in the evening he was still at his post at the bar counter. One afternoon in a crowded bar, his new wife came in weeping and red-eyed and tried to reason with the swaying drunk. He shouted and swore and tried to hit her and fell off the bar stool. A week or two later, news came he had dropped dead from a liver aneurism. We often prayed – 'there but for the Grace of God go I'.

Early that New Year at Nuanetsi it was exceptionally hot and dry. The fan and water method of sleeping was in use. Then the inspector in Ft Victoria running PATU phoned me again. Large gangs were pouring across the south-west boundary. PATU patrols had to be increased. What did I think about taking out a stick with three patrol officers recently out of Depot? There were no other men who could make up a stick. Could I cope? So again it was with deep resentment I took a patrol out. The orders were to report to a sub-JOC down in the area of Crooks Corner, where South Africa, Mozambique and Rhodesia meet. The Joint Operational Command was made up as usual of army, air force and police. On reporting to the police senior officer, we were referred to the army senior officer. The stick was to join up with a Territorial Army company from Bulawayo who were scouring the area in platoon size units. The incoming gangs consisted of large numbers of men. Now the PATU was being used to bolster army patrol numbers. This could not work in so many ways that I was beyond anger. They found it necessary to patrol in units of twenty or more men and we were only five, with three rookies.

The task given to us was to quarter the ground looking for tracks and to call for support if any fresh ones were found. The second morning, when reporting the stick position, the army officer reprimanded me for not using code. On being informed that police did not carry army code sheets, we were ordered to meet up with an army stick and obtain the code. Then he reprimanded me again. The stick was not covering enough ground. At least twenty kilometres had to be covered. The temperature was in the forties; water in bottles was too hot to drink. The best way of finding tracks or insurgents, the way our training dictated, was to go slowly and carefully; to see before being seen. But the army orders were followed and the stick did the required bit, but my way; getting up in the dark and forced marching till midmorning. Then the deep shade of an evergreen was camp for the day, and late afternoon a bit more ground was covered. Several times the tracks of a gang were easily found, the area being uninhabited, but the signs said the tracks were days old. The tyros were barely keeping up; the heat, the distance and fear was dragging on them.

The Shangaan tribe are stockmen. They do not mistreat cattle. In this area there were isolated kraals near the river. The river had the normal sand bed, with the odd holes in the sand where water holes had been dug. The banks were thickly covered in evergreen trees and undergrowth. At intervals, while patrolling parallel to the river, small side streams had to be crossed. There had been some hard rain about ten days back. Some of the side streams had come down in flood, and sandy walls had built up where the stream joined the main river. Behind that wall, water and mud had been trapped. In the heat-haze morning the stick reached another stream. Stuck deep in the mud of the stream bed were two cows. The animals had walked into the mud of the stream bed to reach drying pools of water. The mud was half way up the bellies of the unfortunate animals. One cow was dead, the other still struggling weakly. There were multiple maggot trails to the animals across the black mud; they were being consumed by millions of maggots, even the one still alive.

It was very clear to me and the tracker that the terrorist gangs had been in the area. No Shangaan would have left the animals stuck in the mud unless compelled to do so for a good reason. They would not be lost animals, as again no Shangaan herder could lose his stock. It was a terrible thing to see, that near-dead cow with a million maggots eating it, covering the eyes and mouth and ears. It was a mistake and dangerous given the terrorist situation, but it was not possible for me to leave the animal suffering. I put up my rifle and shot it behind the ear. The shot echoed in the still, hot morning air. The stick went on along the riverbank, and the tracker watching the ground fixedly. He did not approve, but understood it was necessary to fire a shot.

An hour later, the sun was becoming unbearably hot and it would soon be time to stop. Then movement on the far bank of the river attracted my eye. The last three men of a gang of terrorists were moving up the bank on a path, having crossed the river from our side, and were vanishing into the green of the trees. In one movement my pack was shrugged off and the rifle went up; the response was automatic and my magazine was half empty before the last man made it to the concealing trees. The range was about a hundred metres, but there was no indication that any of the gang had been hit. The other four men of the stick had not seen what was being shot at and stood still, unsure of what to do. A few seconds later, three machine guns opened fire from the vegetation on the other bank of the river. The entire stick dived for cover, the other men still wearing the heavy packs. Close on the chatter of the light machine guns came the hollow cough of a mortar firing, and then the whistle of the bomb and an explosion in the bush beyond us. Multiple AK 47s now joined the mortar and machine guns, all firing blind from the distance in the general direction of the PATU stick. There must have been more than twenty of the enemy. The PATU stick was also firing blindly into the opposite bank trees; at least the tracker and I were. The three tyros were out of my line of sight and the noise of my rifle and that of the tracker blocked all other sounds out.

In a minute or two the firing from the gang began to come from further. They were running away from the river line, and then the firing petered out and stopped. The most urgent thing needed now was to cross the river and hunt them down at the run. The tracker caught my eye as I stood up and he inclined his head towards the other three men. Each of them was laying spread-eagled and with faces buried in the ground, and for a moment I thought they had been shot. Then the sound of one of the men crying came, and I saw the other two were trembling violently in shock. There had been a lot of noise and loud bangs but no hiss of near bullets or the whizz of shrapnel. Quickly bending down and touching rifles barrels to test for heat confirmed neither of them had fired a shot. All three were in a complete funk of fear. The tracker again exchanged a disgusted glance with me. To cross the river, half the stick would have to give cover from the near bank, then the men who had already crossed needed to cover the others crossing in turn. The river was at least fifty metres wide, shiny white sand from bank to bank; deep sand that slowed a runner.

At that instant, an overwhelming feeling of loss, anger and doom totally flooded my senses. My body slumped limply down with my head between my knees. How much longer did this inanity have to be endured? Surely there was something I could do to fix things? Was no-one in the country worried about the increasing insurgency? Where were the senior officers? The tracker stood up looking out across the sand, and turned as I finally stood up, with a question on his face. I spread my hands and shrugged. There was nothing to do but go home.

A Land Rover was sent to fetch the stick from the JOC base at my request on the radio. On arrival back there, I reported to no-one, but took another vehicle and drove the stick back to Nuanetsi and sent them on back to Ft Victoria. No words had been spoken between us since the midday contact at the river. From my office at Nuanetsi, the S/O in charge of PATU at District Headquarters was raised on the phone. He was informed that the patrol had come in early and been disbanded by me and that I refused to work any further with untrained men. If any of the gang at the river had been hit I never found out. I had not bothered in my rage to report the contact to the JOC. My anger and disgust was too heavy at the time.

'Also, you can take my name off the PATU list.'

'What you mean? You can't just stop being PATU.'

'Standing Orders say it is voluntary. I un-volunteer.' I was making that one up. If there were any written instructions I had never seen them. He would not know that.

'Well, I don't know. I'll have to think about it.'

'There's nothing to think about, bloke. PATU is finished. Has been for years. Tell you what; give me four men to train with for two months and I will do PATU again with them. Till then forget it.'

'Well, we have problems getting trained men...'

'Save your breath. My PATU days are over.'

Ken, the member i/c, passed by the office door a few minutes later and hardly noticed me. He also seemed to be unaware that the patrol had been abruptly terminated with days still to run. In fact, the subject was never again brought up or commented on. After more than ten years of PATU work no-one noticed my absence. It was humiliating, but not unexpected. The entire concept had for many years not being working as it should. Some rural stations had Police Reserve PATU sticks and those functioned as they were originally designed to do. The constant change of personnel in the regular force made it almost impossible. Anyway, the fruitless patrolling was a thing of the past for me. I had made up my mind on that. The only time I walked the bush now was when I went hunting on the weekends. Ken took two months leave just then. Temporarily I was left in charge. The promotion to inspector had still not come and there were just three other men left on the year's list.

The phone rang one morning and it was the officer commanding, district. When I heard his voice hope flooded though me. Finally, he was calling to advise me of promotion.

'Well good to hear you are fine,' he said. 'Look, I want you to do me a favour. There really is no-one else. The other available S/Os have declined.

What would you say to posting to Salazar?'

'For how long, sir?' Villa Salazar was then nothing but an armed fort, defended by the army. That was common knowledge.

'No longer than a six-month tour of duty. But you must promise me you won't resign over it.'

'That bad? No, sir, I won't resign.' Did it really matter where I lived? Anyway, I was curious.

'That's the spirit. Look, you will have free rations as part of the deal. The quartermaster here in Fort Vic will send you whatever you order. Let me know if there is a problem.' Not a single word about the long overdue promotion.

# 11
# The final count

In 1977, Villa Salazar was on the front line, if there was any front line. The training camps where thousands of terrorists were encamped were all fairly near the border settlement. That border was porous and unmarked. The railway line that ran from Rhodesia to Lourenço Marques was now shuttling hundreds of enemy to near the border and they crossed on foot both sides of the settlement. The Mozambique Army in Malvernia supported the insurgency and constantly attacked the Rhodesian side. The daily situation reports kept local district police stations informed of the situation at Villa Salazar. The police hierarchy and the politicians did not want to be seen as giving up one inch of territory to the insurgency and so the police station was kept open and manned. And so, yet again, it fell on me to keep the flag flying for the policy-makers in comfortable offices.

The road to Villa Salazar ran along the railway line from Rutenga, a small siding and settlement of a few railway houses on the Ft Victoria to Beit Bridge road north of Nuanetsi. Both the road and the railway were nearly without bends or inclines of any sort as the land was flat mopani scrub. It was a track mostly of sand. It was simple and easy to lay landmines on that road, and the thick forest gave good cover to ambushers. Traffic on the road was by then purely military. A mine-detecting vehicle led and all the vehicles behind it were mine-proofed and armoured. Even then landmine detonations often caused casualties. Convoys to Villa Salazar and the garrison there were at two-week intervals. The next one going down would take me.

My batman, who had been with me for over ten years by then, enjoyed the constant transfers. It gave him a chance to see places he would never have been able to see. This time I explained to him that it would be dangerous and there would be lots of shooting, but he had no doubts that he wanted to go too. Most of my personal goods were left at Nuanetsi and only spare clothing packed in the one iron trunk, along with bedding. The batman also carried his own smaller trunk. A few days later, another S/O arrived to take over Nuanetsi till Ken returned from leave. The trunks were put in the back of an armoured truck and the two of us given seats in a mine-proofed Land Rover. That afternoon the convoy rolled through the gates at the Villa Salazar police station. It was the year of 1977 and it was over a decade since Support Unit days had brought me to the same place. It was twenty years since the school days elephant hunt. The vast sea of mopani bush had not changed; the wild animals had changed little. The size of settlement had changed a lot since the first time, but only a little since Support Unit days.

Early Villa Salazar had been three houses and a tin hut on the border. One housed customs, the other immigration, and the third the animal health inspector. In the Support Unit days there had been a large collection of round and oval tin huts at the police camp for the administration of detainees' affairs. There was the large cold room and a clinic building and similar tin huts for the African police, a pre-fabricated house as single quarters and nearby the large tin barracks of the detention camp. Also nearby were another collection of tin huts and a bigger thatched roof hut, Nkomo's hut, where the original detention camp had been and where Support Unit in my days had quartered.

The new police camp had added a large brick under tile single quarters with a swimming pool and fountain on the lawn. The charge office was also a large brick building with the main office and wooden counter at one end and three offices along the corridor. There was also another large brick building used as a garage and storerooms. Both the single quarters and the office had a rare commodity in this area, water-borne toilets. The normal toilet in the bush was a hole in the ground with a small grass fence round it and a crude wooden seat. The large cold room still functioned. It was a tall tin building of two stories; the upper one carried the cooling plant. The power for the plant and charge office came from a diesel generator in the garage building. There was a smaller generator that ran the lights at night. The mess kitchen and bathroom ran on gas, with five, fifty kilogram gas bottles in an iron box along an outside wall. As one emptied it was sent for refilling, so there were always four in reserve.

The settlement was in a dip of land with a high ridge between it and the village of Malvernia across the border with that border running along the highest ground. From Malvernia none of the police camp's housing was visible, only the top section of the police radio mast. The mast was the usual thirty metre high steel triangular latticework with an iron-rung ladder going to the top crow's nest. The mast was a very important part of the present camp. It ensured that the police radio had contact with other stations. But during my tour, the army's SAS commandos mounted a video camera on the crow's nest one night. It was motor-driven to swivel and dip and zoom the lens focus in or out. Then a large excavation was dug at the base of the mast, which became a command room roofed with railway tracks covered deeply in sandbags. The soldiers who provided aiming information to the heavy mortars had detailed maps of the entire cross-border area on the walls of the command room. In the command room was also the small TV screen on which camera images were shown and the controls for the camera. The enemy positions across the border could be accurately plotted on the control room maps to within a metre or less.

The entire police camp was now ringed by a complicated set of barbed wire and heavy diamond-mesh fences, with trip mines scattered between the fences. Behind the mess, on the side facing the border and Malvernia, were seven revetments for the 82mm, long-barrelled heavy mortars. The revetments were wide circular pits in the ground, with a section of the pit roofed and sandbagged. The ammunition was stored under that cover. The heavy tubes sat on solid steel base plates, canted towards Malvernia and propped on bi-pod support legs. The side of the revetment facing the border had a wall of sandbags rising two meters to stop incoming bullets, and over which the mortars fired. There was an army mortar company in the police camp. The camp was an armed fort. The police were there merely to show the flag for the politicians.

The alternative accommodation for the member i/c was a large dug-out at the edge of the mess lawn, on a slope facing the rear gate and facing away from the border. It was a large pit, also roofed with steel tracks and sandbags, the bags piled six or more deep. Steps cut in the earth led down to a large room furnished with a carpet, easy chair and bed. Shelves had been cut into the earth walls on one side. Above the bed were a police and an army radio, night-vision binoculars and paraffin lamp. There was also a box of grenades and another of spare rifle ammunition. The land outside where the dug-out was, sloped fairly steeply and there was a window cut at one end of the room which opened out on a view of the heavily-chained rear camp gate. The actual road to the gate was not mined by the army, although the verges for some way back were. A LMG 7.62mm, belt fed, on a bi-pod was mounted in the dug-out window and was the only defence against an attack on the gate. The army had night sentries out on duty, so the machine gun was hardly likely to be needed. The night-vision glasses came in handy on dark nights when things went bump near the gate. My spare clothing remained in the tin trunk next to the bed.

My batman had a smaller version of my dug-out, but without the window. It was right outside the mess kitchen door and the steps down took an S-bend, giving protection from nearby explosion. There were two gas-fuelled chest-type deep-freezers in the kitchen. Both were full of foil-wrapped fruit cake. In the mess pantry there was also a large carton full of woollen balaclavas and mittens. Women's voluntary groups from round the country had repeatedly sent the cakes and cold gear to the police 'on the border'. It was one of the hottest places in the country and there were only two officers in the mess. The fruit cakes arrived in batches of ten or more. When unfrozen by being warmed in an oven for a while they were good as freshly baked. The supply never flagged even through cake was served several times a day to army NCOs.

The mess was still functioning, but nights were spent mainly underground. Long periods of day were also spent underground. The village across the border was manned by a Mozambique army infantry battalion and an artillery battalion. Large numbers of terrorists were brought by train from camps further inland to near Malvernia and then sent on foot into Rhodesia. It was probably one of those gangs contacted on my last PATU patrol. The Mozambique armed forces were not constrained by small matters such as there being no state of war between their country and Rhodesia. Day and night they bombarded Vila Salazar with small arms, artillery, rockets and mortars. The Rhodesian heavy mortars were brought into action to silence incoming fire. The mortar company commander was not allowed to pre-empt strikes on the Rhodesian side. He had to be under fire first and then request permission to fire back. Usually when permission was granted, the number of mortar rounds allowed to be fired was specified.

On the rare quiet evenings, the mess facilities were used. The incoming convoy brought rations for the army and police. The police rations were free as promised, so every two weeks I ordered two bottles of vodka and orange crush which always arrived. The district OC had kept his word on free rations, but I have often wondered what would have happened if I had ordered larger stocks of liquor. The army issued a daily beer ration and the cold room was always full of cold beer. Each soldier was rationed to two beers a day. The non-commissioned officers – there were no commissioned officers – had been given permission to use the mess bar and lounge by a previous member i/c. That permission was still in place. After a hot bath, my vodka was poured and a game of back-gammon started. It was hot and dry day after day: a soldier needed more than two beers. Their allocation of two bottles was gone in minutes. Then the envious glances at my full glass with ice from the freezers. And then the week's ration of one bottle was gone the first night: a bottle does not go a long way shared with five others. So by the second night after the ration run the vodka was finished. The beer, however, was strictly counted and rationed and there was none to spare for policemen so the nights left till the next ration of vodka came were many and dry.

The army NCOs were also given permission to use the mess toilet. The other ranks used the communal long-drop. The police mess building was L-shaped. The army had covered the space outside between the two wings of the mess, and built a kitchen and dining area there. The army gas stoves and heavy pots on trestles were next to the mess wall, right under the toilet window. During one of the numerous attacks on the camp a small explosive shell landed near the mess building, bounced off the ground and exploded against one of the army gas stoves. The concussion of the explosion destroyed pots and pans. It also shattered the bowl of the toilet inside the police mess. That stray shell destroyed one of only two working flush-toilets within several thousand square kilometres. As the NCO traffic to the mess toilet had been heavy, the one at the charge office had been reserved for police only use. Now a roster of booking had to be brought in for the office toilet use and all day there was a queue. It really was wartime.

There was no regular police work at all. There was a P/O at the station by the surname of Hood, a strange small man. He had volunteered for the duty and had been at the camp for a long time. He was a quiet man who had a battery-powered tape recorder and spent each bombardment recording the pyrotechnics with glee. The tapes were in great demand by the soldiers at the camp. There were also two constables who barricaded themselves in the quarters at the old police lines. During the bombardments they fired hundreds of rounds blindly into the nearby bush. Eventually, I rationed their ammunition supply and forced them to be more careful. We policemen hardly saw or talked to each other; we were all too preoccupied with our own problems. I was the only one who kept office hours or bothered to go to the office at all and I saw no reason to enforce police discipline. Each morning the flag was raised, and then the daily broadcast on the district radio network was done. A mail bag came in with the army convoy and rations every two weeks. There was seldom any mail other than routine stuff. The queue for the toilet reached down the corridor almost to my office, where I fiddled with odds and ends.

It had been a long-standing ambition of mine to learn to play a musical instrument. Sometime previously a tenor recorder and simple practice music sheets had been bought for that purpose. After the few minutes of official work in the morning, taking the broadcast and so on, it was time to find something to do. Out came the practice sheets and the recorder, 'The Miners Daughter', 'The Grand Old Duke of York', 'Peas Pudding Hot' and other simple ditties over and over, trying to hit the right notes and set a rhythm. And the soldiers outside in the corridor tapping heads with a finger and passing snide remarks about the bush-happy cop. At 4.30pm, the flag came down and if there was any vodka left, it was over to the mess and a few nips in the lounge and backgammon or darts. The generator was switched off at 9pm, and the night sentries began patrolling then. The army tried at first to incorporate me into sentry duty, but I refused point blank. The police did not fall under the army command. Hostilities ceased at sundown anyway. The enemy saw no reason to work overtime.

There was a swimming pool outside the mess. The camp water had been supplied by pipeline from a pan about two kilometres away via diesel engine and pump. The pumping was done by a Public Works Department employee who had a hut at the pan. That man had long since vanished, abducted by terrorists or gone to join them, so the army took over the pumping duty. The camp water tank on a high metal stand was full of bullet and shrapnel holes. The mess swimming pool had been taken over as the reservoir for the camp water. A ladder had been pushed across the middle of the pool and standing on edge, canvas pulled over the ladder covering the pool. The canvas was meant to stop the water evaporating and dirt falling into the pool.

One morning, an incoming mortar scored a fluke direct hit on the ladder. That set the canvas alight. After the bombardment had stopped, the burnt canvas revealed the water in the pool was contaminated with drowned and decomposing rodents, snakes and hordes of frogs and insects. The canvas had merely hidden the awful state of the water. The water from the pool had been fed directly into the camp pipes and everyone had drunk it un-purified. There was a scramble to clean the pool and then pump it full of fresh water. Purification and sterilizing chemicals were ordered and a large clear plastic pool cover put in place instead of the canvas.

The same mortar barrage, which had come down when many men were on the lawn of the mess playing volleyball, had landed a bomb on the sandbagged roof of the command post, under the mast. A soldier had been at the start of the stairs going down when the bomb landed just above his head. The thing failed to detonate and the hot projectile bounced up off the sandbag and the hurrying man below caught it in his hands as he scrambled down into the command post. The projectile was hot and he juggled it. The other men in the command post looked up as he came in and a mighty communal scream from them turned him around and chased him back to the surface with his bomb. The offending object was tossed up onto the sandbags and then he returned to safety underground.

It was winter. That meant endless days of cloudless sky; still, windless days with the sun pleasantly warm and just a nip of chill at night. There were many days when nothing unpleasant happened. On those days, the volleyball court set out on the mess lawn near the defunct water feature came into play. Getting a tan was part of Rhodesian culture; everyone wanted to be tanned deep brown. There was no good reason why an overall tan should not be pursued at the camp and so the volleyball teams played stark naked and the watchers, waiting a turn to play, sat and lay around naked as well. That was why there had been many men on the mess lawn that day of the unexpected mortar barrage. Normally, a mortar firing makes the sound of a 'ridge door slamming and there is a gap between the firing sound and the whistle of the incoming bombs. But if the firing point is very far off, then the bombs arrive before the firing sound. The exploding mortars had caught the players off guard. On another day, the volleyball court was again in full use when one of the fence's trip wires detonated a claymore.

The claymore was a shrapnel bomb which fired all its projectiles in one direction. It was a curved steel receptacle like a disc harrow, a shallow basin into which the explosive went and then the shrapnel. Most of them were locally made in army workshops. They were concealed next to a path the enemy might use and a trip wire fired them when the target was in the killing zone. Scores of the devices ringed the camp outside the fence, fastened to scrub bushes and small trees. There were plenty of small buck, rabbits and other game in that scrub and at fairly regular intervals a claymore was detonated by an unfortunate animal. That particular morning I was emerging from my dug-out and just as my head was at ground level, a mighty explosion ripped through the still morning. It was not wise to wait and see if the explosion was a claymore or incoming rockets or mortars.

The volleyball teams were in full gallop in a split second. From my low viewpoint, a lot of floppy male bits could be seen as still pale backsides fled towards dug-outs at full speed. The ball had just been served deep and it was still in flight as the bobbing backsides scuttled down into nearby holes. As the ball hit the ground, the last man vanished from sight.

When orders were given to fire back with the mortars, all the soldiers first dressed correctly in combat kit. It just seemed to be very wrong to fire heavy stuff at the enemy while naked in tanning mode. When claymores did go off, a patrol went out from inside the fence to investigate and that was delicate work as the other trip wires had to be avoided. Sometimes a dead buck made good eating; sometimes it was a crow or other inedible wildlife. The men sent out to check trip wires also went fully dressed. Funny how naked men feel secure in thin clothing.

One quiet day, curiosity took me to see the old restriction camp where the Support Unit had been billeted in the wild days of drinking at Chico's and the Cockroach Club. There were only the concrete bases of the tin huts left, and the burnt, charred framework of the big hut which had once been Nkomo's. The Support Unit had built a bar counter with a wall of cemented glass beer bottles and that still stood although the wooden counter top had been burnt by the same bush fires that destroyed the hut. There was still a scruffy patch of Kikuyu grass where the lawn had been. In the middle of that patchy grass was a wide circle that was barren of any plant growth. That was where, more than a decade back, I had regurgitated Piggy's Pickles and a variety of rot-gut wine. Obviously, the PH of the soil had been changed for good by the acid load deposited after that night so long ago. Nostalgic stuff.

Ian Smith, the Prime Minister and Van De Byl the Defence Minister arrived one day on a visit. The press came with them and the objective was to assure the public that nowhere in the country had the terrorists taken control of any land. The party flew in to Boli airstrip that was about five kilometres back down the road from the police camp. The PM owned a cattle ranch at Nuanetsi and it had been on the police patrol list. Several times my patrols at Nuanetsi had taken me there and a long, slow tea and sandwiches session with him and his wife was always the order of the day. The entire touring party was nervous, and the bodyguards wanted to be assured no incoming stuff would happen during the visit. The opposition was not provoked and so nothing happened for the two hours they were there. My batman outdid himself in making excellent tea and coffee using the mess crockery, and then served up several refreshed fruit cakes from the supply in the deep-freezer. When asked, I said the batman had baked them. The cake vanished at an alarming rate into the greedy maws of various high-ranking officers and I signalled to my man to stick more in the oven. A big dent was made in the vast supply that morning, with the large press contingent coming in uninvited afterwards to clean up as well.

Apart from a lot of noise, the incoming ordinance caused little damage, most being very badly aimed. One 150mm rocket did land on the lawn and the explosion broke one windowpane in the mess. A mortar landed near the garage and shrapnel blew a hole in the sump of a station landmine proof seven-tonner. The next convoy brought in a new sump plate and repairs were easily made. The worst damage, the most serious, was to the cooler room. In the one barrage, a large calibre shell ricocheted off the angled tin roof of one hut and struck the cooling plant above the cool room, the explosion dismantling the motor and gas pipes. This was the worst possible blow of all. Without the cold room, the meat ration would soon go off. Game could be shot to replace meat. But the warm beer that would soon result was a major catastrophe. Cold beer was not negotiable.

The mortar company were from the Rhodesian Regiment battalion in Matabeleland, most of them from Bulawayo. They were Territorial Reserve men, called up from their civilian work many months of the year. There was a mixed bunch of trades in the mortar company at that time on call-up, but no refrigeration mechanic. Also a new cooler motor and gas and copper piping and insulation material were needed. The army radio channel was very busy for a couple of hours. The fridge mechanic in Bulawayo was called up urgently. A shopping list was sent to him, and the army supplied transport to the Bulawayo shops and then to the airport where a Dakota was on standby. That afternoon, the called-up man and material was collected from Boli airstrip and by evening the cold room was running sweetly. The day's issue of beer was cold, in spite of the enemy's best effort.

The Selous Scouts and the Special Air Service came and went on mysterious errands. They were engaged in cross-border raids, finally sanctioned by the government at this late stage. The railway line from the coast was targeted, forcing the insurgents to walk many hundreds of kilometres to the border. The bridges were blown, the railway line smashed and troop trains ambushed. The tide was stemmed, but not stopped. The raids made the Mozambique forces in Malvernia even more hostile. The Scouts and SAS had also been active in the small village at night. The Mozambique artillery and infantry units did not get on well together; the SAS was good at close surveillance and the Scouts raided a smashed train and captured a mailbag. The two rival enemy forces had separate messes and bars. The captured mail was translated and good use made of the intelligence gleaned.

On pay day, when revelling was at its height across the border, the Scouts set up a loud speaker and blasted propaganda across the border. They used the names obtained in the captured letters and read parts of the letters over the loud speaker, but then added in other stuff. This man's wife was leaving him for his brother. That man's house had burnt down and his cattle were all stolen. Another received the news his wife and daughter were pregnant to the same man, an uncle. The distant shouting and laughing in the night fell to a hush as the enemy listened to the false broadcast. Then the wild, angry shooting broke out.

On another payday, when tensions between the two enemy forces were highest as liquor flowed, the SAS crept up to the infantry bar and tossed two hand grenades in the window, shouting as they did so in Portuguese that the grenades were presents from the artillery. The SAS came back to the mess and drank beer while all listened to the prolonged and fierce firefight running through the village across the border. The SAS men were tough professional solders and it was a pleasure to sit and drink with them. If only there had been more of them, things might have turned out differently. There was only one squadron.

A stray donkey was found in the bush near the police camp. All the boreholes near Malvernia had been blown up by Rhodesian Forces, as well as all the water tanks. Water wagons were brought in by train, but with the railway gone for miles back water had to be fetched and carried by hand a long distance. Jerry cans of water were loaded on the donkey and explosives rigged to go off when last can was removed. The donkey was shooed back across the border and the wait was not long. An earth-shaking explosion and distant screams marked the demise of the poor donkey and thirsty men.

Our mortars had for some time been concentrating on removing any infrastructure that made life liveable across the border. The steel water tanks were the first targets destroyed. Then the electricity sub-stations and any structure that held aerials. Then the empty rail trucks and engines at the station were targeted. In the process the massive cathedral-like main building at the station was blown apart. It was hard to watch that happen on the small screen in the command bunker. Chico's orate marble bar had been in that station building and memories of the happy nights spent in revelling there flooded back as the smoke curled skyward black and thick. Then the 'cockroach bar', the railway club, also turned to scattered masonry because it was a rival force mess and gathering place. The camera on the mast picked up all the activity across the border. All points of interest were plotted on the command room maps and the charts used to work out range and direction.

The enemy spent days digging a network of zigzag trenches on the edge of the village and each metre was plotted as it was dug. Some heavy enemy guns were installed in front of the trenches and also a battery of multiple tube rocket launchers. The positions were plotted. When the enemy were satisfied they had a strong well-protected line, they opened fire on Villa Salazar. The mortar company commander sought permission to shoot back and was allocated four rounds per barrel. The centre gun was given range and elevation, read off the previously mapped chart, and told to fire a smoke marker. The marker fell within metres of the target and a small adjustment made, the second fell almost in the trench, near one of the heavy guns firing at us. All eight heavy mortars were told to zero in on the same range and elevation, but with a slight spread. When all had called in ready for action, the order to fire two rounds each rapid fire was issued.

The sixteen high explosive bombs all landed in fractions of a second of each other, all on target. Little stick men flew through the air on the camera screen and smoke mushroomed and flame flared. Men at the receiving-end were crawling and staggering about. A short while later, several heavy trucks arrived through the smoke and the dead and wounded were lifted on. The commander in the bunker ordered the eight guns to fire the remaining eight shells allocated. The enemy trucks took direct hits and for hours new smoke spiralled black and oily. The dead and wounded were left unattended till nightfall. It was a strange thing that the enemy never suspected the mast and the camera as the culprit. They did begin to search for forward observers, still not having worked out that it was the camera at the top of the mast and the mortar commander watched the patrols going and coming and plotted those on his maps as well.

There were days of hiatus when no firing took place on either side. If the interval stretched too long the mortar men became impatient for action. In the walk-in safe at the charge office was a two inch mortar and boxes of bombs for it; possibly a capture in some long-forgotten contact with a terrorist gang, but it was British Army issue so might have been from something else. In the still times, the army senior staff asked me to stir up a fight with the small mortar. It was stood up without a base plate, aimed hand-held and fired by toggle in the general direction of the town across the border. Soon after the first round hit the ground, the retaliation began. Then permission was at once sought to reply to the unprovoked attack.

A company of Rhodesian artillery took up a position about two kilometres back from the police camp and border. There were five WWII twenty-five-pounders, the only heavy artillery type the Rhodesian Army used. They had come to practise, hone-up on skills. While they were there, they too were ordered not to initiate any firefight. So each still day, the artillery commander also called me on the radio and asked for a few mortar shells to be fired to stir things up. When the incoming fire heated up, the artillery commenced firing practise on live targets. The old guns were deadly accurate and they fired on map co-ordinates given to them from the mortar control room, from where the shell strikes were also corrected with the mast camera. It took very few artillery shells to cower the enemy. The shells fired whooshed over the police camp and it was easy to sympathise with those on the receiving end. Sometimes the high explosive was substituted with shrapnel. And so the weeks went by.

The police mailbag brought in by army convoy gave me the information that my promotion to inspector had not happened, and as the full year had passed some elements of the examination had to be redone. Then my name would be re-added to the present year's awaiting promotion list. This was a major blow to me. There was no reason given to me at any time why I had been passed over. No-one had given me any idea that I would be relegated to one of the bottom achievers or that problems had arisen. The lack of promotion seemed to be a combination of never having been on any station long enough to make an impression on the member i/c, and being out of sight and out of mind at Nuanẹtsi, and now Villa Salazar. Combined with the growing sense of impending doom at the present situation where we were forbidden to make war on those making war on us, being passed by for promotion made me deeply unhappy with my circumstances.

The refresher course was set for four days starting on a Monday, in Gwelo, a full day's drive from Nuanetsi. To attend would mean first going back to Nuanetsi, collecting full dress uniform and my car, and then driving to Gwelo via a secondary road past Shabani Mine. The army convoy ran only every two weeks and to attend the course it was vital to get on the next outgoing convoy. A week before the convoy was due it was cancelled and put back three days. Things were desperate as waiting for the convoy would mean missing the set dates for the exams. The examinations only came up once a year. A relief section officer was to come in with the convoy to take over from me for the times I was away but would also be too late arriving now. On an impulse I fuelled the police mine-proofed and partly armoured seven-ton truck. The FN rifle was handed to the batman riding in the back as the armoured cab had only room for the driver. The rifle was cocked and put on safety. The batman had never fired a gun. He was shown how to press the safety lever off and then told to put the rifle over the armoured side and repeatedly pull the trigger if we were ambushed. We would drive on through.

The station keys would have been handed over to P/O Hood but he had gone on a month's leave, so they were left in a drawer of a desk. The relief S/O would be told where they were on the radio. Normally the contents of the safe would have been counted and signed for. There was just over two hundred dollars in the safe, used mainly for field allowances. Present circumstances did not allow for that handover. That morning's three-hour drive along the dirt road next to the railway to Rutenga seemed to be several days long. Each metre a landmine was anticipated. If one hit, the truck wheels could be lost and help would have to be called for and then while waiting it was one rifle against any attackers. When Nuanetsi was reached my body was drenched with sweat, and on standing up to open the hatch, stomach muscle cramp crippled me. The refresher examinations were passed. On return and while at Nuanetsi, the reliving S/O at Salazar called on the radio to ask where the cash from the safe had been hidden as he wanted to draw travelling and subsistence allowance.

For weeks after returning to Salazar angry questions and hopeful answers flew back and forth. Numerous written reports were posted off. The gist of it was the OC demanding to know why normal handover was not done and it did not matter how many times it was explained that it was impossible. Orders were issued to report to the Mabalahuta Airstrip as the district OC was coming to personally interview me. An army escort of three trucks and twenty men went with me on the three hours' drive to that airstrip. The Dakota landed and the OC got out and stood waiting for me to go to him. The plane's engines were kept running.

'Look here S/O Smith,' he said returning the salute, 'why was no handover done?'

'Sir, I have put in several detailed reports. As I told you on the radio yesterday, there was no-one to hand over to.'

'But a relief detail was sent, was there not?'

'I left before he arrived, as my reports explained.'

'Well why was that?'

'I told you on the radio. The course was due to start before the army could get the relief man to the station.'

'Oh, yes, that's right.' He stood thinking for a moment and could find no more questions. 'All right then, you can carry on. I will go back to Ft Victoria now.' He climbed back into the Dakota and it flew away.

'Well, Smithy, I will be buggered if I put up with that sort of shit.' The sergeant in charge of the convoy said. He had heard the exchange. 'Does the little shit not know we drove three hours down landmine alley to get here and still have to go back? Are troopies cannon fodder, then?'

'Sorry Sarg'. You know how the brass works at times.' The rage was hot in me as well.

Shortly after leaving the airstrip and inside the Gonarezhou Game Reserve, I stopped the convoy and shot a kudu bull; an act of rebellion. A dozen men quickly loaded it into a truck and back at Salazar the carcass was taken into the nearby trees and butchered by two qualified blockmen who were on that call-up of the mortar company. The shot would have been heard by the rangers and they would follow up. All the men in Salazar were warned by me to keep the meat out of sight in the trees until the expected visit was over. Hardly an hour passed before the game ranger was at the back gate.

'Hello. Come in for some tea. Let's sit in the kitchen.' We went in. 'Want some cake?' The deep-freezer was opened and he looked in casually. 'Let me get the milk out the fridge. Just unfrozen this morning so should be fresh.' The door was opened wide and he tried not to make it obvious he was looking.

After tea we wandered to the back of the house where the army kitchen was. 'I wonder what they are cooking' I said and lifted the lid of each big pot, one at a time. 'Tell you what, let's get some cold water from the cool room. We keep stocks of it there. Better on a hot day than warm water.' He walked in with me and looked hard, but there was nothing to see except army rations.

'Look,' he said as he climbed in to his truck, 'just be straight with me. You did shoot a kudu, didn't you?'

'Well, yes of course I did.'

'Did you really?'

'I really did, but you find no evidence and if anyone else asks I will lie.'

'Bastard. Thanks for the tea. Bloody nice fruit cake. Come visit sometime.'

'See you.' And he drove off with a rueful grin. The kudu meat was hung in the cool room shortly after he had left.

And more months rolled by. The heavy enemy firing became part of everyday life. No-one our side was ever killed or wounded. It was all a dream, not real. At night, sometimes when sleep would not come, the night-vision glasses were used to scan the bush behind the bunker. The glasses registered heat so where a buck or rabbit had walked silver footprints remained slowly fading. Roosting birds glowed silver as if gilded. The area round the wood-fired water boiler glowed brightly, all the nearby trees and grass, silver. Insects flying left a light trail following after the insect that only slowly faded.

The OC district called me on the radio. My allocated stint had been stretched to two, and now he wanted me to please stay on for another. He reminded me that I had said I would not resign if sent to Salazar and to please remember that promise. That was the instant that made my mind up; I would resign, not right then but soon. No, I would not remain any longer. That, said the OC district, put him in a fix as no other officer could be found for the posting. So I would remain at Villa Salazar until one was found; the OC would contact me again shortly.

That evening when the flag was lowered, there was a bombardment in progress but it hardly registered on my senses. It was all bangs and cordite smell, merely big fireworks. The enormity of leaving the force was all my mind had room for. For nearly fifteen years it was something never even remotely considered. The service to pension had been upped from twenty years to twenty-five shortly before I signed on, so my age at retirement would have been forty-eight. That was time enough to start a new career and collect a second pension. Less than ten years to go; but it was certain the way the war was going that massive changes were due in the country before my pension was due. It would be pointless going on in the police. Part of my mind refused to believe the country was lost, but deep down a dread filled me. I had been close to where the war was being conducted and that worked to convince me all was lost. Losing home is traumatic for man and beast.

A few weeks later, there was a radio message to take down, the one and only concerning just Salazar and not all stations. The district quartermaster from Fort Victoria and a team would arrive with the next army convoy to close down the station. All police equipment would be removed and the police station abandoned. The feeling of doom deepened. So the collapse had started. A dozen or more police trucks arrived with the regular army convoy and all movables were quickly loaded by a score of hands who were anxious to get away from the place and so worked hard. Normally there would be comprehensive lists to be checked and signed, but as no-one was taking over, the equipment was just taken out of the building and packed on the trucks. There were a dozen or so old dockets of unsolved murders, dockets that were never closed, filed in the safe and they also went to Ft Victoria to be stored there.

While I was rooting through the old papers in the big strong room, a top secret manual appeared. It was the South African Police manual on all the ANC big shots. The attached handover sheet on the manual showed it to be the very one that had been handed to me by the SAP after the terrorist was captured a decade back at the DC's camp at Tsoropadzi. The document they had virtually accused me of stealing. It was funny now, if not then. The document had been lying abandoned for years, locked in this remote strong room. The quartermaster staff made a big dent in the remaining fruit cake and the rest was donated to the army. When the army convoy with police trucks attached left one morning, heading for Rutenga Junction, my tin trunk, my batman and I were part of it. The Nuanetsi station Land Rover was waiting at the Rutenga JOC and half an hour later my tin trunk was being unpacked in the sauna of the section officer's quarters.

Ken, the member i/c station had been transferred in the time, nearly a year, I had been at Salazar. Our service together at the station had been less than two months, although we had both been officially stationed there longer, just never there at the same time. The station was still being used as a staging base for the Bright Lights; the police reserve national service men. At least once a week, one of the guarded farms came under attack in the night. Rocket grenades and automatic rifle fire was directed at the house from the safety of the nearby bush. The attacks achieved nothing as the enemy ran as soon as fire was returned, hurried away to put distance between any following trackers and themselves. Several farmers were killed during the day though. The terrorist gang would wait in ambush at a gate in a fence and when the farmer stopped to open the gate, they opened fire. So gates were no longer closed. Stock strayed and was stolen.

With all the terrorist activity in the area, the circuit court at the station was closed down. Arrested prisoners were taken to Ft Victoria and the trials were held there as well. The tennis court and new small clubhouse and pool were in use most of the day by off-duty Bright Lights. The normal quota of crime also dropped. Tribesmen were no longer going out on poaching trips as the risk of being press-ganged was high. Wildlife-related crimes had been the stock-in-trade at the station. Now and then a normal murder came up with usually liquor or women involved. There were daily murders by the terrorists, but most of them were dealt with by CID or Special Branch, units attached to the Rutenga JOC. They passed on to Nuanetsi police any unrelated to terrorism. It became futile to try and maintain routine police work.

One night while trying to direct the air force to a ranch under attack, so they could assist in driving off the attackers with air-to-ground rockets, the final decision came. It took me off guard. I suddenly realized clearly it was pointless to carry on in the police. Everywhere the country was under siege, not only internally but externally by Britain and international left-wing forces. At the same time it came to me more could be done to help the war effort from outside the constraints of the police. For a decade and half I had tried to stem the tide of insurgency working under the orders of incompetent officers or people who did not fully believe in Rhodesia's cause. As I have previously said many of the BSA Police had been recruited from England and intended to retire back to that country. While loyal to the BSA Police, they were ambivalent when it came to a choice between England and Rhodesia. For a long time that night I stood with radio "mic" in hand without hearing the traffic between the planes and the homestead guards.

In the morning, the fan blowing on the flapping mosquito net woke me as the dawn chorus of birds woke the day. Stripped to the waist and carrying the FN over my shoulder, I ran along the path that led along the banks of the river, through thick vegetation. On all sides, herds of buck, mostly impala were going down to the sand pools to drink. Giraffe watched over treetops, silently chewing jaws sideways. It was school holidays all over again; the feeling of freedom. The bush had not changed. The sun came up in an orange sky and the first rays caressed my sweating skin. Two jackals watched me go by and then gambolled along for a while just off the track, playing doggy games. As I ran, my thoughts drifted back to the first days in the force and marvelled at how fast out of necessity the tyro P/O had developed to a fully-fledged policeman. How many murder cases had been taken from report to conviction? How many difficult fatal accidents taken successfully through the courts so that the magistrate commended the work? Plus, hundreds of other minor cases as a matter of routine. And now passed over for promotion for nearly two years. And now classed as one of the worst S/Os in the force. The reason for that was strange, but certainly being an unknown who spent most of his service in remote places had something to do with it. Breakfast that morning after the run and cold shower was thinly-sliced warthog steak on toast, the toast made on a hot plate of the wood stove, which gave it a slightly burnt flavour.

When the resignation was handed to the member i/c, Nuanetsi, it was accepted without comment. He had been my superior for a few months while I was detached to Salazar and we had served only a few days together. There was no connection between us. A week later, orders came that the three months' notice period was to be spent at Ft Victoria Central. The tin trunks were packed and loaded without my help. There were no fond farewells at Nuanetsi as I was virtually a stranger passing through. It was a relief to leave the sweltering low veldt heat and the sauna box quarters and travel to the high plateau of the country. Ft Victoria had been built as a stage on the pioneer route. The fort was the first built by the pioneers up out of the malaria country. It was my birth town where my early memories were of waiting for hours for my uncle outside the Farmers Hall, waiting for a meeting to finish and then driving him back to the farm at Gutu, with him drinking beer. We stopped at the drift at the farm border where he stripped and washed body and mouth to take away the smell of that beer. His wife did not approve of liquor. It was those trips with my uncle as a pre-teen that taught me to how to drive a car.

There were no familiar faces at Ft Victoria Central. A chief inspector showed me to an office with a desk and typewriter. They had nothing for me to do just then. Curious officers passed the open door, but did not stop to talk. Who was this strange section officer? Having served over ten years allowed the accumulation of up to eight months leave and the limit had been reached so I toyed with the idea of swapping leave for three months' notice. Then the OC district sent for me. His office was large and well-furnished and there was a row of filing cabinets along one wall.

'Come in Smithy. How are things going?'

'Fine, sir.' Where was this leading?

'Now look here, man, when I sent you to Salazar you promised not to resign over being posted there. Remember?'

'I have not resigned over that.'

'Well why? We need all the men we can get at the moment.'

'What happened to my promotion?'

'What do you mean? I don't understand.'

'This is the second year I have been overlooked for inspector.'

'Hold on. I don't know about that. Let me get the file.' It was retrieved from a filing cabinet and he flipped through it. 'Well it seems your member i/c at Nuanetsi did not wholly recommend your promotion this year and last year there were not enough vacancies. This is new to me by the way.'

'Well I can't accept that. He was together with me on the station for less than two months. Standing Orders require recommendation for promotion to be done by a member i/c who has known the candidate a minimum of six months.' The damning report had been compiled by Ken. We had been on the station together for no more than about six weeks, if that. It made me very angry as it was so unexpected.

'How could this happen?' he fretted, looking worried. It was his responsibility. He was the final arbitrator. 'I will look into the matter. Do you still want to leave?'

'Yes. Nothing changes. It makes me very angry though. I was not informed. No-one said anything to me about not being recommended.'

'I will definitely look into it. Now look here. Zaka station is struggling with many murders. The dockets are piling up. You have nothing else to do. I want you to go there and help with the docket load. You have done many murder cases I see.' He was feeling guilty and wanted me out of the office.

Zaka was another small remote station with the usual police and internal affairs camp. The station was surrounded by a vast tribal land in a rugged land of granite outcrops and kopjes that marked all south-east Rhodesia. My uncle had once been native commissioner at Zaka and during a short school holiday we had spent a week there shooting baboons in the many crags and caves. The station had the inevitable tennis court. The single quarters mess had a large vegetable garden, with many tree tomatoes. A three-truck convoy took me to Zaka. On the rough dirt track near the station was a procession. A group of men carried a bed on which lay a corpse. The victim had been shot by terrorists and the body was being taken to the police station. It was transferred to the one truck along with two witnesses and the bed was taken up by the bearers to return to the owner.

The police vehicle garage at Zaka had five other corpses in it from previous murders. They were waiting transportation to the government pathologist. The Zaka officers were too afraid to travel with one truck; the three bringing me gave them the chance to send off all six bodies, duly labelled and with the correct forms. Rhodesia forces vehicles were very seldom attacked. The enemy preferred soft targets. At odd intervals, a single police truck had been ambushed but that was rare. It was nerve-wracking to travel down a rough, narrow road through dense trees in a hostile part of the country where the tribesmen watched silently without the usual waving. The police were not soldiers even if they were expected to do duty as soldiers.

On the first morning at Zaka I called the station senior sergeant and spoke to him about the piled-up murders. There were two junior P/Os at the station but it was better to quiz the sergeant who would know all there was to know about the matter. Each of the murders had been by terrorists. The murder scene had been visited and brief statements taken. The P/Os had sent constables out to do the initial investigation, with a sergeant as a driver. In each case the P/O had opened a docket and entered the murders in the crime register. That was all. Till yesterday the bodies had been rotting in the garage. Things were not normal. That night, drinking beer in the mess lounge, that became abundantly clear to me. All six white men, police and internal affairs, at Zaka were living in fear. They had let fear take over and now saw danger everywhere. This was precisely the sort of thing that had caused me to give up on the police.

Next morning, one constable was called to the office. After an hour or so questioning, a docket was made up about the first murder. Most of the statements and drawings were fiction. Then the constable was coached while he did a statement as the investigating officer. The running diary was also a work of fiction. At the end of a morning there were two completed murder dockets. They were nearly total fiction, but based on a few facts gleaned by questioning the constables. The dockets would pass muster when examined by the officer commanding. As no accused would ever be arrested and the dockets would never reach court, it did not matter if they were fiction or not; the post-mortem results would be added in time and the dockets filed away for the life span of witnesses and likely accused, then destroyed. In fact, they were all destroyed when black rule came anyway.

Over the rest of the week, the remaining murder dockets were also fabricated. The constables enjoyed the process and they probably learnt more about murder investigation than they were taught in training in Depot. The senior sergeant called in for tea and a chat one morning and was delighted to find out that I spoke his language and had grown up in the bush just as he had. Then he asked my opinion on the politics of the country, wanted to know what he and the other black policemen should do as it looked as if the white government was going to hand the country to the terrorists. Had they chosen the wrong side? There were no answers I could give him. We were in the same boat. That night when I said I was returning to Ft Victoria in the morning, there was some consternation in the mess. What about the dockets I had been sent to do? Was I intending to do the trip in only one truck? Was if not dangerous? They quietened down when I reassured them the dockets were complete and no-one would be asked to travel with me.

For another week I sat in the empty allocated office at the police camp at Ft Victoria, ignored and unknown, doing nothing. At the weekend, two regular players in the police cricket team went off to a wedding in Shabani with their families. One of the men in the side of that week's opposition, the air force, had played school cricket with me and he put my name forward as a substitute in the police team. On a balmy day a slow game of cricket commenced at the sports club grounds. Without any practise it took some time to get going but then the runs and boundaries began to flow as it all came back. I had not played since Sipolilo and Norton days, but I had captained the school senior team. A century was in sight when there was calling and whistling from the clubhouse. News came that the two team regulars had been in a bad traffic accident on the way back from the wedding and both had been killed. Also killed were some of the family members. The game was at once abandoned.

At nine on Monday morning, I returned to the single quarters from the office. My batman was sitting in the sun polishing a pair of my spare boots. He was told to pack all police uniform in cardboard boxes or plastic sacks, and my civilian clothing in the tin trunks. While he loaded the car with the trunks, the police uniform and badges were taken in a station Land Rover to the quartermaster. The staff members there were disinterested and indicated that the boxes should be left on the ground of the room, and someone would check them later. The rifle they took to lock in the armoury. The truck keys were returned to the board in the charge office and the log book filled in. Wearing a short-sleeved shirt, shorts and sandals, I walked away and across the police camp to my old Mercedes where the batman sat waiting, tin trunks already on the roof rack and in the boot.

After over fourteen years' service I drove away, two months before my notice expired and no-one noticed. Not a single goodbye or handshake. Here in the town where I was born, I was a stranger. Here in a police force I had served well, I was a stranger. The road north was one travelled often in the early days on the way to a hunting holiday, a road that awakened so many happy memories, but now there was only a deep bitterness. There was no destination in mind, but Salisbury seemed like the place to go to. There were relatives of mine there. The final police pay was processed a few weeks later and all ties were cut without further contact from any member of the force.

At Que-Que, where my high school days were spent at boarding school, while filling the car with petrol, I remembered that the schoolteacher from Marandellas now lived with her family in the town. It had been many months apart. My batman was given three months extra pay and a train ticket to his home. After booking in at the hotel in the main street, a phone call arranged a tryst. It was another chapter in the complicated relationship that endures till today. My emotions were strong that night and it had been a long time since any woman had touched me.

That was not quite the end of the story; that came soon enough though as Britain installed Mugabe and Rhodesia was no more. That came about in 1982. Rhodes and Coghlan's dream had come full circle. Winning a war requires more than controlling heart and minds. When I left the BSA Police it was October 1977 and I was rising 40 years old and without work and soon to be without a country. The future is not reachable from today; it can only be experienced by going on to it.

## Related titles published by Helion & Company

*Mad Dog Killers. The Story of a Congo Mercenary*
Ivan Smith
ISBN 9781907677786 (Paperback)
ISBN 9781908916884 (eBook)

*Special Branch War: Slaughter in the Rhodesian Bush. Southern Matabeleland, 1976-1980*
Ed Bird
ISBN 9781909982345 (Paperback)

*Dingo Firestorm. The Greatest Battle of the Rhodesian Bush War*
Ian Pringle
ISBN 9781909384125 (Hardback)
ISBN 9781909384934 (Paperback)
ISBN 9781909384781 (eBook)

*Three Sips of Gin. Dominating the Battlespace with Rhodesia's Elite Selous Scouts*
Timothy Bax
ISBN 978-1-909384-29-3 (Paperback)
ISBN 978-1-909982-44-4 (eBook)

**HELION & COMPANY**
26 Willow Road, Solihull, West Midlands B91 1UE, England
Telephone 0121 705 3393 Fax 0121 711 4075
Website: http://www.helion.co.uk
Twitter: @helionbooks Visit our blog http://blog.helion.co.uk